Gerheart

CONQUEST

America's Painless Imperialism

CONQUEST

America's Painless Imperialism

by

JOHN CARTER

New York

HARCOURT, BRACE AND COMPANY

PRINTED IN THE U. S. A. BY
QUINN & BODEN COMPANY, INC.
RAHWAY, N. J.

"οὐ νέμεσις Τρῶας καὶ ἐϋκνήμιδας Ἀχαιοὺς
τοιῇδ᾽ ἀμφὶ γυναικὶ πολὺν χρόνον ἄλγεα πάσχειν.
αἰνῶς ἀθανάτῃσι θεῇς εἰς ὦπα ἔοικεν."

Foreword

THERE are three particular groups of people to whom
this book is addressed: that section of the American public
which believes that the United States lacks a constructive
foreign policy and that it is usually wrong in any controversy with a foreign power; those foreigners who,
through unfamiliarity with our methods, suspect that the
United States has entered upon a course of imperialism;
and those American officials who have been prevented
from winning a hearing for our national policies by the
public apathy toward our political traditions. If it succeeds
in clarifying the ideas of a single American or foreigner
with respect to the essential character of our rôle in world-
politics, it will have served its purpose.

My preceding work, *Man Is War*, was a diagnosis of
germs of political disease in international society. This
one is offered as a possible remedy, and is designed to
show that our economic expansion and industrial prosperity can be divorced from political expansion and economic imperialism, and that we may have developed institutions capable of promoting the peace of the world and
the political demobilization of the nations.

Much of my information has been supplied by the officials of the Department of State and of the Department of Commerce, who have been courteous and helpful, and for whose coöperation I am deeply grateful, but
it is in no sense to be considered as representing official
opinion. The views developed and the conclusions reached

are, for the most part, individual to myself. So far as they have been modified or expanded, they also represent the critical judgment of my wife, whose wisdom and sense of justice have prevented the expression of several extreme views and dogmatic conclusions. I have drawn freely on the works of other writers for the factual information on which my general opinions are based, but see no occasion for citing authorities or adopting the paraphernalia of critical scholarship in what is intended as a piece of speculative interpretation.

J. C.

June 11, 1928
New York City

Contents

[ix]

Contents

Part One

THE BASIS OF AMERICAN WORLD-POWER

Chapter I

THE PRINCIPLES OF IMPERIALISM

DURING the years which have elapsed since the Armistice, few subjects have provoked more political speculation than has the future of the United States. Our decisive intervention in the World War, followed by our equally decisive refusal to accept an international political obligation under the League of Nations, revealed the growth of our power at the same time that it emphasized our determination to go our own gait in world affairs. Since then the world has tried to read our motives and anticipate the objects of our national policy.

Are we, as so many contemporary critics assume, an Empire? Is our course in Central America and the Caribbean imperialistic? Does the increase of our trade, the spread of our foreign investments, and the construction of a formidable navy portend a bid for world-power like Germany's in the years before 1914? These are the questions which the world is asking about America today. The answer, according to foreign opinion, is invariably in the affirmative.

Yet even that affirmative is qualified by doubts. Why, if we are an Empire, have we failed to demand the slightest extension of our national sovereignty? If we are imperialistic, why have we not annexed the Caribbean and Central American States when it has been within our power to do so? Why, if we are in quest of world-power, do we

[3]

advocate naval disarmament, limit our ability to defend our Pacific possessions, and seek to outlaw war as an instrument of policy? The world is puzzled and irritated by our ambiguous attitude. We are not playing the game in the conventional way. That we are not adverse to wealth and power is obvious. It is not yet obvious that we prefer to acquire wealth and power through indirect, non-political methods.

By its annual trade-balances, its foreign loans, its domestic prosperity, and the huge volumes of its imports and exports, the United States is creating an economic empire over most of the planet. In the conventional Old World sense, it is not an empire at all and is unlikely to become one. It involves no political expansion, menaces the sovereignty of no foreign nation, displaces existing allegiances, languages, flags, and loyalties in no quarter of the globe. Yet year by year, our economic power, operating within the accepted limits of American policy, has grown until the United States now bestrides the Western Hemisphere like a Colossus and casts long shadows over Europe and Asia. While Europe and Asia invoke their policies and their armaments to obtain for them a place in the economic sun, the American empire is intangible, invulnerable, an influence over the minds and customs of mankind which is confirmed every time the world installs an adding-machine, dances to jazz, buys a bale of cotton, sells a pound of rubber, or borrows an American dollar.

Our empire is different from the European type of empire. The Old World has its age-long institutions of political power and its traditions of military glory. American institutions and traditions are the products of a new

[4]

world. More than a century and a half have passed since we broke with Europe's political system; more than a century ago we dissociated ourselves from the European diplomatic system. Using the almost incalculable resources of an undeveloped continent, the United States has built up its distinctive policies and traditions upon economic conceptions, and today stands ready to extend them over the world.

Yet it is the essence of the American conquest that it should be peaceful. Violence and military conquest play no great part in America's economic expansion. The American method is, quite simply, to dispense with politics and to trust to business to settle the question of the survival of the fittest. The convenience, utility and merits of American methods are the only sanctions for their adoption by other peoples. American politics are reduced primarily to the problem of assuring practical equality through the abolition of any privilege—political, social, religious or economic—which might prevent fair play in the free-for-all of American business life.

Hence, though the American Government—like all others—exists to promote the security and wealth of its own people, it alone has found it possible to do so without direct reference to political means. In consequence, the American is not politically but economically minded. This brings him into conflict with the European, for he will not admit the validity of political obstacles to his economic welfare. This psychological difference results in two irreconcilable conceptions of foreign policy. For the European, the object of national policy is political power; for the American, the object is economic prosperity.

In this light, even war and peace assume entirely different aspects. To the American, war is an institution and peace an economic process. To the European, peace is an institution and war a political process. Accordingly, America's policy has been economically acquisitive and only incidentally warlike. Our present political power is based, in European eyes, on our two recent wars—the Spanish-American and the World War—but our economic strength rests, in our own interpretation, on the policies of peaceful assimilation developed in the first century of our national life.

The history of that century is the story of the conquest of the North American Continent. The Revolution, the development of the Northwest Territory, the Louisiana Purchase, the War of 1812, the Florida Purchase, the annexation of Texas, the Mexican Cession, the Oregon Agreement, and the Gadsden Purchase are mile-posts in a policy, half of war and half of negotiation, which has based America's present prosperity and power on the unexploited wealth of the richest portions of a virgin continent.

The Spanish-American War served merely to reveal America's power in the Caribbean, conferring upon the United States effective dominion over Cuba, Porto Rico, Santo Domingo, Haiti, Panama, and the other Central American republics, while expanding American economic influence in Mexico, Colombia, and Venezuela. The same war also revealed our growing Pacific power, giving us Hawaii, Samoa, Guam, and the Philippines. Our participation in the World War gave us no territory, but showed for the first time the full extent of a national strength which had learned to prefer the substance of economic power to the forms of political dominion.

[6]

America, accordingly, values political power principally as a means of protecting existing economic interests against actual menace. Therefore her domestic institutions depend rather on their own economic fitness than on their immediate means of defense. But without the ability to protect them—whether expressed in armaments or implied by economic resources—the United States could not long maintain her provocative tariff and immigration policies, her republican institutions, her territorial integrity, her monopoly of coastwise commerce, or her exclusive control of the world's trade that passes through the Panama Canal. For the reason that her actual strength is greater than her political power, America's policies are as much affirmative as they are defensive. Her own political institutions, in fact, rest on the principles of the Declaration of Independence and the Monroe Doctrine, behind which the United States has developed its experiment in federal government and its congenital code of self-determinant nationalism.

American policy has been, therefore, more concerned with the formulation of general principles than with the protection of specific interests. These principles underlie and give form to material interests, which, in turn, motivate and give effect to national principles. In administering this policy, the Democratic Party, from Monroe to Woodrow Wilson, has excelled in the formulation of national principle; while the Republican Party, from McKinley to Coolidge, has shown a more practical conception of national interest. Only in conjunction can the two political traditions create an harmonious national policy, for the ruin of Wilson's European program suggests that pure principle is dangerous to national interest, while the wreck of Knox's "Dollar Diplomacy" showed that mere self-interest is perilous to national principle. An intelligent combination is the best assurance of a fruitful national policy. For moral ideas wither as the force which supports them is withdrawn; and material interest is dissipated unless controlled by principle.

Political power is, accordingly, to be valued as the handmaid of principle and interest: it supports principle and defends interest. But power may not safely be pursued for its own sake or for the sake of prestige. Power so acquired is likely to be used recklessly in the name of national honor, or frivolously abandoned in the name of economy. Only that power which is the direct and simple expression of national ideals and interests is to be considered, since national policy can be developed and the national domain peacefully extended only through the coordination of principle, interest, and power.

Foreign policy and world-power are thus built on the triple foundation of principle, interest, and force. It follows that these principles and interests are the national principles and the national interests. British policy is not an attempt to endorse Patagonian principles or to foster Roumanian interests; French policy is not solicitous to enforce Italian ideals or Russian institutions; in a world of competing policies, the American Government does not concern itself with anything but the application of American principles and the protection of American interests. The United States holds no brief for any power, temporal or spiritual, save that of the American people.

In the broadest sense, therefore, foreign policy is the export of domestic institutions, methods and ideas. American foreign relations involve the export to other countries of democracy, free popular education, the abolition of privilege, the separation of business and state, Federal Republicanism, Prohibition, reserve banking, chain-stores, mass-production, high wages, installment selling, cafeterias, Mary Pickford, Emerson, Poe, Whitman, Charlie Chaplin, Sinclair Lewis, skyscrapers, cheap automobiles, chewing gum, the *Saturday Evening Post*, central heating, open plumbing, vacuum cleaners, fireless cookers, portable typewriters, multiple switchboards, the single standard of morality, and the one-crop farm.

Similarly, we are constantly importing the institutions of other countries. Great Britain sends us the Prince of Wales, the Church of England, the Irish question, free trade, Bond Street clothes, social distinctions, Oxford and Cambridge, naval supremacy, hands across the sea, English country houses, Shakespeare, five o'clock tea, whisky and soda, Shaw, the Stephenson Rubber Act, lecturers, novelists, playwrights, critics, *Punch*, and *The London Times*. From France we get perfume, military efficiency, the sexual prestige of French demimondaines, logic, the Beaux-Arts, the Latin Quarter, sidewalk cafés, champagne, tips for waiters, women's fashions, wines, *La Vie Parisienne*, Anatole France, Voltaire, Rabelais, and debt cancellation. From Italy come Caruso, chianti, Vesuvius, spaghetti, Dante, and Mussolini; from Russia, vodka, ikons, caviare, the Little Father, the knout, Dostoievsky, Tolstoi, Lenin, secret police, Siberia, smocks, Bolshevism, and Balieff. From Germany we import sausages, beer, Kant, Goethe, chemicals, sauerkraut, pedantry, and kartels; from Japan, the Samurai, silk, wood-cuts, toilet-paper, and fire-crackers. And so on.

In the face of this competition the maintenance of

essential American institutions is the first line of national defense. This cannot be achieved by government but depends on the character of the American people and their understanding of our institutions. The politically-minded European has a highly developed national consciousness which prevents the assimilation of foreign ideas. The English are not interested in the United States; French culture considers itself all-sufficient and unique; even humiliated Germany is loath to imitate her victors. National consciousness in America is weak, but what might be called "national unconsciousness" is strong, inasmuch as nationality is determined quite as much by the things which are taken for granted as by the things which are professed. Americans are very curious and receptive toward the ideas and institutions of other peoples. They do not regard all of their institutions as perfect, complete, or final, and are willing to try almost anything once. But if an alien idea runs counter to American ideals or is subversive of America's economic interest, the "national unconsciousness" of the Americans is aroused and the foreign idea is emphatically and conclusively repudiated. Thus the Americans are willing to spend money as tourists in Italy and will contribute to relieve famine in Russia, but evince no enthusiasm for the political principles of Fascism and no approval of the economic practice of Bolshevism. Americans do not advertise the fact in every department of their daily life, but their national character is of as distinct a quality as that of any other race. Alone of all the nations, the American is not yet standardized into a final national type. His nationality is, nevertheless, an established fact.

The Principles of Imperialism

The arena of American foreign policy is the entire planet. No portion of the world may be ignored in formulating our national principles or in developing our national interests. America's international relations are controlled by the facts of political geography.

These facts are simple. There is one large Eurasian continent, the largest single mass of land on the surface of the globe. It consists of a central country, Russo-Siberia, bordered by three peninsulas, on the east, the west, and the south, which have approximately equal areas and populations. Europe, China, and India each contain about 1,800,000 square miles and 300,000,000 inhabitants. These are the vital regions of the Eurasian world.

To the west and east of Eurasia, commanding its maritime communications, lie two island groups, Great Britain and Japan, also approximately equal in area and population. Flanking the Indian peninsula on the south are two tropical pendants, Africa and Australasia, which are ruled by the European nations. Africa is a compact mass of land, and is split into ten different sovereignties. Australasia is a frayed-out archipelago of peninsulas, islands, and subcontinents, under six different sovereignties.

Floating like two huge islands in the oceans which surround this orderly arrangement of land and water lies the Western Hemisphere. Anglo-Saxon America—the United States and Canada—contains half of the total area and more than half of the population of the entire hemisphere. To the south of them lies another tropical pendant

[11]

—Latin America—divided among twenty different sovereignties. Since the completion of the Panama Canal in 1914, North America has been effectively an island, which commands the world's interoceanic communications exactly as Great Britain and Japan command the maritime communications of Europe and of China, respectively.

The Indian Ocean is the heart of the Eastern Hemisphere and the center of the British Empire. If a circle is drawn on a 7,000-mile radius from Cocos Island—the little-known cable station where the German raider *Emden* was destroyed—it will include the lion's share of Britain's territorial domain: India, southern Persia, Iraq, the Sudan, Arabia, Tanganyika, the Union of South Africa, New Zealand, Australia, and the East Indies.

This fact is the underlying motive in British sea-power, as the Indian Ocean is the greatest symbol of British commerce. Where one ton of cargo moved a century ago in the seas lying between India, Africa, Malaya, and the Tropic of Capricorn, three hundred tons are moved today, two-thirds of them in British vessels. Admiral Ballard of the British Navy, therefore, observes in his *Rulers of the Indian Ocean* that "for such a development of industry it is essential that Britain should hold the naval supremacy not only of the Indian Ocean but of the world." The British Admiralty surveys with suspicion any development which may threaten so rich a prize. In justification, Ballard quotes the letter to Manuel I of Portugal from Francisco Almeida, first European Viceroy to the Indies:

Let it be known to your Majesty that if you are strong in ships the commerce of the Indies is yours; and if you are not strong in ships little will avail you any fortress on land.

This view of the Indian Ocean is important, for it serves to remind the facile critic of Britain's naval policy of the stubborn fact underlying her sea-power, that the Indian Ocean is the commercial heart of the Empire and that the Imperial Government will do everything possible to maintain this ocean as a British lake.

The only real threat to their ascendancy comes from Russia. A circle drawn on a radius from Tomsk to Vladivostok defines the natural limits of the great land-empire of the Eurasian world. There is a zone where the limits of Russian land-power and of British sea-power intersect. It includes the Middle East, northern India, and China. That area is today, as in the past, the scene of a tremendous, steady, and irreducible conflict, between two mutually incompatible powers—summed up, for the present, in Soviet Russia and the British Empire—for the land-power of Russia cannot thrive without free access to the sea, and the sea-power of Britain cannot survive without free access to the land.

Another point to be remembered in considering American foreign policy is that the world is round. If you go east or west from North America, you will strike the Eurasian continent. Similarly Eurasia can reach America either through the Atlantic or the Pacific. Actually, however, the prevailing currents of policy run from east to west. Asia presses on Europe, Europe presses on America, America on Japan, and Japan on Asia.

There is one very important qualification to this easy statement. A glance at the currents of the sea, the trade winds, the isotherms, and the lay of the lands and waters on the face of the globe, shows that the continents and oceans do not lie due east-and-west, like a chess-board, but follow a strong northeast-southwest trend. Thus, while the physical world revolves on an axis, the political world revolves on a diagonal. Traced on a Mercator projection, this diagonal runs from Great Britain, through Panama, to New Zealand.

The direction of sea-power is parallel to this line. Thus, prior to the destruction of the Spanish Armada, Latin sea-power, working from a naval basis which stretched from the North Sea to Cape Verde, influenced the Western Hemisphere from Florida to Cape Horn. Later, English sea-power, working from the broader base of Iceland to Gibraltar, gave the English the predominance in North America. Similarly, American sea-power, working from a base stretching from the Panama Canal to Alaska, is giving the United States a dominant position in Japan, Manchuria, the maritime provinces of Russia, eastern China, the Philippines, the Dutch East Indies, Australia, and New Zealand. In precisely the same way, Japanese sea-power presses heavily on Korea, North China, the Philippines, the East Indies, and Malaya.

In estimating the real influence of sea-power it may be taken as an axiom that the dominant naval power of any continent wields the entire sea-influence of that continent. Great Britain speaks to America with the naval prestige of all Europe. The United States speaks in the Pacific with the naval power of all North America. Only in the case of Japan does sea-power work from a very narrow base and without political substance. Finally, it must be observed that British sea-power interferes with American sea-power in the Caribbean, that American sea-power interferes with Japanese power in the South China Sea, but that British sea-power is subject to no control and hence predominates.

Land-power, on the other hand, runs from northwest to southeast, following the actual distribution of land. Europe's political base extends from Riga to Gibraltar, thus assuring European domination over Africa, the Near East, India, and the East Indies, making Singapore the natural eastern limit of European colonial power. America's political base extends from Norfolk to San Diego, giving the United States the hegemony over the Caribbean, Mexico, Central America, and South America. On the other hand, Japan, working from the broadest political base possible to her—Sakhalien to Formosa—can threaten only the Pacific islands, New Guinea, and a portion of Australia. Until Japanese sea-power acquires the Philippines and Malaya, Japan will be impotent to conquer an Australasian empire.

There are three modern centers of world-power where a broad physical base is combined with sea-strength: Western Europe, which is dominated by Great Britain; eastern Asia, which is partly controlled by Japan; and the eastern and central United States, which is independent. These are the regions which, being free to adopt their own course of action, determine the course of world-events. In practice, no world-power avails itself of this freedom, being restrained by foreign power in the region most vital to its practical independence.

The key to Western Europe is European Russia, without which Europe's political control of India and the Near and Middle East is without substance. The key to eastern Asia lies in Korea, Manchuria, and Japan. Here

Russia and Japan are in conflict, and American sea-power, based on Alaska, nullifies Japan's freedom of naval action. The key to North America lies in the quadrilateral formed by Bermuda, the Hudson Valley, and the Valley of the St. Lawrence. The sea-communications of this area are strategically controlled by Great Britain, while the land-power resides in the United States. Without full control of this region the United States is powerless to extend America's political power across the Atlantic.

Not only are the centers of world-power controlled by key areas, but their political influence is modified by secondary zones of sea-power. Thus the British navy controls the North European zone of sea-power, extending from Helsingfors to Cape Finisterre, from Spitzbergen to Iceland. In the past, Spain, Holland, France, and Germany have attempted to conquer the sea-power of this region. They have failed. The political expansion of Western Europe is conditioned by sea-power in the eastern Mediterranean and Red Sea area, where France, Spain, Italy, and Russia contest Britain's solid naval control. This control has given the British power over Egypt, the Sudan, East Africa, Arabia, and the Suez entrance to the Indian Ocean. The American world-power is barred on the southeast by the Caribbean zone, in which the British contest an American supremacy which is actually more political than naval. Between eastern Asia and the tempting prizes of Australasia lie the China Seas. This is the area of the world's greatest tension, being contested by American, Japanese, British, French, and Dutch sea-power. Its possession assures entrance to the Indian Ocean. It lies in the full sweep of American and Japanese sea-power. It is the farthest and most lightly held outpost of European sea-power. It is the only region of the modern world where a political upset is likely to occur and to have decisive influence on the world's future history.

It is the object of American policy and power to prevent any considerable upset in this region, for disturbance of the balance of power in eastern Asia will prevent the United States from exploiting the full possibilities of her geographic position.

America can exert political dominion over the entire Western Hemisphere, once her control of the Caribbean is complete. With complete strategic control of the vital St. Lawrence-Hudson-Bermuda zone of sea-power, her political influence will predominate in western Africa from Tangier to Durban. With control of the China Seas, her sea-power can assure the primacy of American commerce in eastern Asia and the East Indies. Working in both directions—southeast and southwest—the United States might ultimately secure political and naval access to the Indian Ocean and its rich commerce. America is, however, powerless to exert any decisive influence over Europe, East Africa, or inland Asia. Japan, Korea, and Malaya may fall within her commercial periphery, but inland China, Russia, India, Persia, and central Asia lie forever beyond her scope.

In developing this world-dominion, America must depend upon her economic no less than her geographic base. The number, character, intelligence, and discipline of her people; her industrial organization, her fueling and transportation systems; her raw materials—coal, iron, minerals, oil, her broad agricultural resources, and her ability to produce food: all these will enter into her future bid for control of the world's destinies.

[17]

More than economic resources are needed for American empire. It must rest upon a moral basis, a conquering idea. The broader the moral base, the bigger the empire; but without a broad physical and economic base, American moral ideas will merely merge with a general civilization. Force alone has never created or kept an empire. America, to achieve world-power, must possess some moral or economic attribute which will transform her adherents into willing partners in American policy. A conquering idea is indispensable for durable dominion, a technique of life which will impose itself and subdue humanity to the service of superior organization. Without this moral attribute, American empire will be transient and inglorious, a mere incident in the history of the eternal race for power.

Chapter II

THE CHARACTER OF EMPIRE

EMPIRE may be good, bad, or indifferent, and imperialism may be brutal, admirable, or simply the only practical course open to a nation. It should be conceded at the outset that the empires of the modern world have, in varying degrees, justification for their existence.

Imperialism is, at its best, a suave blending of economic prosperity and moral ideas. At its worst, it is the forcible imposition of political control over alien races and nations. Thus empires may be created by force, but they can never be maintained by that method alone; and when force becomes the only element in an empire, that empire is doomed. No amount of clever administration and military prestige can long restrain subject peoples, without the moral and physical benefits which healthy imperialism confers upon them.

An examination of history shows that imperial power has stayed longest with those nations which had most to offer to their dependents. Rome is the great exemplar of Western imperialism, but the age which thinks of Rome in terms of legions and Caesars is apt to forget the Rome of the roads, the security and the economic activity which sprang up in the legions' wake. Less than one hundred and fifty years after Caesar had conquered Gaul, there were great and flourishing cities at Lyons, Vienne, Marseilles, Narbonne, Toulouse, and Bordeaux. It was quite as much through imitation as through subjugation that the Romans created the Italian, French, Spanish, Portuguese, and Roumanian peoples of Latin Europe, and so produced the germs of modern Europe. Within the borders of the Roman Empire there was an economic activity quite comparable to that of modern times:

The second century after Christ was in fact the age of the greatest prosperity and happiness which the countries governed by Rome were ever to enjoy. This was the effect of many causes, immediate and remote, of the profound peace which with some insignificant exceptions prevailed in the interior; of the natural process of repair which had begun in the provinces in the preceding century, and of which the beneficial effects were now mature; of the roads, the diminished variety of languages, weights, measures, and coinage, the assimilation of manners ["Standardization"?], the canalization of rivers throughout the empire, the efficient policing of the seas, the closer relations with Rome, the army itself—all these created and favored new currents of exchange which brought into mutual contact the most widely separated regions and in each produced knowledge of new habits and new commodities, and at the same time new wants and new activities. Everywhere were opened factories for textiles, weapons, and dyes. The industries of the East, the manufacture of purple, of glass and jewelry, flourished exceedingly, having found new and rich markets in the less civilized provinces of the west. Even the parts of Europe which had remained longest barbarous, such as northern Italy, Gaul, and Spain, began with some success, although not without imperfection, to imitate the products of oriental industry. Innumerable merchant ships plowed the Mediterranean, great commercial expeditions explored new rivers and coasts, and pushed as far as remote India and China in search of silk and pearls, of rice which was then used as a medicament or a highly luxurious article of food, and taking with them in addition to the gold and silver which these very remote countries accepted in payment for their goods, the few products of the Mediterranean, such as wine, which were consumed there.[1]

In addition to economic prosperity, the Romans disposed of a moral idea which still influences the world: the Roman law. With prosperity, law, and order in the track of her invincible armies, the Roman Empire became an institution so solid and natural that when it fell, for a thousand years mankind could think of nothing to take its place.

The next great imperial power, after Rome, was Austria, built by the Habsburgs on two entirely sound principles: the physical principle of convenience which is summed up in Palacky's famous phrase, "If Austria did not exist, it would be necessary to invent her;" and the dynastic principle which won for the Habsburgs the saying, "Tu, felix Austria, nube!" and built up an empire by prudent marriages. The first Habsburg ascended the throne of the Holy Roman Empire A.D. 1273. Two centuries later, the Habsburg dominions included Austria, Carniola, Tyrol, Carinthia, and most of the Burgundian possessions—including, in the bond of a common feudal loyalty, French, Dutch, Flemish, Walloon, German, Slavic, and Italian peoples. This process of matrimonial imperialism came to a climax in the middle of the sixteenth century under Charles V, who inherited from his mother the Spanish and Italian dominions of Ferdinand of Aragon and the Kingdom of Castile, and from his father the hereditary Habsburg possessions and the lands of Mary of Burgundy. Long after this remarkable ag-

[1] Ferrero and Barbagallo, *A Short History of Rome.*

glomeration of territories had been broken up, the Austro-Hungarian Empire survived because it served the interest of Europe as a counterpoise to Russia and Prussia and as a buffer between Europe and the Turkish Balkans. It required the greatest war in modern times to destroy it.

With Charles V the imperial scepter passed to Spain, which rapidly acquired, through discovery and conquest, a great colonial empire in the western hemisphere. It has long been fashionable to sneer at the Spaniards as bad colonists; yet it is noteworthy that the Spanish-American colonies held their allegiance a full century longer than the British colonies. Before dismissing the Spaniards as incompetent, it is also advisable to note that alone of European nations, they have succeeded in imposing their civilization on alien and Oriental races. Long after Spanish rule over America terminated, Spanish civilization, culture, language, and religion remained to attest the permanence of the Spanish conquest.

Spain's engines of empire were twofold—the Roman Catholic faith—a moral idea—and the Spanish system of municipal home rule—a physical technique. The colonies were under the direct supervision of the Council of the Indies, which nominated both the temporal and spiritual authorities of New Spain. Spanish rule in America was thus a diarchy, much of the burden of administration being borne by the Church.

The evolution of the political institutions of Spanish America . . . presents certain interesting analogies to the mediaeval constitutional development of the different Christian kingdoms of the Iberian Peninsula, as the territory was slowly recovered from the Moors. In both cases the first output of the conquistadores was the municipality, with all its inherited traditions of self-government; in both it was gradually superseded and over-shadowed by the more extensive and despotic authority of the central power and its representatives.[1]

The colonial municipalities enjoyed extensive powers, electing a majority of their own magistrates. They even had some authority over the surrounding country. The fine traditions of Spanish urban democracy seemed destined to be revived and planted in the new world. When these early liberties had disappeared it was their memory to which men appealed in the revolt of the colonies against the mother country. The political life of contemporary Latin America is still influenced by Spain's distinctive contribution to the democratic ideal.

Contemporaneous to Spain, the Portuguese created in Brazil and the East Indies a different type of empire, naval and commercial, which they were not strong enough to hold against their Dutch rivals. For the Dutch devised a new organ of imperialism—the commercial company. After their revolt against Spain in the Reformation had deprived them of their rôle as "waggoners of the sea" for the Spanish Empire, they set out to win from Portugal what they had lost from Spain—the carrying trade of Europe. Holland became the cradle of the modern commercial empire.

Following the Portuguese, in 1595 Cornelis Houtman discovered the secret of the Cape of Good Hope route to the spice islands. Four years later, the Dutch had secured so complete a monopoly of the spice trade that they were able to raise the price of pepper from $0.75 to $2.00 a pound. In 1602, the Dutch East Indies Company began

[1] R. B. Merriman, *The Rise of the Spanish Empire.*

operations in India, Ceylon, Sumatra, Java, and the Moluccas. A system of factories, trading-posts, and forts was employed to constrain and facilitate trade. In 1621, the Dutch West Indies Company was established, which incidentally settled Manhattan Island in 1623 as part of its system of fortified trade-operations. In 1630, it acquired Pernambuco and held the north coast of Brazil from 1636 to 1644.

This empire was based on the false premise that mere commercial activity justifies dominion. The Dutch company was simply an armed instrument for extracting wealth. Their colonies subserved domestic interests primarily, and the Hollanders were shrewd monopolists and ruthless exploiters of native labor. Even today, in the Dutch possessions there is small effort to do more than promote the material prosperity of the region. The Dutch have no "conquering idea," and their present empire, like that of the Portuguese, exists by grace and permission of Great Britain.

It remained for the British to take over the Dutch imperial technique and to breathe a new spirit into it. Beginning with the instrument of the trading company and naval power, they discovered that the principles of British freedom supplied a moral basis for their empire. Magna Charta, the Petition of Right, the Habeas Corpus Act, and the Bill of Rights, have led, step by step, to the Irish Free State Act, the establishment of Dominion self-government, and the fostering of local autonomy and parliamentary self-rule throughout the Empire. This has been a tremendous contribution to the political history of the world—the United States itself is derived from the traditional liberties of the Briton and the political traditions of his government. It is the greatest monument to the genius of British imperialism.

On the side of economic prosperity the British contribution has been equally great. Through a shipping supremacy based on naval power, on political victories over Spain, Holland, France, and Germany, on strategic fueling and naval bases throughout the world, on control of commercial communications through radio and wireless monopolies, all backed by an industrial organization which was supreme for a hundred years, British domination has meant an increased movement of goods, the fostering of world-commerce and the spread of free trade in one-fourth of the area of the globe. Virtual free trade was established by the British in a series of treaties with China, Siam, Turkey, Morocco, and Persia, and was urged upon the world as a positive moral principle. This commercial basis of the British Empire has been abandoned, with the adoption of protective tariffs, first by the Dominions and then by Great Britain herself. It remains to be seen whether maritime supremacy alone will suffice to hold the Empire together.

The empires of Spain, Portugal, Holland, and Great Britain were predicated on sea-power: in France, Russia, Germany, and Japan a different type of imperialism was developed.

In the case of France, French civilization supplied the moral basis of her "civilizing mission." French rationalism—Descartes, Montesquieu, Voltaire, Rousseau, Siéyès, and Diderot—built an empire of the mind which has not crumbled yet. The Code Napoléon has been to modern Europe, Latin America, and Japan what the Roman law was to the ancient world. The physical instrument of

French empire has been military power and glory, from the time of Louis XIV and Napoleon down to that of Foch.

In the case of Russia, the spiritual side of empire has depended on Orthodoxy, whether Tsarist or Marxian, while the physical implement of control was absolute monarchy administered by a bureaucracy. This served to cement into a cohesive whole the greatest single land area under one sovereignty. The principle of Christian orthodoxy was used by the Tsars to free Serbia, Greece, Roumania, Bulgaria, and part of Armenia from the Turks, while today Moscow aspires to a protectorate over the Communists in China, Mexico, Great Britain, India, etc. Power under the Soviets is even more centralized and bureaucratic than under the Tsars, and the autocratic principle, with its soothing effect on politically immature minds, still suffices to keep a fantastic diversity of races in an administrative unit.

The Germans based their claim to empire on the moral merits of German Kultur, especially their powers of discipline, coördination, and scientific thoroughness and efficiency. On the spiritual side they also offered a superb example of social organization—clean cities, minimum wages, social insurance, wholesome popular recreation, administrative integrity, and general orderliness. On the material side, Germany had achieved primacy in the technical and chemical arts, a close-knit and harmonious industrial organization with a productive capacity which enabled her to undersell her British rivals in the markets of the world. The downfall of Germany was an absolute tragedy for the Germans, for without war their industrial achievements would have given them the first place in the world. Right or wrong, Germany's appeal to force cost her the opportunity which comes but once in the history of a nation.

The basis of Japanese imperialism is peculiar. As with all true empires, it is both spiritual and material. It is, however, so special and so narrow that it is difficult to imagine it as a principle of world-dominion. On the material side, Japan offers to Asia the example of "Westernization." She has shown that it is both expedient, possible, and profitable for an Oriental people to adopt and adapt the civilization of the West. This is a tremendous economic achievement, but Westernization is a single process which, once accomplished, merely adds to the number of the modern nations without contributing anything distinctive to the world's economy. On the spiritual side Japan offers even less as a basis for empire. Her political ideology is bound up with the Shinto superstition of emperor-worship, an idea which cannot expand except as the race increases. Shinto is really spiritual seclusion. It is a tribal belief, inculcated by the authorities as a state religion, to embody the principles of reverence and patriotism, and to lead the people to respect the emperor and to be obedient to his will. By its tenets, the Japanese emperor is the lineal descendant of the sun and moon, and for a Japanese subject to refuse to honor the emperor's ancestors is disloyal.

[Shinto] inculcates ideas of the unique sanctity and moral authority of Imperial rescripts, together with special regard for the "peculiar dignity and superiority of the Imperial House of Japan," and the assurance that "the national ideal of Japan is unsurpassed and impregnable." In such a way the protection afforded Japanese institutions by the Tokugawa exclusion policy, which was disrupted by the arrival of the "black ships" of Perry in 1853, is now secured by a psychological, educational program that attempts to strengthen the inner spirit rather than to put a wall of seclusion about the land.[1]

Shinto, ancestor-worship, and the reckless procreation which it engenders, the Samurai code of chivalry and self-effacement—these may be satisfactory moral conceptions for the Japanese, but they are not the broad moral principles which make for permanent or successful empire. The creation of the Japanese empire has, therefore, been achieved primarily through force, and that empire is now maintained by heavy armaments—that fatal principle of violence which has destroyed all empires that have relied on it to counterbalance their own spiritual inadequacies.

AMERICA'S IMPERIAL ADJUNCTS

In considering the phenomenon of American expansion it is immediately evident that ours is a political society of highly acquisitive powers. Our economic and political institutions possess an exquisitely prehensile character which has enabled the United States, in the scant century and a half of its national independence, to assume a powerful and almost paramount economic position in the modern world.

The bare facts of American expansion are impressive. Ours is a story of big figures, rapid growths, unprecedented developments. In 1790 our area was less than 900,000 square miles; today it is nearly 3,750,000 square

[1] D. C. Holtom, *The Political Philosophy of Modern Shinto.*

miles, with an additional 700,000 square miles in outlying possessions. At the first census our population was less than 4,000,000 people; today it is about 120,000,000, with 14,000,000 more in our possessions. In 1850 our national wealth was computed at $7,000,000,000; today it is over $320,000,000,000. In 1790 our foreign trade was $100,000,000; today it is nearly $10,000,000,000, and our annual favorable trade balance amounts to almost $1,000,000,000 a year. Our yearly trade with Europe amounts to $3,500,000,000; we do $2,000,000,000 worth of business each year with both Asia and North America; our South American trade is worth $1,000,000,000.

Figures alone cannot give a proper sense of America's economic importance to the world. We supply one-fifth of all the imports of Great Britain; one-fourth of the imports of Italy, Russia, Japan, the Argentine, Bolivia, Chile, and Brazil; one-half of the imports of Colombia; two-thirds of the imports of Canada, Santo Domingo, Cuba, and Ecuador; three-fourths of all Mexican imports, and four-fifths of the imports of Haiti and Honduras. We buy one-third of the exports of Ceylon, Canada, and Peru; nearly one-half of Japanese exports; half of the exports of British Malaya; three-fourths of the exports of Cuba, Mexico, and the Philippines; and nine-tenths of the exports of Honduras and Panama.

Since the war we have been lending our money abroad at the average rate of $1,000,000,000 a year; in 1927, more than $2,000,000,000 of American money was invested in foreign securities. Not counting the $10,000,-000,000 of war-debts due the United States Government from its former associates in the war against Germany, our private investments abroad amount to about

$13,000,000,000 and bring in about $750,000,000 a year in interest. We have invested $3,000,000,000 in Europe, $4,500,000,000 in Latin America, and $3,000,000,000 in Canada.

Back of this outpouring of money and goods lies America's distinctive economic adjunct, a business system based on two very simple conceptions. The first is the idea of individualism and competition, which has discouraged monopoly, encouraged the rapid development of economic resources, and made for low prices to the consumer. The second is the separation of business and state, which is implicit in the Fourteenth Amendment to the Constitution and which operates to keep business free of Government control and to keep the Government out of business.

Coupled with immense natural resources, this separation has operated to the advantage of American economic life. Five industries produce goods and services worth $1,000,000,000 a year; there are five $2,000,000,000 industries; two $3,000,000,000 industries; two which produce $4,000,000,000, two which produce $5,000,-000,000, and one which produces goods worth $7,000,-000,000 every year. These industries represent a total investment of over $100,000,000,000 and give employment to 11,500,000 workers, while the basic business of farming employs over 10,000,000 people, represents an investment of $60,000,000,000, and produces goods worth $17,000,000,000 annually.

Another factor enters the fabric of American prosperity: the payment of high wages, which makes labor an important element in consumption. Wages are, on the average, double what they were in 1913, though hours of work are less and retail prices are only 50 per cent. higher than the 1913 level. This combination of competition, separation of business from government, and the payment of high wages to the workers, provides the United States with a formidable equipment for economic expansion.

On the political side, the United States disposes of a moral adjunct which is, in its way, as great a contribution to the world as was British parliamentary government and British freedom: it is the principle of autonomous nationalism or self-determination. This is tempered by a system of Federal Government, a balance between the States and the central authority, which is an original contribution to political thought. It has been imitated in the British Dominions and is today affecting the political evolution of Europe in the League of Nations, the British Commonwealth of Nations, and the Russian Union of Soviet Socialist Republics. The whole system is vitalized by the American endorsement of democracy, which has been called "the political form of the humane ideal." The triple principle of self-determination, federalism, and democracy is a moral factor in the expansion of American influence which may become highly important to the world at large. It means that America, unlike the imperial powers of the past, will have no fear of the nationalism which is the disruptive element in empire. American advocacy of Federalism avoids the eternal temptation to "Divide and Conquer!" for the principle of "Unite and Prosper!" Finally, the entire American theory of government is based on the theory of equality and popular sovereignty, which means the renunciation of the principle of autocratic force, the abolition of po-

[31]

litical privilege, and the subordination of the state to the liberty of the individual. The self-governing nations of the world have nothing to fear from the political expressions of American power. American battles are not to be fought by the conscripts of subordinate nations. American citizens outside of the United States are not to enjoy special privileges not shared by the peoples, dependent or otherwise, of the other portions of the world.

In American economic and political institutions resides the power to remake the world in a new pattern. That the process is largely unplanned and unconscious is the most eloquent argument for its ultimate success. America's power will expand only if it is convenient to the world; her civilization will be imitated only if her methods are successful, and her influence over the destinies of the world will be tolerated on the sole condition that she make herself indispensable to the world's peace and welfare.

Chapter III

THE POLITICS OF AMERICAN EXPANSION

AUTONOMOUS NATIONALISM

THE policies of the United States are based on the North American Continent; the principles of American expansion are based on the western hemisphere. These are not metaphors, but facts. In a federal republic, stretching from the Atlantic to the Pacific, embracing every variety of climate and resource, without formidable neighbors and without the restraint of international hostility, policy and principle must be stated in terms of the Continental common denominator, not, as with less extensive or less favored nations, in terms of narrow interest or immediate defense.

The policies of the United States are broad and acquisitive, but they are not exclusively or avowedly designed for aggrandizement. Like all sound political devices, they are as much defensive as they are offensive. They were established in a period of national weakness and were designed, originally, to defend and maintain American interest. In their development they have become susceptible of aggressive motivation. They have, thus, a positive and a negative character, and they represent, in their totality, the political and the economic interests of the western hemisphere.

These principles, for the sake of convenience, may be

summed up in six major policies: autonomous nationalism, the Monroe Doctrine, the freedom of the seas, the open door doctrine, diplomatic disassociation, and the separation of business and state. That the United States has other policies, it would be foolish to deny. We have a Caribbean policy, an eastern Asiatic policy of the integrity of China, an immigration and tariff policy which affect our relations with the rest of the world, and so on. But the six mentioned above are fundamental to the protection and expansion of American interests and institutions.

Our entire political system is based on the principle of autonomous nationalism. This self-determinant principle is, however, qualified by the practical reservation that it is not enough to proclaim independence—the ability to maintain it must be demonstrated. In this reservation lies the chief justification of a principle which would otherwise be wantonly subversive of established political order throughout the world.

The American nation comes by self-government legitimately. The early colonies were English joint-stock companies, and the voting rights of stock-holders underlay the later acceptance of the ideal of self-administration. Before the colonies had been established for three generations, this joint-stock ideal of business began to appear as the ideal of government. James Truslow Adams finds the Rev. John Wise of Massachusetts writing in 1700 his *Vindication of the Government of the New England Churches,* in which the Puritan clergyman anticipates the Declaration of Independence by asserting that government is "the effect of human free-compacts and not of divine institution"; that "all power is originally in the people"; that the only end of government is to promote "the good of every man in all his rights, his life, liberty, estate, honor," and that "it is as plain as daylight, there is no species of government like a democracy to attain this end."

The affirmations of the Declaration of Independence have become hackneyed and platitudinous, but at the time of their enunciation they were shockingly radical. So worn are the phrases that we are inclined to forget that the real basis of our theory of government is contained in the statement that

We hold these truths to be self-evident, that all men are created equal, that they are endowed by their Creator with certain unalienable Rights, that among these are Life, Liberty and the Pursuit of Happiness. That to secure these rights, Governments are instituted among men, deriving their just powers from the consent [not "acquiescence"] of the governed. That whenever any Form of Government becomes destructive of these ends, it is the Right of the People to alter or to abolish it, and to institute new Government, laying its foundation on such principles and organizing its power in such form, as to them shall seem most likely to effect their Safety and Happiness.

But no student of politics can fail to regard the qualification, "that a decent respect for the consideration of mankind requires that they [revolutionists] should declare the causes which impel them"—in this case, the subversion of autonomous institutions by royal authority.

It was upon the basis of the Declaration of Independence that the American federal republic was established, with its—at that time—unique division of powers and its balance between State and Federal government. In this development, three major steps must be noted: The Articles of Confederation, which were in effect a treaty of alliance between the several States; the Constitution of 1789, which subordinated the States to the people in the establishment of a central government; and the Civil War of 1861-65, which attested the permanent and indissoluble character of this union.

The Articles of Confederation, drawn up in 1777, contemplated a "Confederation and Perpetual Union" between the States then in revolt. The essential character of this document, which is that of a treaty, is borne out by the second and third articles:

Article II. Each State retains its sovereignty, freedom and independence, and every power, jurisdiction and right, which is not by this confederation expressly delegated to the United States, in Congress assembled.

Article III. The said States hereby severally enter into a firm league of friendship with each other, for their common defence, the security of their liberties, and their mutual and general welfare, binding themselves to assist each other, against all forces offered to, or attacks made upon, them, or any of them, on account of religion, sovereignty, trade, or any other pretence whatever.

It was, in fact, an American League of Nations. It lasted ten years. In the autumn of 1787, a new Constitution was ratified and declared in force the first Wednesday in March, 1789. The preamble of the new Constitution set forth its popular, as distinct from its diplomatic, character:

We, the people of the United States, in order to form a more perfect Union, establish justice, insure domestic tranquillity, provide for the common defence, promote the general welfare, and secure the blessings of liberty to ourselves and our posterity, do ordain and establish this Constitution for the United States of America.

This Constitution destroyed the old autonomy of the States by providing that "No State shall enter into any treaty, alliance, or confederation" and that "No State shall, without the consent of Congress, lay any duty of tonnage, keep troops or ships of war in time of peace, enter into agreement or compact with another State, or with a foreign power, or engage in war." The whole was freed of the imputation of tyrannical centralization by the so-called "Bill of Rights," the first ten Amendments to the Constitution, adopted in 1791, which established the principle, among others, that "The powers not delegated to the United States by the Constitution, nor prohibited by it to the States, are reserved to the States respectively, or to the people." This, the Tenth Amendment, is the true basis of all subsequent extensions of American sovereignty and political power.

The test of the permanent character of this Union was caused by the secession of the Southern States in 1860 and 1861. The issue was between the theoretical sovereignty of the several States and the actual sovereignty of the American nation. The South Carolina convention, on December 20, 1860, declared that "the union now subsisting between South Carolina and other States under the name of 'The United States of America' is hereby dissolved." And when the Southern Confederacy was established at Montgomery, Alabama, on February 4, 1861, the preamble read, "We, the deputies of the Sovereign and Independent States." But such disruptive principles

[37]

could not stand the test of war. Even in the Confederacy, defense required the abandonment of the principles which had occasioned the need for defense, and the matter was settled at Appomattox Court House early in 1865. The Union is, politically speaking, indissoluble.

The strain of theoretical autonomy, tempered by the practical expediency of Federalism, runs through our entire history and is today, after a century and a half of freedom, the dominant principle of our national life and our international policy.

Before the British Commonwealth of Nations was dreamed of or ever the Russian Soviet Union was conceivable, the United States solved the problem of territorial expansion without harm to its political theory. America's colonies lay within her own borders, at the outset, and by the development of fresh territory into States, she perfected the method of an indefinitely extensible Union. Even the Articles of Confederation contained a clause for the admission of Canada on equal terms, and the Northwest Ordinance of 1787 established, before the Federal Constitution, an equivalent method of expansion for the new territories north of the Ohio River.

This Ordinance extended the provisions of the common law to the territories subject to the United States, established a method of territorial government subject to the jurisdiction of the central government, and provided

for extending the fundamental principles of civil and religious liberty, which form the basis whereon these republics, their laws and constitutions, are erected; to fix and establish those principles as the basis of all laws, constitutions, and governments, which forever hereafter shall be formed in the said territory; to provide, also, for the establishment of States, and permanent government therein, and for their admission to a share in the Federal councils on an equal footing with original States, at as early periods as may be consistent with the general interest.

It was the device embodied in this document which enabled the number of American States to be expanded from fourteen to forty-eight without dislocation of our political institutions or modification of our political theory.

Indeed, it will be seen that the theory of delegated and reserved powers, as embodied in the Constitution and clarified by the Tenth Amendment, makes possible an indefinite development of federative democracy. This principle, as stated in the Platt Amendment to our Treaty with Cuba—delegating certain Cuban powers to the United States and embodying this delegation of powers in the Cuban Constitution—supplies the key to American policy in Central America and the Caribbean.

The issue of autonomous nationalism was brought to the front by the revolt of the Spanish-American colonies. In 1815, the United States was the only republic in the western hemisphere; by 1822, almost all America was free of European control. It was here that the ability to maintain free governments became the qualification of our endorsement of the theory of self-determination. Although the final successful revolt of Latin America began in 1817, it was not until 1822 that Monroe's message to Congress declared that Argentina, Chile, Peru, Colombia, and Mexico, were "in full enjoyment of their independence, of which there was not the most remote prospect of their being deprived," and that they had "a claim to recognition by other powers, which ought not to be resisted." Recognition and diplomatic relations followed with Colombia, Mexico, Chile, Argentina, Brazil, Central America, and Peru, in the next four years, in all but the last two cases, before the promulgation of the Monroe Doctrine. It is apparent, therefore, that the mere declaration of independence does not entitle any state to our recognition, but that the ability to remain independent is the final test of our policy.

This is true even in the case of the recognition and annexation of Texas by the United States. As early as 1827 we tried to purchase Texas from Mexico. Both Adams and Jackson endeavored to buy the territory, but in vain. In 1835, a revolt of Texas was successfully accomplished by a group of colonist-filibusters. In 1837, an American chargé d'affaires was appointed. In 1843, we proposed annexation to the Texas chargé at Washington. In the meantime, France and Great Britain, which had recognized the Republic of Texas, had arranged for an armistice with Mexico and were preparing for a treaty. On March 3, 1845, by authority of a joint resolution of Congress, President Tyler invited Texas into the Union, after it had maintained independence of Mexico ten years.

Similarly, our provocative recognition of Cuba in 1898 was qualified by a disclaimer of annexationist intentions:

The people of the island of Cuba are, and of right ought to be, free and independent. . . . The United States hereby disclaims any disposition or intention to exercise sovereignty, jurisdiction or control over said island except for the pacification thereof, and asserts its determination, when that is accomplished, to leave the government and control of the island to its people.

The annexation of Hawaii affords another instance of the cautious extension of our jurisdiction. In 1893, an

Hawaiian revolution overthrew the native monarchy and established a provisional government. A delegation was sent to Washington to petition for annexation. President Cleveland came into office in time to block the treaty of annexation. He then attempted to reinstate the Queen of Hawaii and informed the provisional government that the Queen should be restored to her throne. President Dole of Hawaii refused and inquired whether American force would be used to overthrow the Hawaiian Republic. On May 31, 1894, the Senate approved Hawaiian independence. Eventually, five years after Hawaii had achieved practical independence, a joint resolution of the House and Senate in 1898 provided for its annexation.

So far, the American doctrine of autonomous nationalism had been used solely as a defensive or an acquisitive device. It remained for the World War to reveal its uses as an offensive weapon. Wilsonian self-determination was best stated in his message to the Provisional Russian Government, on June 8, 1917:

The position of America in this war is so clearly avowed that no man can be excused for mistaking it. She seeks no material profit or aggrandizement of any kind. She is fighting for no advantage or selfish object of her own, but for the liberation of peoples everywhere from the aggressions of autocratic force. . . .

We are fighting for the liberty, the self-government and the undictated development of all peoples, and every feature of the settlement that concludes this war must be conceived and executed for that purpose. . . . No people must be forced under sovereignty under which it does not wish to live. No territory must change hands except for the purpose of securing those who inhabit it a fair chance of life and liberty. No indemnities must be insisted on except those that constitute payment for manifest wrongs done. No readjustments of power must be made except such as will tend to secure the future peace of the world and future welfare and happiness of its peoples.

In January, 1918, the Fourteen Points were laid down, providing, among other things, for autonomous developments in Poland, Austria-Hungary, and Turkey. And on October 5, 1918, when the German Government requested Wilson to end the war, it was on the ground that his principles were in accord with the "general ideas cherished by the new German Government and with it the overwhelming majority of our people." This was after Wilson had previously rejected the Pope's peace message on the ground that "we cannot take the word of the present rulers of Germany as a guarantee of anything that is to endure, unless explicitly supported by such conclusive evidence of the will and purpose of the German people themselves as the other peoples of the world would be justified in accepting." The German Republic is, accordingly, the creation of American diplomacy.

Nor was Germany the only republic to emerge from the cauldron of self-determinant nationalism thus seasoned by Wilsonian principles. Czecho-Slovakia, Poland, Latvia, Lithuania, Esthonia, Finland, Armenia, Georgia, and the Irish Free State—not to forget the republics of Austria and Hungary and the federal kingdom of the Jugo-Slavs—were among the fruits of this American policy. It is important to note that of these, only one— Czecho-Slovakia—was recognized before the armistice, and then only as an hostile act against a country with which we were in a state of war. Recognition of the republics carved from former Russian territory was conditioned by prior Russian recognition of these same republics. Georgia was never recognized, and our recognition of Armenia was purely *de facto*. In the case of British dominions and dependencies, our attitude was dependent upon British initiative. Thus recognition of Egypt came only after the Anglo-Egyptian Treaty establishing the Kingdom of Egypt. Relations with the Irish Free State and with Canada followed the reception at Washington of Irish and Canadian ministers accredited by King George.

While encouraging the spread of autonomous nationalism in Europe, our policy has been to improve the quality of republican institutions in this hemisphere in an effort to keep democracy respectable. Thus, as early as 1913, we find Colonel House writing to Ambassador Page at London:

It is to be the policy of this Administration henceforth not to recognize any Central American government that is not formed along constitutional lines. Anything else would be a makeshift policy. As you know, revolutions and assassinations in order to obtain control of governments are instituted almost solely for the purpose of loot and when it is found that these methods will not bring the desired results, they will cease. The President [Wilson] also feels strongly in regard to foreign financial interests seeking to control these unstable governments through concessions and otherwise. This, too, he is determined to discourage as far as it is possible to do so.

Wilson's moral mandate for the maintenance of respectable republics was elaborated ten years later by Secretary of State Hughes into the reasonable support of established and constitutional governments which marks the present stage of development of our policy. It carries with it a self-denying clause, as first stated by Wilson in his speech at Mobile, on October 27, 1913:

> The United States will never again seek one additional foot of territory by conquest. She will devote herself to showing that she knows how to make honorable and fruitful use of the territory she has, and she must regard it as one of the duties of friendship to see that from no quarter are material interests made superior to human liberty and national opportunity.

In the Central American Treaty, signed at Washington early in 1923, under the aegis of the State Department, it is affirmed by the five signatories that

> they declare that every act, disposition or measure which alters the constitutional organization in any of them is to be deemed a menace to the peace of said Republics, whether it proceeds from any public power or from their private citizens.
>
> Consequently, the Governments of the Contracting Parties will not recognize any other Government which may come into power in any of the five Republics through a *coup d'état* or a revolution against a recognized Government.

This principle, of supporting established constitutional governments, is the key to American policy toward Latin America since 1913, and is already imposing a further duty—not yet formulated as a policy—to see that the republics supported effectively guarantee the practice of democratic methods in their domestic politics. We have begun to supervise elections in Central America. We may be compelled, eventually, forcibly to inculcate self-government throughout the western hemisphere. Page called it "shooting men into self-government."

The Politics of American Expansion

Although really secondary to our doctrine of self-determination, the Monroe Doctrine is generally considered our major foreign policy. It is, in essence, simply a declaration of our desire that the Americas should be for the Americans. It was adopted to forestall the threat by the allied powers of Europe to reconquer the revolted Spanish colonies for Spain. Having learned that England was also opposed to the forcible restoration of Spanish rule in the Americas, the United States felt free to proclaim as a policy what had already become a deep-seated motive in American diplomacy: that the western hemisphere should be politically disassociated from Europe. Inasmuch as European wars had already involved the American colonies in no less than six struggles, the expediency of this disassociation was obvious. Knowledge that he would be supported by the naval power of England emboldened President Monroe to deliver his message to Congress on December 2, 1823, in which he laid down the following principles:

the occasion has been judged proper for asserting as a principle in which the rights and interests of the United States are involved, that the American continents, by the free and independent condition which they have assumed and maintain, are henceforth not to be considered as subjects for future colonization by any European powers. . . . In the wars of the European powers in matters relating to themselves we have never taken any part, nor does it comport with our policy so to do. It is only when our rights are invaded or seriously menaced that we resent injuries or make preparation for our defense.

With the movements in this hemisphere we are, of necessity,

more immediately connected, and by causes which must be obvious to all enlightened and impartial observers. The political system of the allied powers [the Holy Alliance] is essentially different in this respect from that of America. This difference proceeds from that which exists in their respective Governments. And to the defense of our own, which has been achieved by the loss of so much blood and treasure, and matured by the wisdom of their most enlightened citizens, and under which we have enjoyed unexampled felicity, this whole nation is devoted.

We owe it, therefore, to candor, and to the amicable relations existing between the United States and those powers, to declare that we should consider any attempt on their part to extend their system to any portion of this hemisphere as dangerous to our peace and safety. With the existing colonies or dependencies of any European power we have not interfered and shall not interfere. But with the Governments who have declared their independence, and maintained it, and whose independence we have, on great consideration and on just principles, acknowledged, we could not view any interposition for the purpose of oppressing them, or controlling in any other manner their destiny, by any European power, in any other light than as the manifestation of an unfriendly disposition towards the United States. . . .

Our policy in regard to Europe, which was adopted at an early stage of the wars which have so long agitated that quarter of the globe, nevertheless remains the same, which is, not to interfere in the internal concerns of any of its powers; to consider the Government *de facto* as the legitimate Government for us; to cultivate friendly relations with it, and to preserve those relations by a frank, firm, and manly policy, meeting, in all instances, the just claims of every power; submitting to injuries from none.

But in regard to these continents, circumstances are eminently and conspicuously different. It is impossible that the allied powers should extend their political system to any portion of either continent without endangering our peace and happiness; nor can any one believe that our Southern brethren, if left to themselves,

[46]

would adopt it of their own accord. It is equally impossible, therefore, that we should behold such interposition, in any form, with indifference.

This is the substance of the Monroe Doctrine as it exists today, a one-sided statement of interest conditioned on American abstention from European affairs. Thrice since the original emergency has it been invoked to protect Latin-American states from Europe: once in 1865, when Secretary Seward demanded unconditional withdrawal of the French troops from Mexico; once in 1895, when President Cleveland urged arbitration of a boundary dispute between Venezuela and Great Britain; and once in 1902, when, with Great Britain, Germany and Italy blockaded Venezuela, Roosevelt assembled the American fleet and gave Germany twenty-four hours in which to arbitrate the issue.

Unfortunately for the peace of mind of foreign critics of American policy, many executive actions have been interpreted as extensions of the Monroe Doctrine. Thus J. W. Garner in his highly partisan *American Foreign Policies* voices the discontent of those who object to any American foreign policy of an independent character, in describing these "extensions":

No Latin-American state may voluntarily transfer its territory by sale, lease, or gift to any non-American state without the consent of the United States; in case of a boundary dispute between an American state and a European power possessing territories in America, which cannot be settled by diplomacy, the United States must be the virtual arbiter of the dispute; no non-American "corporation or association" may acquire a harbor on the American continent, if it is so situated that its occupation for military or naval purposes might threaten the communications or safety of the United States and if such corporation or association is subject to "the practical power of control" of such non-American government; that the United States does not look with favor upon the granting by Latin-American states of economic concessions and franchises to non-American capitalists or companies to exploit their resources; that the United States has a "right" under the Monroe doctrine to intervene in the domestic affairs of Latin-American states to prevent European powers from themselves intervening for the purpose of obtaining redress for wrongs to their nationals (in short, to exercise a sort of "international police power" over them); that, in case of internal political strife and revolution in a Latin-American state, the United States has a right to support, by military and naval power, the government which it has recognized as the legitimate one; that when, in the judgment of the United States, a Latin-American state is unable to maintain domestic order and discharge its international obligations the United States may assume financial and political control of such state; and, finally, the disposition to deduce from the Monroe doctrine the special privilege of the United States to treat certain Latin-American states as an exclusive preserve for North American economic exploitations.

This is a fair summary of all the evil that has been imputed to the Monroe Doctrine by other nations. It is, however, inaccurate to describe all American policies or actions toward Latin America as manifestations of the Monroe Doctrine. Thus Roosevelt, in 1904, did not make any reference whatever to the Monroe Doctrine in laying down the specific principle that

If a nation shows that it knows how to act with reasonable efficiency and decency in social and political matters, if it keeps order and pays its obligations, it need fear no interference from the United States. Chronic wrongdoing, or an impotence which

[48]

results in a general lowering of the ties of civilized society . . .
may force the United States, however reluctantly, in flagrant
cases . . . to the exercise of an international police power.

This is not the Monroe Doctrine; it is a simple statement that the United States, under certain circumstances,
might combat anarchy and impotence. Under this general
"international police power," the United States has intervened thrice in Cuba, five times in Panama, five times in
the Dominican Republic, six times in Nicaragua, twice in
Mexico, once in Haiti, six times in Honduras, once in Colombia and once in Costa Rica. This summary includes
every occasion on which diplomatic, military, and political
pressure was brought to bear on neighboring governments
for the purpose of promoting or safeguarding general
American interests. To the European and the Latin American, this is the Monroe Doctrine; actually it has as much
to do with the Monroe Doctrine as British suppression of
the African slave trade had to do with England's naval
policy.

If one would find the true course of the Monroe Doctrine, it must be sought in the record of the Pan-American
Union and the effort to establish an "American system"
of international law and political organization in the
western hemisphere. The first Pan-American Conference
was held at Washington in 1889, the latest at Havana in
1928. At the end of the first conference, Secretary Blaine
made clear its character by asserting that the abolition of
war and the substitution of arbitration was "the first and
great fruit of the International American Conference."
Since that day no wars have been waged between the
major American republics.

Between the ultimate ideal of inter-American coöperation and the practical necessities of American "police duty" in the Caribbean region, lies a middle course which expresses itself in the growing tendency of Argentina, Brazil, and Chile to coöperate with the United States in the broader fields of inter-American stability. Thus, the "A.B.C. Powers" offered to mediate between the United States and Mexico in 1914; as a result they joined the United States in urging Huerta to leave Mexico. So Pershing's Sonora expedition of 1916 was undertaken with their full approval. President Wilson in a speech to Latin-American journalists on June 7, 1918, carried the principle still further, in urging "a common guarantee, that all of us will sign, of political independence and territorial integrity. Let us agree that if any one of us, the United States included, violates the political independence of any of the others, all the others will jump on her."

This self-denying attitude on the part of the United States, coupled with repeated pledges to seek to annex no further American territory, has encouraged an illusive sentiment for the "mutualization" of the Monroe Doctrine, pledging the United States not to intervene in the domestic affairs of Latin-American countries without prior consultation with other Latin-American countries. It was disclosed at the Havana Conference in 1928, however, that Latin America was so split into hostile and discordant groups that consultation would serve no practical purpose save to make action impossible. An alternative tendency, whereby Mexico shall join Argentina, Brazil, Chile, and the United States in regulating inter-American affairs, seems to be more immediately practicable. In any event, the Monroe Doctrine is not involved, for that is a declaration which any American power is free to make—namely, that European or Asiatic interference with the self-governing nations of the western hemisphere is an unfriendly act to any and all of the American republics. America for the Americans, Europe for the Europeans—that is the Monroe Doctrine.

Chapter IV

AMERICAN COMMERCIAL DOCTRINES

THE FREEDOM OF THE SEAS

If the political principles of American diplomacy repose on self-determination and the Monroe Doctrine, our commercial policy is intimately bound up with the ideal of the freedom of the seas.

This doctrine is most explicitly stated in that Magna Charta of American commercial policy, the Treaty of Amity and Commerce negotiated with France and ratified by Congress on May 4, 1778. Article XXIII of this instrument sets forth, in the stately diplomatic language of the period, that

It shall be lawful for all and singular the subjects of the Most Christian King, and the citizens, people and inhabitants of the said United States, to sail with their ships with all manner of liberty and security, no distinction being made who are the proprietors of the merchandizes laden thereon, from any port to the places of those who now are or hereafter shall be at enmity with the Most Christian King or the United States. It shall likewise be lawful for the subjects and inhabitants aforesaid to sail with the ships and merchandizes afore-mentioned, and to trade with the same liberty and security from the places, ports and havens of those who are enemies of both or either party, without any opposition or disturbance whatsoever, not only directly from the places of the enemy afore-mentioned to neutral places, but also from one place belonging to an enemy to another place belonging to an enemy, whether they be under the jurisdiction of the same

Prince or under several. And it is hereby stipulated that free ships shall also give a freedom to goods, and that everything shall be deemed to be free and exempt which shall be found on board the ships belonging to the subjects of either of the confederates, although the whole lading or any part thereof should appertain to the enemies of either, contraband goods being always excepted. It is also agreed in like manner that the same liberty be extended to persons who are on board a free ship, with this effect, that although they be enemies to both or either party, they are not to be taken out of that free ship, unless they are soldiers and in actual service of the enemies.

This doctrine, that "a free ship makes free goods," has been the contention of the American Government from the earliest stage of our national independence. It was a principle forced on us by the restraints imposed upon our commerce by the Napoleonic wars. While conceding the right to close blockade and of contraband, we have steadfastly asserted that a belligerent has not the right to seize goods of enemy origin or consigned to an enemy, except contraband, upon a neutral ship.

The freedom of the seas is, therefore, a principle which is put into effect only by the existence of a state of war, there being no occasion for its enforcement in time of peace. In practice, however, the American Government has observed that the respect paid to our interpretation of this doctrine is in direct proportion to our own naval power. Infringements upon our lawful commerce in time of war have, accordingly, provoked naval construction by the American Government, and naval power has slowly won a hearing for the principles underlying our interpretation of maritime rights.

The origin of the American navy, in fact, was the

[53]

treaty of 1793 between Portugal and Algiers (negotiated by the British Consul-General), opening the Atlantic to Barbary pirates who were subsidized to prey on American commerce. On March 27, 1794, the President signed a bill for the construction of six frigates, and the policy of protecting our commerce by force, then undertaken, was pursued until, in 1815, we compelled the Algerian pirates to sue for peace, having previously broken the power of the Bey of Tripoli. The destruction of the Barbary corsairs was the first contribution of American naval policy to the world's commercial stability.

At the same period the French, who were at that time our allies, began to seize American vessels, leading to a naval conflict between the United States and France which was ended by a treaty in 1801 after three years of sea warfare. With Great Britain we were not so fortunate. By the imposition of sundry restraints upon American commerce, "paper blockades," impressment of American seamen, and capture of American vessels, the British Navy all but strangled American trade with Europe during the Napoleonic wars. "In the Orders in Council of November 11, 1807, so far as Britain could effect it the ruin of American commerce was decreed."[1] The American Government attempted retaliation through an embargo, which was ruinous to American interests but not fatal to British trade. Neglect to construct a formidable navy, with the British fleet in undisputed command of the seas, meant that when war was declared on Great Britain in 1812, American commerce was doomed. American warships won isolated engagements with British vessels, but the British won the naval campaign and were enabled to

[1] Sears, *History of American Foreign Relations.*

[54]

raid the American coasts, burn the Capitol at Washington, and undertake the invasion of Louisiana, unopposed at sea.

The long period of peace which followed the Napoleonic wars left the question of the freedom of the seas an academic theory. It was not until 1856, after the Crimean War, that the powers of Europe drew up the famous Declaration of Paris, the first codification of sea law, with the following provisions:

1. Privateering is, and remains, abolished.
2. The neutral flag covers enemy's goods, with the exception of contraband of war.
3. Neutral goods, with the exception of contraband of war, are not liable to capture under enemy's flag.
4. Blockade, in order to be binding, must be effective; that is to say, maintained by a force sufficient really to prevent access to the coast of the enemy.

This Declaration was accepted by all the powers of the world, except the United States, which objected to the abandonment of privateering so long as the principle that "free ships make free goods" was not affirmed. However, on the outbreak of the Civil War the American Government was prepared to ratify, when, at the last moment, the British Government qualified the convention with a reservation which was unacceptable to Washington:

In affixing his signature to the convention of this day between Her Majesty the Queen of Great Britain and Ireland and the United States the Earl Russell declares by order of Her Majesty that Her Majesty does not intend thereby to undertake any engagement which shall have any bearing direct or indirect on the internal differences now prevailing in the United States.

In other words, the British Government was not prepared to forbid privateering to the Southern Confederacy.

In consequence, Southern privateers were fitted out in British shipyards, and one of them, the *Alabama*, put to sea over the protests of the American minister at London. They virtually swept American shipping from the seas. Finally, by the Treaty of Washington (May 8, 1871), Britain consented to arbitrate the *Alabama* claims. By the Geneva award of 1872, Great Britain was condemned to pay $15,000,000 damages for the ruin of American shipping by British-equipped Confederate cruisers.

If the Declaration of Paris was useless to America in an emergency of her own making, it proved no stronger than its weakest link—the definition of contraband—in the emergency of the World War. The Declaration of London, drawn up by a conference of naval experts in 1908 after the Second Hague Conference, endeavored to define contraband, but its findings were not ratified by any Great Power.

In 1914, when war broke out, the American Government tried to hold Great Britain to the Declaration of London, but its effort was fruitless, and the next three years saw persistent violation of American maritime rights by both sides in the European conflict. The first American protest to Great Britain was made on October 30, 1914. To German efforts to dissuade America from shipping munitions to the Allies, our Government replied, "It is the business of a belligerent operating on the high seas, not the duty of a neutral, to prevent contraband from reaching an enemy." After the sinking of the *Lusitania*, in May, 1915, the American government proclaimed that

"The rights of neutrals in time of war are based upon principle, not upon expediency, and the principles are immutable. It is the duty and obligation of belligerents to find a way to adapt the new circumstances to them." Nothing availed. In January, 1915, Great Britain declared grain and flour conditional contraband. United States mails were searched, business correspondence ransacked, checks and money orders impounded, and business secrets explored, by the agents of the British blockade.

The answer, as a hundred years before, was the expansion of the American navy. The 1916 program contemplated the construction within three years of a battle-fleet ostensibly able to cross the Pacific and to maintain station in eastern Asiatic waters, and had the program been completed after the war it would have given us what Wilson loosely termed "incomparably the most adequate navy in the world"—naval supremacy by 1925.

This supremacy was abandoned at the Washington Conference in 1922, when America destroyed fifteen new battleships, as against seven new Japanese and four new British battleships. For five years no effort was made by the United States to engage in naval building, until the failure of the Conference at Geneva made it evident that the other parties to the Washington Conference would not scrap their navies to correspond with the reduced American fleet. Then a determined effort was made by the General Board of the American navy to launch the first five-year section of a twenty-year building program, to cost $2,500,000,000, designed to give the United States a well-balanced fleet, especially strong in fast, heavy cruisers.

At the same time, the American mercantile marine had been reorganized and expanded, having risen from 5,893,000 tons in 1915 to 14,879,000 in 1926, of which nearly 8,000,000 were engaged in foreign trade. Although slightly reduced in gross tonnage and relative importance since 1923, the American merchant marine is still a formidable element in the world's trade and a valuable adjunct to our commercial and naval policy. Half the vessels using the Panama Canal are of American registry; about a third of our total foreign trade is carried in American bottoms. When one considers that in 1913 our total mercantile marine (lake, coastwise, and foreign) was smaller than our present merchant fleet engaged in foreign trade alone, and that before the war less than a tenth of our foreign trade was carried in American ships, it is obvious that a mercantile revolution has taken place.

For the events of the last European war have forced Americans to the conclusion that the principle of the freedom of the seas, to be effective, must be institutional. It presupposes an American merchant fleet capable of carrying American goods without deference to the shipping facilities of other commercial powers, and it also presupposes an American navy strong enough to protect American trade and American merchant vessels from injury or unlawful restraint by other naval forces. The creation, the maintenance, and the appropriate expansion of the American merchant marine and of the American navy is creating the only institution by which the doctrine of the freedom of the seas can be justified and enforced. It is this sentiment which underlies the entire naval policy of the United States.

American Commercial Doctrines

THE OPEN DOOR DOCTRINE

It is generally supposed that the open door doctrine originated with American diplomacy under John Hay. In his circular telegram of July 3, 1900, Hay declared that the United States, in the negotiations regarding China, desired

to seek a solution which may bring about permanent safety and peace to China, preserve Chinese territorial and administrative entity, protect all rights guaranteed to friendly Powers by treaty and international law, and safeguard for the world the principle of equal and impartial trade with all parts of the Chinese Empire.

Hay's "principle of equal and impartial trade" received the title of the Open Door.

Actually the policy underlying it dates from the beginning of American diplomacy, as the "most favored nation" principle, and had been a traditional American policy. The object of the Open Door is simply to insure that the merchants of one nation do not receive special or undue privileges in the territory of another, weaker nation. The "most favored nation" principle simply demands that no favors be granted to other nations which are not shared equally by the United States. The two principles, taken together, are the foundation of American commercial policy. For it is useless to promulgate a theory of the freedom of the seas, to operate merchant shipping, and to maintain naval power, if American merchandise is liable to discriminations in favor of the merchandise of other exporting powers.

The Treaty of Amity and Commerce with France in 1778 established the principles of American commercial policy which, with slight modifications, are valid today. The object of the treaty being to establish "in an equitable and permanent manner" the rules governing the commerce of the two countries,

His Most Christian Majesty and the said United States have judged that the said end could not be better obtained than by taking for the basis of their agreement the most perfect equality and reciprocity, and by carefully avoiding all those burdensome preferences which are usually sources of debate, embarrassment and discontent. . . .

The two parties, therefore, in the second article of this fundamental document, agree

mutually not to grant any particular favour to other nations in respect of commerce and navigation, which shall not immediately become common to the other party, who shall enjoy the same favour, freely, if the concession was freely made, or on allowing the same compensation, if the concession was conditional.

This stipulation is the very heart of American commercial policy.

The entire bent of this policy is against special privilege in any form. Competition on fair terms was all that we desired. For a century and a half we maintained the most favored nation principle on a reciprocal basis: that is, for special concessions to one party we demanded equivalent compensation from any nations desiring to share equally in the reduction of duties. The Fordney-McCumber Tariff Act of 1922 eliminated the practice of reciprocity from our commercial relations, thereby imposing a new policy upon our diplomacy.

Since 1922, therefore, the United States has reversed

its traditional policy and insists on interpreting all "most favored nation" treaties as unconditional. Under the old policy, concessions had to be mutual; under the new policy, concessions are automatic and special or reciprocal agreements are no exception, for the "most favored nation" clause entitles the United States to share in the benefits of a tariff reduction without rendering compensation. In consequence, we now enjoy unconditional "most favored nation" privileges in our treaties with Albania, Brazil, Czecho-Slovakia, the Dominican Republic, Egypt, Estonia, Finland, Germany, Greece, Guatemala, Haiti, Honduras, Hungary, Latvia, Lithuania, Morocco, Nicaragua, Poland, Roumania, Spain, Turkey, and Salvador. Our former conditional treaties are now regarded as unconditional—save with Cuba, whose special political relation to us is recognized in a mild reciprocity treaty—and in the case of France, which is the only European power, apart from Russia, which has failed to negotiate with the United States a commercial treaty based on the unconditional "most favored nation" principle.

The open door doctrine is, in practice, nothing but insistence on the "most favored nation" idea in dealings with oriental or dependent states. The change in the status of trade occasioned by Europe's partition of Africa and her forcible imposition of commercial relations on China caused anxiety lest these changes should result in a deliberate discrimination in favor of European as against American commerce.

The very fact that the United States followed Great Britain in China—"crawled behind British guns," as the contemptuous phrase still runs among the "old China hands"—supplied our competitors with a reason for not regarding American interests too seriously. However, the United States more than evened the commercial score by her success in opening Japan, in 1854, and Korea, in 1882, to the commerce of the world. If America followed Europe in securing commercial privileges in China, Europe followed America in securing equivalent privileges in Japan. As a strict matter of fact, the open door doctrine was first definitely called into play well before 1842, when the British imposed the Treaty of Nanking on the Chinese Government. In Formosa, Madagascar, and elsewhere it had already become obvious that American diplomacy must oppose the effort of European commercial interests to obtain a privileged position in trade.

The incident which crystallized our traditional open door policy into an international doctrine was the so-called "Battle of Concessions" in the Far East, when Europe, for the ten years following the defeat of China by Japan, attempted to divide the Chinese empire into a set of European spheres of influence. Hay's doctrine was invoked to combat the certain economic consequences of this tendency. He secured the assent of the Powers to the open door principle, and in 1922 the obligation to maintain the principle of "economic liberty without inequality" was accepted in the Nine-Power Treaty by Japan, Europe, and by the Chinese government itself.

Since then, with the League of Nations mandates, American diplomacy has secured "complete economic, commercial, and industrial equality" in Africa and the Near East. Only in the Pacific has the open door principle been discarded by the League powers. Thus New Zealand maintains a tariff preference in Samoa, while on the island of Nauru there is a British monopoly of phosphates. The United States did not receive "most favored nation" status in the German and Turkish territories conquered during the war, until 1925. Years of diplomacy eventually succeeded in achieving a group of treaties with France, Belgium, and Great Britain, in which these countries recognized America's claim to the open door as based on the fact that

the United States of America, by participating in the war against Germany, contributed to her defeat and to the renunciation of her rights and titles over her oversea possessions. . . ."

This formula was embodied in the treaties with France over the Cameroons and Syria, with Belgium over East Africa, and with Great Britain over Palestine. It is of interest to note that it is not embodied in the treaties with Great Britain over East Africa, the Cameroons, or Togoland. In the case of Iraq the United States has stated formally to the British Government that upon the conclusion of a Tripartite Treaty "with respect to the rights of the United States and of its nationals in Iraq," it would "recognize Iraq as an independent state." This was subsequent to the disposal of the oil resources of Iraq.

Events in contemporary China and Manchuria have kept the Far Eastern open door ajar. The principle of commercial equality is a counsel of perfection which has little practical bearing on conditions in a land ravaged by banditry and disorganized by civil warfare. Through diplomatic and financial pressure, the American ideal has been underwritten by the Great Powers, but every effort to translate it into action—whether in 1909, when Knox endeavored to internationalize the Manchurian railways, or in 1928, when a partner of J. P. Morgan and Company proposed a loan to help the Japanese operate the same Manchurian railways from which they had excluded American capital twenty years before—has failed to make the open door more than a pious hope. For no matter what political or commercial undertakings are subscribed to, their execution depends entirely upon the outcome of the disorders in China.

In the future, the American doctrine of commercial equality—expressed in the open door and "most favored nation" principle—will depend less upon its economic justice than upon American power and the extent to which American power is expressed in American policy. As formulated, the open door is only the aspiration of a weak nation; American ability to substantiate it as the policy of a strong nation will be the test of its ultimate fitness.

Chapter V

TWO DIPLOMATIC SAFETY-VALVES

DIPLOMATIC DISASSOCIATION

THE support of such bold, far-reaching policies as self-determination and the Monroe Doctrine, on the political, and freedom of the seas and the open door, on the commercial, side might be mischievous and provocative were it not for the adoption of two equally broad principles in our international conduct: that of diplomatic disassociation, which prevents the irresponsible exploitation of self-determination and Monroeism, and that of the separation of business and state, which protects our commercial relations with the world from the diseases attendant on concession-hunting diplomacy.

The policy of diplomatic disassociation—the avoidance of entangling alliances—is the most misunderstood of all our policies. It contemplates no isolation, merely a detachment; no Oriental exclusiveness, merely political insularity; it does not spell refusal to deal with the world; merely refusal to deal with the world on the basis of national favoritism. Far from prohibiting alliances, it specifically admits their occasional desirability. It simply means that America has scrapped the traditional European methods of alliances, counter-alliances, ententes and enmities, and the balance of power which these methods involve. It is, moreover, a policy which minimizes inter-

[65]

nal discord arising from the composite national origins of our population.

The defensive character of this doctrine was clearly established by Washington in his Farewell Address of 1796:

> As avenues to foreign influence in innumerable ways, such attachments [devotion to a favorite nation] are peculiarly alarming to the truly enlightened and independent patriot. How many opportunities do they afford to tamper with domestic factions, to practise the arts of seduction, to mislead public opinion, to influence or awe the public councils!

It was in this Address that the principle of disassociation as a national policy was first laid down:

> The great rule of conduct for us in regard to foreign nations is, in extending our commercial relations to have with them as little *political* connection as possible. So far as we have formed engagements let them be fulfilled with perfect good faith. Here let us stop.
>
> Europe has a set of primary interests which to us have none or a very remote relation. Hence she must be engaged in frequent controversies, the cause of which are essentially foreign to our concerns. Hence, therefore, it must be unwise in us to implicate ourselves by artificial ties in the ordinary vicissitudes of her politics or the ordinary combinations of her friendships or enmities.
>
> Our detached and distant situation invites and enables us to pursue a different course. If we remain one people, under an efficient government, the period is not far off when we may defy material injury from external annoyance; when we may take such an attitude as will cause the neutrality we may at any time resolve upon to be scrupulously respected; when belligerent nations, under the impossibility of making acquisitions upon us,

will not lightly hazard the giving us provocation; when we may choose peace or war, as our interest, guided by justice, shall counsel.

Why forego the advantages of so peculiar a situation? Why quit our own to stand upon foreign ground? Why, by interweaving our destiny with that of any part of Europe, entangle our peace and prosperity in the toils of European ambition, rivalship, interest, humor, or caprice?

It is our true policy to steer clear of permanent alliances with any portion of the foreign world, so far, I mean, as we are now at liberty to do it; for let me not be understood as capable of patronizing infidelity to existing engagements. I hold the maxim no less applicable to public than to private affairs that honesty is always the best policy. I repeat, therefore, let those engagements be observed in their genuine sense. But in my opinion it is unnecessary and would be unwise to extend them.

Taking care always to keep ourselves by suitable establishments on a respectable defensive posture, we may safely trust to temporary alliances for extraordinary emergencies.

Washington is generally considered as the founder of the conservative party in American politics; his principle of diplomatic disassociation is, however, equally endorsed by the founder of the Democratic Party. Thomas Jefferson in his First Inaugural Address, in 1801, coined the phrase which is usually attributed to Washington.

About to enter, fellow-citizens, on the exercise of duties which comprehend everything dear and valuable to you, it is proper you should understand what I deem the essential principles of our Government, and consequently those which ought to shape its Administration. I will compress them within the narrowest compass they will bear, stating the general principle, but not all its limitations. Equal and exact justice to all men, of whatever state or persuasion, religious or political; *peace, commerce, and honest friendship with all nations, entangling alliances with none.* . . . These principles form the bright constellation which has gone before us and guided our steps through an age of revolution and reformation. The wisdom of our sages and blood of our heroes have been devoted to their attainment. They should be the creed of our political faith, the text of civic instruction, the touchstone by which to try the services of those we trust; and should we wander from them in moments of error or of alarm, let us hasten to retrace our steps and to regain the road which alone leads to peace, liberty, and safety.

Avoidance of diplomatic entanglements is, therefore, a non-partisan theory, and one which has been maintained through many vicissitudes. Since the abrogation of its Revolutionary Treaty of Alliance with France, the United States, while participating in many international undertakings and in three European wars, has never signed an alliance.

Extraordinary efforts were made by our statesmen to avoid being drawn into the Napoleonic conflicts. Washington, Adams, Jefferson, and Madison alike tried to steer clear of European complications. Washington negotiated an unpopular treaty with England to preserve the peace. Adams enforced the drastic Alien and Sedition Laws to prevent subversion of American neutrality. Jefferson attempted to combat the Napoleonic decrees and the British Orders in Council against American commerce by the ruinous Embargo and Non-Intercourse Acts. It was in vain. The impressment of American seamen, the seizure of American ships, British incitement of the Indians, and the profitable purchase of Louisiana from the French, inclined our policy to favor Napoleon. Eventually we were drawn into the war and paid for it by a disastrous and galling impotence in the face of British sea-power.

Subsequent to the War of 1812, an effort was made to draw us into the web of Continental policy in the shape of an invitation from Tsar Alexander I in 1818 to join the Holy Alliance. To this embarrassing overture, John Quincy Adams, the Secretary of State, replied:

To stand in firm and cautious independence of all entanglements in the European system has been a cardinal point of their [the United States'] policy under every administration of their government from the peace of 1783 to this day. . . . In proportion as the importance of the United States increases in the eyes of others, the difficulty of maintaining this system, and the temptations to depart from it, increase and multiply with it. . . . As a general declaration of principles . . . the United States not only give their hearty assent to the articles of the Holy Alliance, but will be the most earnest and conscientious in observing them. But . . . for the repose of Europe as well as of America, the European and American political systems should be kept as separate and distinct from each other as possible.

It was John Quincy Adams who, five years later, endeavored to establish in the Monroe Doctrine a permanent "American System" of international politics distinct from that of Europe. The principle had been asserted, however, as early as 1808, when Jefferson opposed the tendency on the part of Great Britain to secure dominance over the revolted Spanish colonies:

If they [the Spanish colonies] succeed, we shall be well satisfied to see Cuba and Mexico remain in their present dependence but very unwilling to see them in that of either France or England, politically or commercially. . . . We consider their interests and ours as the same, and that the object of both must be to exclude all the European influence from this hemisphere.

[69]

The United States, however, lacked the power and prestige to make the Monroe Doctrine the basis for an American System, and the possibility was deferred for sixty-six years—until Blaine created the Pan-American Union.

The Spanish-American War of 1898 provided the first test of American power as independent of that of Europe. When the *Maine* incident made war inevitable, the Vatican intervened on behalf of peace with Spain, and a six-power protest, signed by Germany, Austria-Hungary, France, Italy, Russia, and Great Britain, advised us not to attack the Spanish Empire. We found, however, that in the conflict we could count on England's friendship. Ambassador Hay wrote from London:

I do not know whether you especially value the friendship and sympathy of this country. I think it important and desirable in the present state of things, as it is the only European country whose sympathies are not openly against us. We will not waste time in discussing whether the origin of this policy is wholly selfish or not. Its existence is beyond question. . . . If we wanted it—which, of course, we do not—we could have the practical assistance of the British Navy.

German resentment at our acquisition of the Philippines strengthened this sentiment into a firm Anglo-American friendship, which lasted from 1898 till the outbreak of the Mexican troubles in 1912. During this period Roosevelt worked in informal partnership with Great Britain in the general interest of world peace. The first Anglo-Japanese Alliance of 1902 included the United States as a silent partner and insured American support of Japan in the Russo-Japanese War. The Treaty of Portsmouth

(1905), negotiated as a result of Roosevelt's mediation, was "the first effort made by the United States to stand as an equal at the side of the great nations of other continents." The Algeciras Conference of 1906 was held as a result of Roosevelt's pressure on France and led Ambassador Jusserand to remark:

It is the simple and literal truth to say that in my judgment we owe it to you more than to any other man that the year which has closed has not seen a war between France and Germany, which, had it begun, would probably have extended to take in a considerable portion of the world.

The second Hague Conference, in 1908, was in reality called by Roosevelt. In a word, it had been demonstrated that the United States could play its part in world politics without recourse to alliances and favoritism.

The history of the World War showed, however, that disassociation was no final guarantee against becoming involved in European quarrels. In 1914 Colonel House was sent to Europe on a mission to stave off the war which was clearly impending. He failed, and Wilson was forced back to a restatement of American disinterestedness:

I venture, therefore, my fellow countrymen, to speak a solemn word of warning to you against that deepest, most subtle, most essential breach of neutrality which may spring out of partisanship, out of passionately taking sides. The United States must be neutral in fact as well as in name during these days that are to try men's souls. We must be impartial in thought as well as in action, must put a curb upon our sentiments as well as upon every transaction that might be construed as a preference of one party to the struggle before another.

[71]

America did not protest the violation of Belgium and did not concern itself with any of the incidents of the German and British blockades save as they impinged upon American interests. In 1916 a second confidential American peace mission requested a statement of belligerent aims and suggested that the United States might help the side which put forward the best case. And when German intrigues against us in Mexico and Japan, coupled with the German submarine war, had driven us to war, even then we fought only as an associate, not as an ally, of the Entente Powers.

When the war ended, Wilson hoped through the League of Nations to make impossible a similar jeopardy to American interests arising from European quarrels. His original conception of the League was similar to that of the American Federal Constitution. But the League, from the start and even with the United States as a member, was destined to be a European organ. Lacking Russia, with Chinese membership only nominal and Japanese membership purely diplomatic, the League assumed the complexion of a European Alliance against the vanquished (among whom Russia was included), and, so far as its writ ran in the Orient, of an Anglo-Japanese encirclement of the Near, Middle, and Far East in despite of the United States and Russia. The United States refused to join, a decision which has been reënforced by the practical withdrawal of Argentina, Brazil, Bolivia, Costa Rica, and by the abstention of Mexico and Ecuador from the European League of Nations.

America's subsequent course has been equally circumspect. Our government has coöperated with the League in all broad international administrative problems, such as disarmament, commerce, radio, opium, etc., but has resolutely refused to deal with the League powers on a basis of political commitments and guarantees, and when approached by France for the outlawry of war between the two countries—which would have made America in effect an ally of the French European policies—we proposed instead that the undertaking be made general to the great nations of the world.

Efforts to induce or compel us to abandon our traditional disassociation have been numerous, persuasive, and intense, but there is as yet no indication of any will at Washington or among the people for the surrender of a principle which at once serves our national interest, preserves our domestic tranquillity, and expresses our political philosophy. Only an overwhelming fear of national disaster or an utter subversion of Europe's traditional political system could effect so radical a change in our resolution to free our destiny from minor European complications.

THE SEPARATION OF BUSINESS AND STATE

Exactly as our policy of diplomatic disassociation prevents our two positive political doctrines—autonomous nationalism and the Monroe Doctrine—from becoming meddlesome, so the division between the American Government and American business prevents our two positive commercial policies from degenerating into a mischievous advocacy of individual American interests.

There have been few to recognize that America's most notable contribution to the nineteenth century was the complete separation of business and state. It was not any mere *laissez faire,* but a perfectly definite separation, a reformation as important to the modern age as the separation of church and state was to the preceding one. It did not preclude business influence over government any more than the earlier reform precluded ecclesiastical influence, but it meant that the influence must be indirect rather than organic and thus created a type of the general system which the United States may eventually extend over the rest of the world.

The American business principle is largely at variance with the practice of other nations, where commercial interest and political power are still lawfully wedded. In banking, trade, and industry, the nations of Europe extend political support and political control. Even so liberal a state as England inclines to the European method of government predominance in economic matters. Such legislation as the Stevenson Rubber Act and the British Cinematograph Films Act, with their minute solicitude for particular business interests, would be impossible in the United States. In the field of shipping and transport, telegraph and telephone systems, and other appurtenances of the modern state, Europe is dedicated to the theory of government ownership, operation, or subsidy, and it may be taken as axiomatic that the diplomacy of Europe will seek for its nationals any business or economic advantage which is available and will lend the full support of national power to the aspirations of individual banks, firms, and companies. The history of the battle for concessions in China and in Turkey before the war shows every Great Power in Europe pressing through diplomacy for the enrichment of its subjects.

The United States did not arrive at its present policy

without a long and bitter struggle. The founders of the Republic were influenced by the political ideals of their time, which were marked by a far more exclusive nationalism than is current today. The monopolistic United States Bank was a type of the economic institutions of the eighteenth century and was not overthrown without a struggle which lasted until the fourth decade of the last century. Following the abolition of financial monopoly, various expedients were tried—State banks and National Banks—until the creation of the Federal Reserve System in 1913 made possible the orderly development of our financial resources. The vast growth of our wealth since 1914 and the enormous volume of our loans to Europe caused the State Department to impose a supervision of individual flotations, by informal agreement with private American bankers. This effort by our government to prevent the utilization of our wealth contrary to our national interests has, naturally, provoked opposition; but in the summer of 1927, Secretary Hoover, in addressing the Pan-American Commercial Congress, advocated the extension of this government control to assure that loans for none save productive purposes were made.

The basic idea of the American business reformation is simple: no government ownership. Keep the government out of business unless private interests are incompetent to run that business. Let the government use its regulating power merely to preserve competition and to prevent monopoly. Thus the Sherman Anti-Trust Law of 1890 declares that "Every contract, combination in the form of trust or otherwise, or conspiracy, in restraint of trade or commerce among the several States, or with foreign nations, is hereby declared to be illegal."

This principle of regulation has had interesting vicissitudes, ranging from the dissolution of the Standard Oil in 1911 and the American Tobacco Trust in 1912 to the endorsement of the United States Steel Corporation in 1920, and to the prosecution of French potash and Dutch quinine producers as violators of the anti-trust law. The law has been modified in two important particulars, by the Webb-Pomerene Export Trade Act of 1918, which permits American manufacturers to pool their products in foreign trade operations, and the Farm Coöperative Act of 1922, which exempted farm coöperatives from anti-trust legislation. Early in 1928, an act to permit American importers to pool their purchases of products controlled by foreign monopolists was, however, defeated by Congress.

If the government is kept out of business, business is itself given a charter of liberties in the far-reaching "Due Process Clause" of the Fourteenth Amendment to the Constitution, adopted in 1868:

No State shall make or enforce any law which shall abridge the privileges or immunities of citizens of the United States; nor shall any State deprive any person of life, liberty, or property without due process of law, nor deny to any person within its jurisdiction the equal protection of their laws.

As every corporation is a legal "person" and as ease of incorporation is a dominant feature in all State commercial codes, the effect of this clause has been an enormous stimulation to business. Government regulation is uncontested. Through the tariff the Government accords protection to American industry and agriculture. Railway legislation, shipping legislation, tariff rates, industrial legislation, are handled by such government bureaus as the Interstate Commerce Commission, the United States Shipping Board, the Tariff Commission, and the Federal Trade Commission, but the main current of American business is untouched by government save through tariffs and taxation, and has developed an independent status which renders possible a peaceful and coördinated development of economic and political life.

The whole is made coherent by the use of a firm American business diplomacy, the object of which is to encourage American trade generally and to protect individual American interests in their duly acquired rights, but not to promote the advantage of any single American firm or business. Thus the State Department has acted to protect American oil and commercial rights in Mesopotamia and in China under the open-door doctrine and has similarly protected American owners of Mexican land and oil-wells, but has refused resolutely to request particular concessions in behalf of its nationals. The only alleged successful instance of an American diplomat recently obtaining a concession for an American firm was rewarded by that diplomat's recall.

On the other hand, the American State Department has endeavored to incorporate the "due process" principle as an international doctrine, and in its dealings with Russia, China, and Mexico, has stood firm on the right of every person, whether legal or actual, to own property, until deprived of it by due legal process. President Coolidge in an address to the United Press in 1927 made the statement that the national domain includes American citizens and American property abroad and that the American Government, by implication, is bound to protect them, while abroad, in their rights under the American Constitution.

Such a statement marks the beginning of a new phase in American commercial policy—the effort to extend domestic conceptions of legal right to international problems. Coupled with the prosecution of foreign companies for violation of the Anti-Trust Law, with the despatch of treasury agents with power to discover, under threat of tariff retaliation, the cost of production of articles manufactured abroad, and with the examination of prospective immigrants at the port of embarkation for the United States, it marks a very definite tendency to extend American jurisdiction over the rest of the world.

It is for this reason that the separation of business and state must be considered as a major foreign policy of the United States. For the conceptions which underlie it are being exported to foreign countries and the actual course of our foreign relations is in large part controlled by the effort to render these conceptions acceptable to other nations.

Chapter VI

INFANTILE IMPERIALISM

AGRICULTURAL IMPERIALISM

NATIONS, no less than individuals, pass through a series of childish diseases. In the case of the United States, there were three serious attacks of infantile imperialism before America discovered the true course of her international power. Between 1783 and 1854 a first spasm of agricultural imperialism ran its course, backed by the feverish impulses of slavery and Northern pioneering. There followed a casual period during which the United States picked up a few unconsidered trifles, like Hawaii, Alaska, Porto Rico, and the Philippines. Between 1900 and 1927 a third formula for expansion was followed, with ever-increasing success, making the region of the Caribbean an American jurisdiction without perceptibly extending American sovereignty. Eventually a type of painless imperialism was to emerge, the promise of a world-dominion which rests chiefly on economic power.

In the light of the later methods of American expansion, the crude enthusiasms of the early pioneers and the hip-hurrah spirit of the acquisitive 'nineties, seem no more than nationalistic whooping-cough or imperialistic measles, diseases of political immaturity which had to be experienced before sound national health could be assured. It was, in fact, a century and a quarter before

America discovered the real character of her international destiny and realized that the United States could achieve a world-power *sui generis,* unique and distinctive, no more like British imperialism than British imperialism had resembled Spanish imperialism.

No one knows how many Indians were living in American territory at the time of the founding of the English colonies, but it is estimated that not more than 300,000 could be supported by the type of nomadic life which they had developed. The North American Indians were a cruel, savage, courageous race of warriors. They knew the wilderness. They owned the land. The English settlers outfought them and took away their land in a series of Indian wars which began with the settlement of Jamestown in 1607 and ended with the Sioux and Apache wars of the 1870's and 1880's.

The story of the Indian wars is a saga of heroism, stratagem, surprise, massacre, treachery, fraud,. and revenge. No sooner was the Revolution won than the Americans discovered that the British planned to create from the Northwest Territory an Indian buffer state between Canada and the United States. In 1791 an American army under St. Clair was ambushed and destroyed by the Miamis. Three years later "Mad Anthony" Wayne advanced into Indian territory and avenged St. Clair at the battle of Fallen Timbers. By the Treaty of Greenville (1795), Wayne brought Indian peace after twenty years of fighting. Then William Henry Harrison was appointed superintendent of the Northwest Indians. Between 1795 and 1809, Harrison secured, by "treaties" with the Indians, 48,000,000 acres of land for the pioneers. Then came the anti-alcoholic and Canadian-inspired confederacy of Tecumseh, in alliance with the powerful Creek tribe of the south. On November 7, 1811, Harrison defeated Tecumseh at Tippecanoe and made the Northwest safe for the whites.

Two years later the Creeks rose against the Americans. Andrew Jackson was sent against them, broke their power in two battles, and by the Creek Treaty (August 9, 1814), dismembered their territory. To anticipate slightly, between 1829 and 1837 it became Jackson's policy to remove the Southern Indians to the Trans-Mississippi region. This process of expropriation caused the Black Hawk War of 1831, and the Seminole War, which lasted until 1842 and cost the United States $20,000,000 and 1,500 lives. The Cherokees in Georgia were driven from their lands by force, and the last of them settled in Indian Territory by 1838. The wars with the Plains Indians came later. Custer's defeat at the Battle of the Little Big Horn in 1876 was the last real victory for the Indians. Ten years later the Apaches of the Southwest gave up the hopeless struggle, and the long contest for the possession of the North American continent came to an end.

Working from the fringe of colonies on the Atlantic Coast, the agricultural domain of the Americans was steadily enlarged. Five new States—Vermont, Kentucky, Maine, Texas, and West Virginia—were admitted to the Union, and thirty territories were developed into States. The long course of agricultural imperialism came to an end in 1853, with the Gadsden purchase from Mexico, after having added to the United States the territories of the Louisiana and Florida purchases, Texas, the Oregon territory, and the Mexican cessions at the end of the brief war of 1847.

The method by which these lands were incorporated in the American Union was established by the Ordinance of 1787. The Northwest Territory had been claimed by Virginia, Massachusetts, New York, and Connecticut, under their original charters. As early as 1780, however, the Continental Congress voted that the Western Territory "shall be settled and formed into distinct republican States, which shall become members of the Federal Union, and shall have the same rights of sovereignty, freedom, and independence as the other States." Between 1781 and 1785, the contesting States ceded their titles and jurisdiction to the nation, and the Ordinance of 1787 devised an intermediate system of territorial government for the unpopulated lands, with the proviso that as soon as the population of one of the territories amounted to 60,000 free inhabitants,

such State shall be admitted, by its delegates, into the Congress of the United States, on an equal footing with the original States, in all respects whatever; and shall be at liberty to form a permanent constitution and State government; Provided, the constitution and government, so to be formed, shall be republican, and in conformity to the principles contained in these articles.

The title to the public land reposed in the Federal Government, however, even after the admission of the new State to the Union. Until the passage of the Homestead Act of 1862, with its liberal terms to settlers, the question of free lands disturbed the national councils. A system of Federal Land Offices was established, and provision was made by the Act of 1796 for the sale of sections of 640 acres at $2 an acre. Popular pressure forced the minimum down to the low unit of 160 acres, and made the national domain available to the individual as well as to the speculator and capitalist. Government lands suitable for agriculture ran out in the 1880's. The frontier ended. The age of the pioneer was over.

It was the American pioneer, an individual remote from his kind and unprotected by his government, who supplied the force behind the demand for fresh territory. With ax and rifle he forced the surrender of one European claim after another. Thus Louisiana, which had been founded by France, had been ceded to Spain in 1769. In 1800, by the secret Treaty of San Ildefonso, Spain retroceded the province to France. A year later President Jefferson got wind of the deal. Napoleon had sent an army to San Domingo to overthrow Toussaint l'Ouverture, the "Negro Napoleon." His plan was to make Louisiana the base for a great French empire in the New World. Jefferson was alarmed, for he saw that "The day that France takes possession of New Orleans . . . we must marry ourselves to the British fleet and nation." In 1802 the dummy Spanish government withdrew the trading privileges which Americans had enjoyed at New Orleans. What Jefferson feared was in sight: the western pioneers were being cut off from the sea. He pushed through Congress a $2,000,000 appropriation for "diplomatic expenses," and in April, 1803, our minister at Paris approached Talleyrand. On April 30, 1803, in return for 60,000,000 francs and the claims of American citizens, Napoleon sold the Louisiana territory to the United States. The American title was defective: the province was still in Spanish hands, its sale was illegal under the French treaty with Spain, and its purchase unauthorized by the Constitution of the United States. However, on

November 30, 1803, the Spanish handed over the province to a French prefect, who three weeks later transferred it to the United States. The American people did not raise any constitutional objections to the acquisition of 827,987 square miles at a cost of three cents an acre.

The next move of the western pioneers was a hopeful effort to conquer Canada. There had been constant trouble with Great Britain over the Indian territory, British officials had equipped and encouraged anti-Yankee scalping-parties, and the pioneers wanted more land. Almost as nomadic as the Indians they displaced, they exerted a constant pressure which led to Indian wars. Until 1808, the pioneers were kept quiet by government purchase of Indian land, but after the Tecumseh rising and the battle of Tippecanoe, the frontiersmen felt that Great Britain was inciting the Indian tribes. The "war-hawks" of the West—Henry Clay of Kentucky and John C. Calhoun— boasted that Canada could be conquered in six weeks, and in the vote on June 18, 1812, all but one of the Congressional delegations from the frontier States of Vermont, Ohio, Kentucky, and Tennessee, were for war.

The result was disappointing to their hopes. General Hull invaded Upper Canada, retreated, and surrendered at Detroit on August 16, 1812. An invasion of Canada at Niagara was defeated because the New York militia refused to leave their State and allowed their comrades across the river to be shot down, surrounded, and captured under their eyes. Militia under Dearborn marched twenty miles north from Plattsburg and then refused to go any farther. General Harrison advanced to the recapture of Detroit, beat the Indian auxiliaries of the British, and took Malden and Amherstburg in Ontario in

1813. Upper Canada was invaded, York—the modern Toronto—captured and burned, and the country devastated. Two American columns advanced on Montreal, but turned back on the first sign of opposition. In 1814, General Brown took the offensive, captured Fort Erie, beat the British regulars in pitched battle at Chippewa, and fought a draw at Lundy's Lane. In August the British under Sir George Prevost invaded northern New York, but retreated after the Battle of Plattsburg on Lake Champlain. The war on the north was a fair draw, and the conquest of Canada had miscarried. Henceforth the American pioneer preferred to fight the Indians and Mexicans.

In the south, the British attempt to capture New Orleans had been repulsed by Andrew Jackson. In withdrawing they sent some colonial troops to Florida, built a fort on Spanish territory, made alliances with the Seminoles and Creeks, and encouraged the latter to break their treaty with the United States. British traders and officials intrigued to prevent the Americans from entering the Creek lands, until Jackson was despatched to clear up the situation. Early in 1818 he entered St. Marks, Florida, hauled down the Spanish flag, hanged the Indian chiefs, and executed two British adventurers. This officially conducted filibuster showed the Spanish that they could not hope to hold Florida. On February 22, 1819, in return for $5,000,000, the Spanish government ceded to the United States all the Spanish territory east of the Mississippi as well as their ancient claims to the Oregon territory.

The Oregon territory was likewise claimed by Great Britain. In 1818 the two countries assumed a joint sovereignty, which was continued in 1827. In time, the

Americans claimed the entire territory up to 54° 40'
north latitude, the southern boundary of the Russian
claims in Alaska. "Fifty-Four Forty or Fight!" became
an effective campaign slogan, but the American Government was entirely willing to continue the actual Canadian
boundary along the forty-ninth parallel to the Pacific. In
1844, the British took up the matter of the Oregon
claims, and in June, 1848, the matter was settled on the
basis of the forty-ninth parallel frontier as far as the
Straits of Fuca, navigation rights for the Hudson Bay
Company in the Columbia River, and the cession of all
Vancouver Island to the British. Despite the aggressive
slogan, there never was the slightest danger of war with
Great Britain over Oregon. The British and Americans
had learned to respect each other as fighters in the War
of 1812, and neither government was anxious to renew
such a struggle.

The real conflict was brewing in the southwest. Hitherto, most of the gains of territory had favored northern
agriculture. The South now wished to acquire fresh slave
territory. The result was the annexation of Texas in 1845.
In consequence, Mexico furiously clamored for war, while
the United States tried to preserve peace. A mission was
sent to Mexico City to uphold the American claim to the
Rio Grande frontier and to offer a graduated series of
prices for more territory: $5,000,000 for New Mexico,
"money would be no object" for California, but $20,-
000,000 was suggested for a boundary which should include San Francisco, and $25,000,000 for one which
should extend from the southern boundary of New Mexico to the Pacific. Mexico formally refused to treat with

the American commissioner on December 21, 1845, and forced his withdrawal.

War followed, due in large part to the fatuity of the Mexican government in failing to anticipate the result of the war which it desired. An unbroken series of American victories made it possible for the United States to gain much more than it had anticipated. On February 2, 1848, the American commissioner, Trist—anxious lest he be superseded and lest an official scheme to annex all northern Mexico be consummated—signed the Treaty of Guadeloupe Hidalgo, which gave the United States full title to Texas, Arizona, New Mexico, and California, in return for $15,000,000 and the assumption of the claims of American citizens.

Five years later a fresh mission, under Gadsden, was sent to Mexico to negotiate for additional territory in the southwest and an outlet to the Gulf of California. He succeeded in paying the maximum price for the minimum territory—$20,000,000 for 30,000 square miles of desert. No port on the Gulf was secured, but Congress, after subtracting $5,000,000 from the sum, ratified the treaty on June 30, 1854, and paid Mexico the balance.

This was the last successful attempt by the slave and cotton pioneers of the South to gain fresh territory. Their enthusiasm for war with Mexico over Texas was hotly denounced as outrageous by the very Northerners who had been clamoring for war with Great Britain over Oregon. The efforts of William Walker to secure fresh slave territory by filibustering expeditions in Nicaragua and Honduras met with failure at the hands of the British, and a prolonged attempt to buy Cuba from Spain was likewise a failure. In 1848, the American minister at Madrid was authorized to approach Spain with a view to purchasing Cuba, and in 1852 the American Government declined to enter a joint guarantee of Spanish rule over Cuba with France and England. In April, 1854, the minister at Madrid presented an ultimatum to Spain on the Cuban project. The Spanish Government refused to deal with him on those terms. The American ministers to Spain, France, and Great Britain then met at Ostend and issued on October 10, 1854, the "Ostend Manifesto," recommending the offer of $120,000,000 for Cuba, and stating that America's duty to posterity called for annexation. Nothing came of this desperate move. The era of agricultural imperialism had come to an end. Until the internal conflict between free and slave agriculture was settled by the Civil War, it was not possible for the American nation again to expand its territorial dominion, and by that time the character of its ambitions had irrevocably altered.

UNCONSIDERED TRIFLES

The years between the end of the Civil War and the beginning of the twentieth century were the palmy period of European imperialism. Between 1865 and 1900 most of Africa and the Pacific was parceled out among the European powers, and tentative arrangements were made for the division of eastern Asia.

During this period the United States was not idle. The full force of commercial imperialism never motivated American policy, but there was a certain instinctive imitation of European methods. The United States continued to fumble its way toward a political formula which might reconcile empire to republicanism. During this period the United States did not acquire much, but what she did acquire was worth having.

The United States annexed, in those thirty-five years, outlying possessions with a total area of more than 800,000 square miles—an area greater than that of the original thirteen American colonies at the end of the Revolution. It is true that much of this was barren arctic waste, but its present population of over 14,000,000 is thrice that of the United States in 1790.

The first step in the creation of this empire was Seward's purchase of Alaska from Russia. The first Russian proposal to sell Alaska was made in 1854, during the Crimean War. In 1857 the matter was taken up again, and the sum of $5,000,000 was offered for the territory. As Russia was more anxious to get rid of it than America was to buy, its final purchase was, in large measure, an act of gratitude to Russia on the part of the United States.

While we were engaged in the Civil War, Russia was also engaged in suppressing a Polish insurrection, and it was thought that England contemplated intervention on behalf of the Poles and of the South—both faced a common peril. Russia was freeing her serfs, America her slaves—both had a common moral principle at stake. In the autumn of 1863, a Russian fleet was sent to Californian waters, thereby taking it out of danger from the British navy and placing it where it could menace British commerce in the Pacific. It was also a practical demonstration of friendship and confidence in the American Government, and in 1864 the Russian admiral actually protected San Francisco from Confederate raiders. Accordingly, in 1866, when the Russian minister pressed for a sale, American gratitude dictated the purchase. The sum of $7,200,000 was agreed upon. Congress attempted to secure some of this money for graft, tried to mulct Russia of $800,000, the transaction was condemned as "Seward's Folly," but the treaty went through, and the purchase was completed in 1868.

Seward contemplated an ambitious policy of expansion, of which the Alaskan purchase was only an element. He foresaw the time when the Pacific would supplant the Atlantic as the chief theater of the world's political events. The opening of Korea, which was accomplished in 1882, and better commercial relations with China, were parts of his program. He arranged for the purchase of the Danish West Indies, but the Treaty was blocked in the Senate. Similar efforts to acquire Santo Domingo and Hawaii were also blocked. Seward was ahead of his time.

The American interest in the Hawaiian Islands—which command the eastern Pacific much as the Bermudas command the western Atlantic—dated back to 1851, when Admiral Dupont noted their strategic and commercial value. In 1874 the royal house of Hawaii died out, and David Kalakaua, the new king, was under American influence. In 1875 a commercial treaty, highly profitable to Hawaiian sugar planters, was negotiated by the United States. In 1887 another treaty gave Pearl Harbor to the United States navy. In 1890 King David died and was succeeded by his sister Liliuokalani. In the same year, the McKinley Tariff annulled the commercial treaty and imposed a duty of two cents a pound on the island product. When this cost the planters $12,000,000 a year, they soon came to the conclusion that their only escape from bankruptcy was annexation to the United States. In 1893, a revolution overthrew the Queen, and American marines were landed to preserve order. The American minister raised the flag and declared that the islands were under the protection of the United States. President Cleveland, however, withdrew the treaty of annexation which he found awaiting him when he assumed office in March, 1893. He endeavored to restore the Queen, but refused to utilize American force to do so, when it appeared that Liliuokalani contemplated decapitating all the rebels. On May 31, 1894, the Senate approved Hawaiian independence, and on the Fourth of July, 1894, Hawaii was declared an independent republic and was recognized as such by the United States. During the excitement of the Spanish-American War, a quiet little treaty of annexation was passed by joint resolution of Congress on July 7, 1898. The change of one small item in the American tariff had added a rich province to the United States.

It was in much the same absent-minded way that Samoa was acquired. In 1872 Admiral Meade secured a treaty for a naval base at Tutuila. Two years later the State Department considered annexing the islands. In 1877 the American consul at Apia actually raised the flag and declared the islands an American protectorate, but he was not sustained. In 1878, we acquired Pago-Pago as a naval coaling station. Six years later a Samoan chief offered the islands to Great Britain. Promptly the German consul raised his flag over Apia, and the American consul followed suit. British, German, and American naval vessels gathered, and a conflict seemed assured, when a tidal wave and hurricane solved the situation by wrecking most of the warships. In 1889 a joint protectorate of the three countries was established after negotiations with Bismarck which drew from Secretary Blaine the comment, "The extent of the Chancellor's irritability is not the measure of American right." Subsequently Great Britain withdrew from Samoa, and in 1900 the American Senate ratified the treaty which divided the islands between the United States and Germany.

Alaska, Hawaii, Samoa—these were trifles in comparison with the Spanish loot which was taken in a few brief months in 1898. The chronic disorders in Cuba burst into revolt in 1895. The atrocities of the civil conflict and the measures taken by the Spanish authorities to suppress the insurrection aroused American indignation. On February 15, 1898, the American battleship *Maine* was blown up in Havana harbor. In consequence of the passions which the incident aroused, war became inevitable, although the Cuban situation was being satisfactorily adjusted through diplomacy. The war began on April 25 and was practically over in July. Burning with indignation to free Cuba, the American fleet destroyed the Spanish fleet at Manila, in the Philippines, 10,000 miles away, a week after the declaration of war. Two months later, the Spanish fleet in Cuban waters was destroyed at Santiago. The island was pacified by July 17; Porto Rico was taken on July 24; Manila fell shortly afterward, and on the twelfth of August a provisional agreement of peace was signed, providing for an independent Cuba, while Porto Rico, the Philippines, and an island in the Ladrones—Guam—were held under United States authority. The peace commission met on October 1, and the final treaty was signed at Paris on December 12. The United States paid Spain $20,000,000 for the territories conquered, while Cuba became free, subject to the restoration of order by the

United States. Incidental to the naval operations of the war, cable stations at Wake and Midway Islands, as well as Guam, in the western Pacific, were also acquired by the United States. The whole affair may be characterized as pretty quick work.

The retention of the Philippines offered a grave problem to the United States, which had never before faced the real issue of empire. The Administration was more than half prepared to let the islands go, when President McKinley came to a sincere and naïve decision which he reported to a body of visiting clergymen:

I walked the floor of the White House night after night and I am not ashamed to tell you, gentlemen, that I went down on my knees and prayed Almighty God for light and guidance more than one night. And one night late it came to me this way—I don't know how it was, but it came. . . . There was nothing left for us to do but to take them all, and to educate the Filipinos, and uplift and civilize and Christianize them, and by God's grace do the very best we could by them as our fellow men for whom Christ also died. And then I went to bed, and went to sleep and slept soundly.

The Filipinos revolted against the United States on February 4, 1899.

The insurrection lasted three years and cost the United States $175,000,000. In 1902 an Organic Law for the Islands was enacted, providing for administration by an American commission. In 1916, Congress passed a new act, stating that the Philippines should eventually be independent, and providing a larger measure of autonomy for the islands. In 1921, General Leonard Wood was sent to repair the wreckage of administration which this

[93]

partial autonomy had wrought. When, in 1927, the Philippine legislature passed a bill for a plebiscite on the independence issue, it was vetoed by President Coolidge on the ground that independence meant economic ruin to the islands. Similarly when, in 1928, Porto Rico, which had been made a Territory of the United States ten years before, petitioned for complete independence, the President answered the petition by proving by trade statistics that independence would bring economic disaster upon the Porto Ricans.

He was right, in both cases. Once such territories were outside the protection of the American tariff, as in the case of Hawaii, economic pressure on the tobacco and hemp industries would drive them back to American sovereignty and the American markets for their products. This condition is, however, the fruit of a subtler conquest than was conceived of thirty years ago.

The annexation of the Philippines marked the end of the brief period of American commercial imperialism on the European model. In the next thirty years, the United States was to develop its own methods of expansion and to exert its power over a new type of informal empire, containing 200,000 square miles and more than 8,000,000 inhabitants, without fighting a war or extending American sovereignty—a political paradox without precedent in modern history.

THE TENTH AMENDMENT AND THE CARIBBEAN

Almost immediately, in settling her future relations with Cuba, the United States discovered in the Platt Amendment an invulnerable method of expansion which has brought under her effective control (in the matters to which she confines her interposition) Cuba, Panama, the Dominican Republic, Haiti, El Salvador, Mexico, Guatemala, Honduras, Costa Rica, Colombia, and Venezuela.

European and Latin-American publicists have stigmatized this control as an American empire and regard American operations in preserving order therein as manifestations of imperialistic aggression. In this they are vigorously supported by many American professors of history, economics, and politics, advocates of the League of Nations, and other internationalists. This view is unscientific. Imperialism is a political action involving an extension of sovereignty on the autocratic principle. American "Caribbeanism" is an economic and administrative policy designed to achieve and maintain stable self-government in the area which is most vital to our national and commercial welfare.

This region contains twelve republics, with a total population of 36,000,000 and a total area of over 1,800,000 square miles. American policy in this region is not based on the Monroe Doctrine at all but on Admiral Mahan's dictum: "One thing is sure. In the Caribbean Sea is the strategic key to the two great oceans, the Atlantic and the Pacific, our own chief maritime frontiers."

The device by which America has attempted to keep the Caribbean safe for the United States is found in the Tenth Amendment to the Federal Constitution, which provides that "The powers not delegated to the United States by the Constitution, nor prohibited by it to the States, are reserved to the States respectively, or to the people."

[95]

The application of this principle to the Caribbean republics was first embodied in the so-called Platt Amendment, offered on March 2, 1901, to the Army Appropriation Bill, by Senator Platt of Connecticut, "in fulfillment of the declaration contained in the joint resolution" which pledged the United States, in making war on Spain, to leave Cuba independent.

Certain powers were "prohibited by it" to Cuba, namely:

That the Government of Cuba shall never enter into any treaty or other compact with any foreign power or powers which will impair or tend to impair the independence of Cuba, nor in any manner authorize or permit any power or powers to obtain by colonization, or for military or naval purposes or otherwise, lodgment in or control over any portion of said island.

That said Government shall not assume or contract any public debt, to pay the interest upon which and to make reasonable sinking fund provision for the ultimate discharge of which the ordinary revenues of the island, after defraying the current expenses of government, shall be inadequate.

Other powers are "delegated" by Cuba to the United States:

That the Government of Cuba consents that the United States may exercise the right to intervene for the preservation of Cuban independence, the maintenance of a government adequate for the protection of life, property, and individual liberty, and for discharging the obligations with respect to Cuba imposed by the Treaty of Paris on the United States, now to be assumed and undertaken by the Government of Cuba.

That to enable the United States to maintain the independence of Cuba and to protect the people thereof, as well as for its own defense, the Government of Cuba will sell or lease to the United States land necessary for coaling or naval stations at certain specified points, to be agreed upon with the President of the United States.

These and other provisions were embodied in a permanent treaty with the United States and were ratified by the Cuban Constitutional Convention, thus becoming part of the organic law of Cuba. In consequence, the United States has intervened four times in Cuban affairs: the original occupation from 1898 to 1902, the Magoon régime of 1906-09, once in 1912, and once in 1917.

The next expansion of this American policy came in Panama. American interest in an isthmian canal dated officially from the Clayton-Bulwer Treaty of April 19, 1850, subsequently modified by the Hay-Pauncefote Treaty of November 18, 1901. Roosevelt had been authorized by Congress to purchase the rights of the French Canal Company and to acquire a canal zone in Panama from Colombia; and the Hay-Herran Treaty of January 27, 1903, had in fact offered Colombia $10,000,000 for the canal zone. It was ratified by the American Senate, but the Colombian Senate failed to accept it.

At this juncture Panama had a revolution—its fiftieth revolt in fifty years—and proclaimed its independence on November 3, 1903. Roosevelt prevented Colombia from suppressing the insurrection and three days later recognized the new republic. Ten days afterward, Panama ceded the canal zone to the United States by the Hay-Bunau-Varilla Treaty, which was ratified by Panama within less than a month of the original revolution. By March 1, 1904, all the principal European nations had recognized Panama.

By the canal treaty the United States guaranteed the

independence of Panama and paid $10,000,000 for the canal zone, as well as an annual bonus of $250,000. Work on the canal was promptly begun, and by August 15, 1914, the new waterway was open to navigation. The total cost, exclusive of fortifications, was less than $113,000,000. The Panama Canal revolutionized the world's history. For the first time, North America became an island in fact as well as in geographical theory. The economic and political consequences of this event are as yet only suspected. Even the immediate effects have been enormously important. For example, in 1927, 5,475 ships of 26,227,815 net tons, half of them of American registry, passed through the Panama Canal, as compared to the 4,980 vessels of 26,060,377 net tons, half of them British, which used the Suez Canal in 1926. As a national, as well as international, asset, the value of the Panama Canal is beyond computation.

To protect it, the United States has frequently exerted its right of intervention in Panama—in 1908, 1912, 1917, 1918, and 1921—and in 1927 the American Government negotiated a new treaty granting the United States extensive powers over Panama in the event of war. This treaty—as a result of anti-American agitation in League of Nations and Latin-American circles—was rejected by the Panama Senate and resubmitted to negotiation.

With the American undertaking on the Isthmus came a renewed sense of the importance of the entire Caribbean to the United States. Santo Domingo had already tempted President Grant, who wanted to establish an American coaling station at Samana, but the Senate had twice rejected his Treaty of annexation. Gross mismanagement of the Dominican finances in 1903 left a total revenue of $500,000 to pay interest of $1,700,000 on a debt of $25,000,000, largely held in Europe. It was a case where either Europe would, or the United States must, intervene. Santo Domingo was urged to invite the United States to do so. The two countries came to an agreement, whereby the United States guaranteed the political integrity of the republic and assumed its fiscal administration. The Senate rejected this agreement, but Roosevelt named a Customs Receiver who was appointed, under naval pressure, by the President of Santo Domingo. The United States intervened in 1903, 1904, 1913, and 1914, and when an armed insurrection occurred in 1916, American marines were landed, and the Republic came under an American military occupation which lasted until 1924, when a treaty of evacuation was signed. The American base at Samana was secured for the United States navy, and the Dominican Government was left safe and solvent.

At the other end of the island, the Republic of Haiti likewise experienced American regulation. As early as 1892, Blaine had pressed for a naval base at Mole St. Nicholas. A revolution in 1915 was threatening to bring French intervention, when prompt American naval action anticipated this, and by a treaty ratified November 11, 1915, Haiti received an American military high commissioner, general receiver of customs, and a financial adviser, as well as an American-directed constabulary. The Haitian treaty, which was renewed for ten years in 1925, closely followed the pattern of the Platt Amendment. Naval bases at Mole St. Nicholas and Cape Haitien were ceded to the United States, pledges not to increase the public debt or to impair Haitian independence were given, and it was provided that

the President of Haiti shall appoint, upon nomination by the President of the United States, a general receiver . . . who shall collect, receive, and apply all customs duties on imports and exports accruing at the several customs houses and ports of entry of the Republic of Haiti.

As a footnote to this far-reaching Caribbean naval design, the United States acquired in 1917 the Danish West Indies, with the harbor of St. Thomas, "the Gibraltar of the Caribbean," for the sum of $25,000,000. With other bases at Guantanamo, Samana Bay, Mole St. Nicholas, Cape Haitien, a fortified canal at Panama, and the rights for another one acquired in Nicaragua, the American naval grip on the Caribbean became predominant.

Nicaragua is a vital element in the strategic situation. The only alternative route to the Panama Canal runs through Nicaragua, and was, for a time, preferred to the Panama route. Nicaraguan politics, moreover, have been turbulent for generations. Unstable governments, dictatorships, and constant revolutions have made the country fair game for any strong power that might be tempted to intervene. After various attempts, between 1907 and 1911, to induce the Nicaraguan governments to preserve order, the Knox-Castrillo Convention of 1911 provided for a United States administration of the customs and supervision of the budget. The Senate rejected this treaty, thus perpetuating disorderly conditions in the Central American republic. Finally, the Bryan-Chamorro Treaty of February, 1916, was ratified, giving the United States

the right to build a Nicaraguan canal, control for ninety-
nine years of the strategic approach to this projected
canal, and a naval base in the Gulf of Fonseca. Efforts to
block this treaty through the Central American Court of
Justice—which had been established in 1907 in the effort
to induce the five little republics of Central America to
unite and prosper—simply led to the dissolution of the
Court, whose jurisdiction was denied by Nicaragua and
the United States. The United States has intervened in
Nicaragua six times: 1899, 1907, 1910, 1912-25, 1926,
1927-28, for Washington has no intention of permitting
political anarchy to flourish in a region so near to the
Panama Canal and so important to its protection.

For exactly the same reason, the United States intervened in Honduras six times (1907, 1910, 1911, 1919,
1924, and 1925), once in Costa Rica (1917), once in Colombia (at the time of the revolution of Panama), twice
in Venezuela (in 1895-96, in support of Venezuela against
Great Britain, and in 1902-03, in support of Venezuela
against Great Britain, Italy, and Germany), and twice in
Mexico (1914 and 1916).

It was with relation to Mexico that two of the most
interesting of our Caribbean interventions occurred—if
Mexico can be ranked as a Caribbean state. Diaz had ruled
Mexico from 1876 to 1911, when overthrown by revolution. At that time American investments in Mexico totaled
$1,050,000,000, whereas Mexican wealth in native own-
ership amounted to only $793,000,000. The disorders of
the revolution, with the changing fortunes of Diaz, Madero, Huerta, Villa, Carranza, and Obregon, were a menace to this paramount economic interest. Every effort was
made by the American Government to protect the Ameri-

can stake south of the Rio Grande. The government of Huerta was considered hostile to the United States and favorable to British and German interests. Ostensibly to maintain American prestige and to compel an apology for an insult to the American flag, on April 21, 1914, the American navy seized Vera Cruz, thereby preventing the arrival of a German shipload of munitions consigned to Huerta. In this action the United States was supported by the powers of Argentina, Brazil, and Chile, which had offered their mediation, but Great Britain's support of Huerta ceased only when the United States agreed not to exempt American coastwise vessels from the payment of tolls in the Panama Canal. Huerta fled his country, but the civil war continued despite the pressure of the United States, the A.B.C. countries, Bolivia, Guatemala, and Uruguay.

In 1916, a raid into American territory by Pancho Villa impelled the United States to despatch a punitive raid into Sonora. This expedition was led by Pershing and remained in Mexico until February 5, 1917, on the eve of the war with Germany. In this intervention, too, the United States received the support of Latin America. The Mexican disorders continued. Carranza had been recognized in 1915. In 1920 he was murdered and Obregon came into power. In 1922, the latter resumed the payment of interest on Mexico's foreign debt and consequently was recognized in the following year, and in 1924, when his rule was menaced by the revolt of De La Huerta, the United States intervened effectively in his behalf, supplying him with munitions and denying them to the rebels. Subsequent revolts against Calles were likewise discouraged by American policy.

The basis of this policy was exactly the same as that pursued in Nicaragua: the maintenance of responsible government and the encouragement of autonomous nationalism. Thus on March 11, 1913, Wilson said: "We can have no sympathy with those who seek to seize the power of government to advance their own personal interests or ambition. We are friends to peace, but we know that there can be no lasting or stable peace in such circumstances."

This "moral mandate" was much ridiculed in view of our own revolutionary origin, but the Washington Government wisely distinguished between a genuine transformation of social and political forms and an armed *coup d'état* by a group of disgruntled politicians or military adventurers.

The sole point on which Washington was adamant toward Mexico was the necessity for bringing its land and mineral legislation into line with the basic assumptions of the American Constitution. Wilson said of the Huerta régime that "The present situation in Mexico is incompatible with the fulfillment of international obligations on the part of Mexico, with the civilized development of Mexico herself, and with the maintenance of tolerable political and economic conditions in Central America." The terms of the recognition of Obregon and the settlement with Calles in 1928 were simply the principle that Americans should not be deprived of life, liberty, or property without due process of law.

In two particulars, the United States has striven to justify its moral position in Latin America. In April, 1921, the Senate ratified a treaty paying to Colombia $25,000,000 in full settlement of the injury done her by American intervention in the revolution of Panama. Hostile critics connected this treaty with the discovery of oil in Colombia, but it is significant that the United States, though strong enough to do as she liked, preferred to conciliate Venezuela. And finally, on repeated occasions, the United States pledged itself against annexations. On October 27, 1913, Wilson declared that "the United States will never again seek one additional foot by conquest." In 1923, Secretary Hughes repeated the pledge and at the Havana Conference of 1928 made its sincerity apparent to the entire Latin-American group of states. However, fear of the United States had been deliberately fostered in Latin America by such publicists as F. G. Calderon, who asserted: "To save themselves from Yankee imperialism the American democracies would almost accept a German alliance, or the aid of Japanese arms; everywhere the Americans of the North are feared."

Despite this attitude of fear and distrust, the fact remains that in thirty years of world-power and political domination of the Caribbean, the United States has not annexed a square inch of Latin-American territory.

Part Two

THE STRUGGLE BETWEEN AMERICA AND EUROPE

Chapter VII

EUROPEAN MENACE TO AMERICA

WOODROW WILSON: A BISMARCKIAN IDEALIST

THE inauguration of Woodrow Wilson, in 1913, as President of the United States, placed in charge of American policy one of the most baffling personalities of modern times. The effort to evaluate his character, and its relation to his policy, will employ the historians for many years. Fortunately, it is not so necessary to understand a statesman as it is to appreciate the actual effects of his policy.

A statesman is not judged by what he says—unless his words are embodied in subsequent governmental policies —but by what he does. Wilson, therefore, must be judged, not as an orator, diplomatic stylist, or political idealist, but as a practical statesman, if one is to appraise his relative importance to the development of American foreign policy.

Judged by this simple test, Wilson—for all that his words breathed a lofty and honorable idealism—was one of the most practical of American statesman. Had he acted coldly on the precept of a Machiavelli who believed only in getting results or of a Bismarck who deliberately reckoned "the imponderables" in his political computations, Wilson would have done no other than he did.

He found awaiting him a general body of American policies, coherent in principle but generally segregated from the actual conduct of our foreign relations; he found America on sufferance with the rest of the world, and the legacy of American traditions listlessly administered by a diplomatic bureaucracy. He boldly seized these policies and, by a bewildering and masterly resort to fixed principles, made them intelligible to the American public and to the world, and achieved results that the most cynical of practical diplomatists might well envy.

One need only examine the state of the world, before and after Wilson; one need only consider America's position—military, naval, financial, commercial, economic, political, as well as moral—relative to Europe in 1914 and 1919 to appreciate that Woodrow Wilson was one of those practical statesmen who know how to reconcile the possible with the public's view of the desirable, in a manner as satisfactory to the nation's moral sense as it is to the nation's pocketbook.

Wilson was a Machiavelli of democracy, an idealistic Bismarck, a thoroughly sincere protagonist of his nation's moral, no less than material, aspirations. Judged by the results of Wilsonism, the American "idealist" takes rank with the world's most ruthless conquerors.

WILSON LEARNS THE ROPES

It was in his dealings with Mexico that Wilson learned the ropes of international policy and learned also the knack of protecting his nation's material interests by reference to general principles, where other governments dealt with specific cases on their merits.

The special interest of America in Mexico centered around oil. Lord Cowdray, the British oil operator, had come to an agreement with Diaz in 1910, when the latter was elected President for the eighth time. Francisco Madero started a revolution against Diaz, and was elected President in 1911. Madero favored the American oil interests. He was overthrown in February, 1913, by Felix Diaz and Victoriano Huerta, and was murdered. Huerta favored Lord Cowdray. Thus matters stood when Wilson came into office.

Wilson, Bryan (his nominal Secretary of State), and Colonel House (his confidential adviser), all believed that the British oil interests were back of Huerta, on the ground that "the Huerta forces have maintained the Diaz policy of antagonism to American oil interests and friendship to Lord Cowdray. . . . On Lord Cowdray's own statements, the firm subscribed to 3 per cent. of the loan floated by Huerta." Instead of encouraging the American oil interests to back another Mexican politician, Wilson proclaimed a "moral empire" a week after his inauguration: "We can have no sympathy with those who seek to seize the power of government to advance their own personal interests or ambition." He advocated an end to fighting, a free election, and the elimination of Huerta.

This brought him into conflict with the British. On November 14, 1913, Wilson told Sir William Tyrrell: "I am going to teach the South American republics to elect good men!" His Ambassador in London, a week later, had a similar conversation with Sir Edward Grey at the British Foreign Office. Ambassador Page described this interview in a letter to Wilson:

"Suppose you have to intervene, what then?" [Grey asked].

"Make 'em vote and live by their decisions."

"But suppose they will not so live?"

"We'll go in again and make 'em vote again."

"And keep this up two hundred years?" asked he.

"Yes," said I. "The United States will be here two hundred years and it can continue to shoot men for that little space till they learn to vote and to rule themselves."

I have never seen him laugh so heartily. Shooting men into self-government! Shooting them into orderliness—he comprehends that; and that's all right. But that's as far as his habit of mind goes.

In order to teach Mexico to elect good men, Wilson established a financial and moral blockade of the country and raised the arms embargo to favor the Constitutionalist movement against Huerta. After the American navy had seized Vera Cruz, in April, 1914, Huerta's case became helpless. He left the following July, and Carranza was inaugurated. A Constitutional Convention assembled in December, 1916, and on February 5, 1917, a new Constitution, providing incidentally for a new oil and land policy, came into effect. Wilson's despatch of Pershing to Sonora in 1916 was designed to protect the United States border from Villa rather than to interfere with political events in Mexico. In a word, Wilson dealt with the Mexican question of his time through the enunciation of moral principles backed by the judicious use of force.

The lesson learned in Mexico was quickly applied in the Caribbean, where he made greater steps toward a control of the entire region than any preceding President. Roosevelt could point to the Panama Canal and fiscal control in Santo Domingo; Taft could point to dollar diplomacy in Nicaragua and Honduras, but Wilson put the United States in actual control of the destinies of Haiti, Nicaragua, and Santo Domingo, bought the Virgin Islands, and dealt out to Costa Rica exactly the same sort of treatment that he had given Mexico.

In the case of Haiti, on December 17, 1914, American marines landed at Port au Prince and seized the specie in the vaults of the National Bank to protect it from revolutionary disorders, the bank being American property. In March and May, 1915, two American missions proposed an American military protectorate over Haiti. On the outbreak of revolution on July 27, 1915, marines again landed and set up martial law so effectively that on August 19, Admiral Caperton reported that "the United States has now actually accomplished a military intervention in the affairs of another nation." By virtue of a ten years' treaty signed on September 16, 1915, the United States collected the customs, organized a constabulary force, and guaranteed the inalienability of Haitian territory. A new Haitian Constitution of June 18, 1917, promoted by the American high commissioner, validated all the acts of the American occupation and permitted foreigners to own land in Haiti. The treaty was subsequently renewed to run for another ten years.

Shortly thereafter, through the Bryan-Chamorro Treaty of February 18, 1916, Wilson acquired for America canal rights and naval bases in Nicaragua for $3,000,000. In 1918, Wilson secured supervision of the Nicaraguan railway, and two years later encouraged a $9,000,000 loan to Nicaragua through Wall Street.

The occupation of Santo Domingo was similar to that of Haiti. On September 9, 1913, Bryan notified the Dominican Government that the United States would discourage revolution and would support the lawful authorities. In April, 1916, an insurrection led to the landing of American marines. On May 4, 1916, a treaty was offered, providing for American control of the customs, treasury, army, and police. The Dominican President resigned in protest. On November 29, 1916, the marines declared martial law, ousted the officials, dissolved the legislature, and forbade the elections, setting up an American military dictatorship which lasted until 1924, despite proposals by Wilson and Harding for its termination. On June 26, 1924, the Dominican Republic ratified the treaty, and the American forces were withdrawn.

While the purchase in 1917 of the Danish West Indies —St. Thomas, St. John, and St. Croix in the Virgin Islands—is important to naval strategists, Wilson's treatment of Costa Rica is most interesting to political theorists, as showing how concrete interests can be protected by general principles. In 1915-16, American companies received oil exploration rights in Costa Rica. In 1917, the Tinoco government came into power, through revolution, and prepared to give the rights to Lord Cowdray's British oil interests. Wilson, in accordance with his theory of teaching Latin America to elect good men, refused to recognize the Tinoco government, and excluded Costa Rica from the peace conference. In 1919, a revolution headed by Acosta restored constitutional government and was accordingly recognized. Acosta canceled the British oil concessions and gave them back to the original American companies.

Not only in Mexico and the Caribbean was the "moral empire" established, but in China as well did Wilson insist on scrupulous propriety. After the endorsement of the open door by the Great Powers of Europe in 1900, the United States had made various efforts to act as though they meant what they said. On being excluded by Russia from Manchuria, we had supported Japan in the Russo-Japanese War. When Japan disappointed her American backers, the United States secured Chinese imperial support for railway and bank projects in Manchuria, but the death of the Emperor and Dowager Empress, in November, 1908, destroyed this hope. On November 30, 1908, after the Root-Takahira Agreement providing for Japanese-American respect of each other's spheres of interest in China, the open door, and the status quo, the Manchurian railway scheme was again pressed by Washington, and in 1909 Knox proposed the internationalization of all the Manchurian railways. In reply, on July 4, 1910, Russia and Japan came to an agreement, in concert with Great Britain, which blocked this scheme to admit American capital to the development of northern China. At the same time, Japan annexed Korea outright and announced the end of the open door in a province which had originally been opened to world trade by the American navy.

In the meantime, the great powers were proceeding with plans for the exploitation of China, and arrangements were made for the participation of America in a Six Power Loan to China (April 15, 1911), to be undertaken by the United States, Great Britain, Germany, France, Russia, and Japan. The Chinese Revolution broke out in the same year and prevented the execution of this so-called Chinese Consortium. The State Department had urged American bankers to take part in the loan, but on

March 18, 1913, a fortnight after assuming office, Wilson withdrew American support on the ground that "the conditions of the loan seem to us to touch very nearly the administrative independence of China itself," leaving the Five Power group to make a loan of £25,000,000 for the reorganization of China. Luck was with Wilson on this point, for the subsequent outbreak of the World War bankrupted Europe and rendered the resumption of the Consortium in October, 1920, conditional on American consent. Japan then proposed the exclusion of Manchuria and Mongolia from its terms, but was overborne. The American monopoly of capital in the years after the war meant in effect that, under the Consortium, all China might become an American sphere of influence and that the open door might be opened in reality. Wilson's moral scruples in 1913—by sheer luck, it must be admitted—prepared for America's material advantage in 1920.

EUROPE IN 1914 AS A MENACE TO AMERICA

The weapons of Wilsonian statecraft were scarcely forged and tested when he was presented with the opportunity to employ them on a world-wide scale.

Those who look at Europe today—divided, impoverished, and economically dependent, despite her feelings, upon American credit—can scarcely realize how great a threat the pre-war Europe was to American institutions. The Europe of 1914 was a standing menace to every American interest. Through the balance of power she deeply compromised American political safety. Integrated in a delicate balance of political forces ready at any moment to precipitate an explosion, inextricably involved in historical, political, and economic hatreds and incompatibilities, pre-war Europe was the antithesis of the American political system.

On one side stood the Triple Alliance. Austria-Hungary and Germany had signed an alliance in 1879, in fear of an attack by Russia. Italy adhered to this alliance in 1882 and renewed her membership in 1887, 1891, 1902, and 1912, and abandoned it in 1915. Roumania had joined secretly in 1883. During the war, Bulgaria and Turkey also became members of this group. On the other side was the Triple Entente. In 1892 France and Russia had signed a defensive alliance against Germany and Italy. In 1904 England and France had come to an "entente cordiale" over Egypt and Morocco. In 1907 an Anglo-Russian treaty had settled rivalries in Tibet, Persia, and Afghanistan. Japan and England were allies since 1902, and had renewed their alliance in 1905 and 1911.

So precarious was the peace of Europe under this explosive grouping of states that war threatened in 1906 over Morocco, in 1908 over the Casablanca incident and Austria's annexation of Bosnia, in 1911 over the Agadir incident, in 1912-13 over the Italo-Turkish and the Balkan Wars, and when, in 1914, a Bosnian student murdered an Austrian Archduke at Serajevo, the deed actually precipitated a world-struggle into which the United States was reluctantly dragged, at great cost to itself and injury to its political tradition against entanglement in the Old World's politics.

Not only was the European balance of power a peril to the United States, but Europe's political institutions were incompatible with American institutions. The autocratic principle, based on the factor of military power, was natural to Europe. Germany, Austria-Hungary, and Russia were, quite frankly, military empires, with huge standing armies and powerful navies, with autocratic administration and sanctions for acts of arbitrary power.

Moreover, Japan, the ally of Great Britain, was itself an autocracy comparable to those of Europe and congenial to the European type. Italy was also a monarchical country, where, as subsequent events have shown, the autocratic ideal is still preferred to self-government. Even democratic England, with her world-wide empire, her incomparable navy, and her demonstrated willingness to conquer non-European territory and hold her title by force of arms, was closer to the European ideal of statecraft than to the American ideal of "demobilized democracy." And in republican France the army and the bureaucracy relieved the people of the burden of political thought. As a sample of the relative armaments of pre-war Europe and America, in 1906 (before the peril of war had become acute), when the United States Army numbered 67,000 men, the British Army numbered 445,000; the Russian, 1,225,000; the Austrian, 410,000; and the German, 610,000. Even now eight European nations and two Asiatic powers maintain larger standing armies than does the United States.

The final point in the count against pre-war Europe was the ominous fact, from the American point of view, that the actual relations of this complex military and political organism were shrouded in secret compacts, informal private understandings, and subterranean alliances. Thus the terms of the Austro-German Alliance of 1879 were not published until 1888. The League of the Three

Emperors (1881), the Austro-Serbian Alliance (1881), the Russo-German Reinsurance Treaty (1887), the British-Italian Agreement (1887), the Anglo-French Entente (1904), all contained secret undertakings, the very existence of which was denied. Thus in 1913 and 1914, Sir Edward Grey twice formally assured the House of Commons that Great Britain was not under any obligation to France, under the Entente Cordiale; yet on the outbreak of the war he argued before the Commons that through the Entente Cordiale England was in honor bound to aid France. Thus the terms of the Treaty of London, which brought Italy into the war in 1915, were kept secret until 1917, when the Bolshevists published the text which they found in the Russian archives. Even the United States, in its dealings with Japan, was forced into this game. The Root-Takahira Agreement of 1908 and the Lansing-Ishii Agreement of 1917 were both kept confidential by the two governments.

The war gave Wilson his opportunity to destroy the threat to America of Europe's balance of power, to mitigate European autocracy and military imperialism, and to call a halt to a secret diplomacy which multiplied national fears and hatreds and which invoked competitive armaments. It is his chief claim to fame that he very nearly succeeded in disinfecting European statecraft.

THE ISSUES OF 1917

When the United States went to war in 1917, it was because virtually every single one of the major American foreign policies was endangered. The freedom of the seas, the open door, the Monroe Doctrine, the principles of federative democracy and of permanent disassociation from European politics, were all involved in the momentous decision of Good Friday, 1917, to declare war on the Imperial German Government.

During the first three years of the European war, American rights had been flagrantly violated at sea by both the British and the German navies. On October 20, 1914, the United States had been impelled to protest against the British disregard of neutral rights, the British blacklist, and the failure of Great Britain to accept the Declaration of London with respect to contraband. Tension of the gravest character was barely averted in the case of the *Dacia*, a ship of former German registry which flew the American flag and was sent through the blockade as a test case. Ambassador Page at London solved the problem by the following suggestion to the British Foreign Secretary, in January, 1915: "Well," said Page, "there's the *Dacia*. Why not let the French seize it and get some advertising?" British and French control of cables and wireless, their censorship of American mail to neutral countries, their arbitrary extensions of contraband, their declarations of blockaded zones contrary to the Declaration of Paris, their Orders in Council, and their general indifference to neutral rights, for a time threatened to compel the United States to undertake reprisals against the Entente.

The only reason why America did not take this step was that the German submarine campaign endangered American life as well as property, where the Allied blockade concerned only property. The sinking of the *Lusitania* on May 7, 1915, brought America to the brink of war with Germany. When the German Government broke its promises to the United States and resumed an unrestricted submarine warfare on January 31, 1917, the United States broke diplomatic relations within three days. Three weeks later Wilson proposed an armed neutrality. Within ten weeks America was in a state of war with Germany.

The Allied and German disregard of American maritime rights led in 1916 to the formulation of an ambitious naval program, providing for the construction—within three years—of ten first-class battleships, six battle-cruisers, and a large number of auxiliary craft. The purpose of this new naval policy, as defined by the General Board of the Navy, was the creation of "a navy equal to the most powerful maintained." On September 25, 1916, Colonel House saw Ambassador Page with a view to discovering whether this program would offend the British:

I asked Page [he wrote] if he thought the irritation apparent in Great Britain had increased because of our naval program, and whether we were not getting in the same position, from the British viewpoint, as Germany. I spoke of the traditional friendship between Germany and Great Britain, which existed until Germany began to cut into British trade and to plan a navy large enough to become formidable; and I wondered whether they did not see us as a similar menace both as to their trade and the supremacy of the seas. Page thought not, and yet he said Great Britain would never allow us to have a navy equal or superior to theirs.

The 1916 naval program was aimed quite as much at the Pacific as at the Atlantic, since Japan, by the presentation of her Twenty-One Demands to China on January 18, 1915, had made a bold bid for the destruction of the open door. The demands, the very existence of which were long denied by Tokyo, were in five groups: First, for China's consent in advance to Japanese disposal of the German rights in Kiaochow and the Shantung Peninsula; second, for Japanese rights to certain mines in southern Manchuria and eastern Inner Mongolia, the right to purchase land and an option on all railway construction and loans in this area, a ninety-nine-year lease on Port Arthur and Dalny, and control of the railways of southern Manchuria and eastern Mongolia; third, for the conversion of the Hanyehping Iron and Steel Company into a joint Sino-Japanese concern which should have a veto on the workings of all mines near its own; fourth, for China not to cede or lease to any third power any harbor, bay, or island along the Chinese coasts; and fifth, for Japanese advisers to supervise China's political, financial, and military affairs, for a joint Sino-Japanese police force, for the purchase by China of one-half of her munitions from Japan, for a Japanese sphere of interest in Fukein province, and for the right of religious propaganda. On May 25, 1915, the Chinese Government agreed to all but the last group, under the pressure of an ultimatum.

China, in effect, seemed about to become a Japanese Egypt or Haiti. In November, 1915, when the Allies had wanted to bring China into the war, Japan had vetoed the proposal. In August, 1917, when American influence made China a belligerent, the Japanese had already received secret promises of support from the Allies. Even the United States was compelled, on November 2, 1917, in the Lansing-Ishii Agreement, to recognize that "territorial propinquity" gave Japan "special interests" in China, as well as to endorse Japan's claim on Shantung.

The reason why the United States gave this unusual support to Japan's aggressive policy, was the Zimmermann note, which attempted to embroil the United States with Germany, Mexico, and Japan. On March 1, 1917, the United States Government published a despatch from the German foreign secretary, Zimmermann, to the German minister in Mexico:

Berlin, January 19, 1917.

On the first of February we intend to begin submarine warfare unrestricted. In spite of this it is our intention to keep neutral the United States of America. If this attempt is not successful, we propose an alliance on the following basis with Mexico: that we shall make war together and together make peace. We shall give general fiancial support and it is understood that Mexico is to reconquer the lost territory in New Mexico, Texas and Arizona.

You are instructed to inform the President of Mexico of the above in great confidence as soon as it is certain that there will be an outbreak of war with the United States and suggest that the President of Mexico, on his own initiative, should communicate with Japan suggesting adherence at once to this plan; at the same time, offer to mediate between Germany and Japan.

Please call to the attention of the President of Mexico that the employment of ruthless submarine warfare now promises to compel England to make peace in a few months.

ZIMMERMANN.

The occasion was propitious for the success of this plan for the encirclement and partition of the United States. The U-boat warfare was in full swing, with a good chance of success. The American navy, though strong in destroyers, was weak in merchant shipping, transports, and trained officers and seamen. Mexico was only half-way through the cycle of revolution unleashed by Madero. President Carranza was personally hostile to the United States, though Wilson had wisely avoided being lured into a serious intervention in Mexican affairs. Japan was doing very nicely in China, after the twenty-one demands. Her share in the war had been limited to the reduction of Kiaochow in 1914, some naval patrol work in the Pacific and the acquisition of Germany's North Pacific possessions—the Caroline, Marshall, and Marianne Islands. Russia had recently overthrown the Tsar and had inaugurated a liberal régime under Kerensky, which may have been a moral gain for the Entente but was certainly a dead loss to its military power. Mexico and Japan nearly accepted this German offer. The price paid was the agreement by the Allies to Japan's retention of her winnings and America's endorsement of Japan's special interest in China.

The Russian Revolution of 1917 involved the American policy of republicanism as well as American policy in China. In July, 1916, Japan and Russia had made a secret treaty for joint action against any attempt by any other power—meaning America—to dominate China. The collapse of Tsardom ended this intrigue, as well as abolishing America's deep aversion to Tsarist Russia. But the collapse of Russia also knocked the bottom out of the military balance of power in Europe and Asia. In the first place it made American participation in the war vital to the success of the Allied cause. In the second place it removed the only effective deterrent to Japanese aggression in eastern Asia. With the advent of Bolshevism, all moral excuse for playing fair with Russia vanished, and the Allies in North Russia and the Japanese in Siberia began to encroach on Russia's territory. Coöperating with China, the Japanese occupied the Russian zone in northern Manchuria and then, in August, 1917, began to invade Siberia. America thought that Japan could be controlled better by an ally than a neutral, but after agreeing to joint Allied intervention with a limit of 7,500 troops for each power, the Japanese rushed 70,000 troops into Siberia and America found her own rôle in Russia to be primarily the protection of that country against the predatory ambitions of her European and Asiatic colleagues.

All these elements influenced America's decision to enter the war, but underlying all, and perhaps stronger than all, was her desire to maintain the political balance of world-power. Russia's offensive on the eastern front had collapsed in 1916. The Allied offensives in France had likewise failed. A negotiated peace seemed so possible that Colonel House at the end of 1916 offered American mediation and requested a statement of the peace terms of the combatants. All refused. However, with Great Britain menaced as seriously to the east as was China to the west of America, it was realized that a German victory meant the end of the British Empire, to which—as the basis of the status quo—the United States was committed. It meant, too, that the United States must prepare for heavy naval and military armaments in anticipation of German rivalry in Latin America and Japanese rivalry in Asia. The spring of 1917 was the last possible moment at which the United States could intervene decisively. France was bled white, England had her back to the wall, Europe was on the road to exhaustion.

America was fresh and fortunate not to have gone to war over the *Lusitania* in 1915, which would have cost her heavy casualties in 1915 and 1916, without materially affecting the military situation.

Wilson had been wise to keep his country out of Mexico and out of the war. For in 1917, had the United States been involved in Mexico, intervention in Europe would have been hampered. Had America been drawn into the struggle previously, her losses would have been multiplied without corresponding advantage to her policies. But Wilson was wisest of all in bringing the United States into the war in 1917. As it was, he was barely in time to save the day for American interests.

Chapter VIII

THE AMERICAN OFFENSIVE

AMERICA DECLARES WAR ON THE EUROPEAN SYSTEM

THE issues and circumstances of 1917 gave the United States an unparalleled opportunity to assert the political principles of Americanism against the European system which had endangered them. America's intervention in the war—in the narrow sense—took the form of actual hostility to Germany; basically, it was a tremendous effort by America to overturn the foundations of European statecraft and to recast Europe in a form less baneful to ourselves. This was shown from the start by America's decision not to ally herself, not to seek territory or expansion, but to "make the world safe for democracy." Wilson's war message of April 2, 1917, began with a sharp distinction between the German Government and people, which augured a new method of warfare, and his ringing periods contained the germs of his highly subversive political program:

We shall fight [he said] for the things which we have always carried nearest our hearts, for democracy, for the right of those who submit to authority to have a voice in their own governments, for the rights and liberties of small nations, for a universal dominion of right by such a concert of free peoples as shall bring peace and safety to all nations and make the world itself at last free.

The American intervention—economic, military, naval, financial, political, and moral—was vigorous and decisive. The American war was based on the North American Continent and upon its manifold resources. The War Industries Board was established July 18, 1917, under Baruch, and enabled the Government to handle raw materials, priority, labor, and army and navy requirements on a big-business scale. Similarly the War Shipping Board, the United States Railroad Administration, Hoover's food administration, and Garfield's fuel administration completed the American industrial mobilization. Espionage and Enemy Property Acts and the Committee on Public Information completed the civil organization for war.

The military and naval mobilization was not so swift. Secretary of War Baker described its beginning as "a happy confusion" and rejoiced that "when we entered this war we were not, like our adversary, ready for it, anxious for it, prepared for it, and inviting it." Inasmuch as America was protected from invasion for some months by the Allied armies and navies, this boast was in doubtful taste. Yet our military intervention was decisive. Congress quickly passed a $4,000,000,000 Army and Navy Bill. A Selective Service Act was signed by the President in May, 1917, to draft the male population between the ages of twenty-one and thirty. This bill added 3,091,000 men to the regular United States Army of 133,000 and to the National Guard of 67,000. At the time of the armistice the regular army contained 527,000 troops, the National Guard 382,000, with the balance in the new National Army. In November, 1918, the entire army consisted of 3,634,000 men, of whom 1,971,000—

or 55 per cent.—were in the American Expeditionary Force. This army was created on precisely the same principles employed in American mass-production. Thirty-two assembly plants—or cantonments—were erected at a cost of nearly $1,000,000,000. Troops were partly trained there and were then despatched like semi-finished manufactures to complete equipment in France.

Officers were prepared in special training camps and later assigned to their commands. Between March and October, 1918, 1,500,000 American troops were rushed overseas. The first comers met the Germans at the battle of Château-Thierry of July 15-18, 1918, of which the German Chancellor said, "The history of the world was played out in three days."

To transport and supply this army an entirely new merchant marine was constructed by similar direct methods. The War Shipping Board was reorganized on July 27, 1917. The first keel was laid July 29, 1917. The first launching occurred November 24, 1917. The first delivery was made January 5, 1918. The Emergency Fleet Corporation built these vessels in four huge shipyards, of which the largest—Hog Island—employed 350,000 workers. On July 1, 1917, the United States had 94,000 tons of transatlantic shipping; on December 1, 1918, 3,246,000 tons. The Shipping Board delivered 1,308 steel and 589 wooden ships. In four months—March to June, 1917—it delivered 870,368 tons of new and reconditioned German ships. The outbreak of war found 104 German vessels in American ports, their machinery so damaged as to render them unworkable. Yet 550,000 American troops were transported in twenty of these German liners, all but two of which made their first trips in 1917. The program of the United States navy had been in 1916 that "The Navy of the United States should ultimately be equal to the most powerful maintained by any other nation of the world. It should be gradually increased to this point by such a development, year by year, as may be permitted by the facilities of the country," and the initial appropriation of the bill of August 29, 1916, had been $312,678,000. This program was postponed by the war, to enable the fleet to coöperate with the British in combating the submarines. The A.E.F. was convoyed to France without submarine losses, a battleship division was stationed with the Grand Fleet, the navy was expanded to 500,000 men, and innumerable small craft and destroyers, bases were established at Gibraltar and the Azores, and a barrage of mines was laid across the North Sea. The simplicity of these naval achievements tends to obscure their significance in the winning of the war.

American financial intervention was lavish. The total war expenditure was $22,000,000,000, or more than $1,000,000 an hour. The Entente Allies borrowed over $10,000,000,000 from the United States Government: Great Britain $4,000,000,000; France nearly $3,500,-000,000; Italy over $1,600,000,000; and Belgium, Poland, Russia, and Czecho-Slovakia lesser amounts. The naval appropriations alone in 1917 and 1918 amounted to $3,833,000,000. The appropriations in 1917 were for $18,897,000,000, but contracts brought the expenditure to over $21,000,000,000. The First and Second Liberty Loans of July and October, 1917, amounted to $8,000,-000,000, and both were over-subscribed 50 per cent. The Third and Fourth Liberty Loans were floated without difficulty at six-month intervals, and netted $9,000,000,-

000 more. Between April, 1917, and October, 1919, the Government raised $11,280,000,000 in taxation. The total direct and indirect cost of the war to the United States was over $35,000,000,000.

It was, however, Wilson's political and moral intervention which was most decisive of all. In his War Message of April 2, 1917, he drove the wedge between the German Government and the German people and stipulated that peace should come with democracy in Germany:

We have no quarrel with the German people [he proclaimed]. We have no feeling toward them but one of sympathy and friendship. It was not upon their impulse that their Government acted in entering this war. It was not with their previous knowledge or approval. . . . Even in checking these things and trying to extirpate them [intrigue and espionage], we have sought to put the most generous interpretation possible upon them because we knew that their source lay, not in any hostile feeling or purpose of the German people toward us—who were, no doubt, as ignorant of them as we ourselves were—but only in the selfish desgins of a Government that did what it pleased and told its people nothing.

Self-governed nations do not fill their neighbor states with spies or set the course of intrigue to bring about some critical posture of affairs which will give them an opportunity to strike and make conquest. Such designs can be successfully worked out only under cover and where no one has the right to ask questions.

On January 8, 1918, he laid before the world the Fourteen Points of his peace program, which provided for open diplomacy, the freedom of the seas, the removal of economic barriers, the reduction of armaments, the impartial adjustment of colonial claims, the settlement of Russia, Belgium, Alsace-Lorraine, Italy, Austria-Hungary, the Balkans, Turkey, and Poland on the basis of self-determination, and the establishment of "a general association of nations . . . for the purpose of affording mutual guarantees of political independence and territorial integrity to great and small states alike."

His program originally contemplated the federalization of Austria-Hungary. On December 4, 1917, in explaining America's declaration of war on the Habsburg Empire, he said: "We owe it to ourselves to declare that we do not wish to weaken or to transform the Austro-Hungarian Monarchy. How it may wish to live politically or industrially is not our concern. We neither intend nor desire to dictate to it in anything. We wish only that the affairs of its peoples, in great things and small, may remain in their own hands." But a month later, in his Tenth Point, he had altered his policy: "The peoples of Austria-Hungary, whose place among the nations we wish to see safeguarded and assured, should be accorded the freest opportunity of autonomous development." Wilson's endorsement of federation in Austria-Hungary died slowly. Eventually he recognized the Czecho-Slovak National Council and the national aims of the Yugo-Slavs, and on May 20, 1918, Secretary Lansing accepted the resolutions of the Rome Congress of Oppressed Austro-Hungarian Peoples. But the American Government saw with misgivings the Balkanization of Central Europe and at the Peace Conference tried vainly to temper it with federal ideals.

However, in the final analysis, it was the moral fervor with which Wilson endowed his political intervention which was the most decisive element of all. He turned the war into a crusade to end war, a struggle against autocracy and tyranny, a battle to make the world safe for democracy and a decent place to live in. In his reply to the

Pope's peace proposals of August 27, 1917, he declared that

The object of this war is to deliver the free peoples of the world from the menace and the actual power of a vast military establishment controlled by an irresponsible government. . . . This power is not the German people. It is the ruthless master of the German people. . . . The American people have suffered intolerable wrongs at the hands of the Imperial German Government, but they desire no reprisal upon the German people, who have themselves suffered all things in this war, which they did not choose. They believe that peace should rest upon the rights of people, not the rights of Governments—the rights of peoples great or small, weak or powerful—their equal right to freedom and security and self-government and to a participation upon fair terms in the economic opportunities of the world. . . .

And when the war was won and the Germans had laid down their arms on the basis of the Fourteen Points, Wilson felt that the victory was to the peoples of the world. On February 24, 1919, he told an audience at Mechanics Hall, in Boston, that

when I speak of the nations of the world I do not speak of the governments of the world. I speak of peoples who constitute the nations of the world. They are in the saddle, and they are going to see to it that if their present governments do not do their will, some other governments shall. The secret is out, and present governments know it.

Wilson believed all this.

THE BATTLE FOR SELF-DETERMINATION

The principle of self-determination, unchecked and undisciplined by its proper federative qualification, was one of the most subversive political forces which have ever been unleashed. It was first invoked as a war measure in dealing with the Central Empires, and even then reluctantly; soon it had burst all bounds and had created dangerous domestic problems for every one of America's associates in the war.

The first development of this dangerous force was in Central Europe and the territory of the enemy states. The Fourteen Points had advocated autonomy for the peoples of Austria-Hungary and had proposed that "the other (non-Turkish) nationalities which are now under Turkish rule should be assured an undoubted security of life and an absolutely unmolested opportunity of autonomous development," and that "an independent Polish state would be erected which should include the territories inhabited by indisputably Polish populations."

However, when it came to recognizing the self-determinant aspirations of a particular state—such as Czecho-Slovakia—Wilson was cold, until convinced by Masaryk of the reality of Czecho-Slovak nationalism. On June 28, 1918, Secretary Lansing expressed a hope for the emancipation of the Slavs; on September 3 the United States accorded belligerent status to the Czecho-Slovak National Council; on October 18, the American Government accepted the Czecho-Slovak Declaration of Independence; but not until April 23, 1919, was an American minister appointed to the Czecho-Slovak republic.

Subsequently, full sway was accorded to the nationalistic aspirations of the Yugo-Slavs, the Roumanians, Armenians, and Greeks of Central and Eastern Europe. In 1919 and 1920 recognition was given to Yugo-Slavia, Poland, Finland, and Armenia, in 1922 to the remaining

Baltic states. Central Europe was smashed. Germany was pared down, and then—in violation of the self-determinant principle—forbidden to unite with Austria. Austria-Hungary and Turkey resolved into their component parts. Vast accretions were permitted to Roumania and Serbia, while Hungary, Bulgaria, and Austria were whittled away. The Arab portions of Turkey were snatched from the Ottomans, and an ephemeral Armenian republic was given *de facto* recognition.

Not only was the principle of self-determination used to wreck the enemies of the Entente, but it was invoked against the latter's former Russian ally. Clemenceau's *cordon sanitaire* against Bolshevism and Britain's less well-advertised system of Baltic states were used to thrust Russia back into Asia and away from the sea. Poland, Lithuania, Esthonia, Latvia, Finland, Georgia, and Russian Armenia were given encouragement and recognition. In 1920 an attempt was made to set up an independent Ukrainian Government, and the province of Bessarabia was forcibly added to Roumania, first by the Supreme Council and later by a formal treaty (October 28, 1920), signed by France, Italy, Great Britain, and Japan. The Soviet authorities had approved the earlier Baltic and Polish states, prior to American recognition, but in the case of Bessarabia no such Russian consent has been obtained, and the United States has consistently refused to endorse Roumanian sovereignty over this province. The efforts of British Indian officials to build up autonomous republics in the Caucasus were regarded as an attempt to cut off Russia from the Near and Middle East, while the interventions in 1918-20 were further efforts to give a special anti-Russian bearing to Wilson's doctrine. Allied and American interventions occurred in North Russia, South Russia, and Siberia. Russian adventurers, such as Denikin, Kolchak, Wrangel, Semenoff, and Yudenitch, were supplied with munitions and credits to overthrow the Soviet régime. It is only fair to state that Wilson did not entirely commit his government to this enterprise and that American troops were in North Russia and Siberia primarily as a check on the Allies. Wilson's Russian policy was stated in his Fourteen Points as

the best and freest coöperation of the other nations of the world in obtaining for her an unhampered and unembarrassed opportunity for the independent determination of her own political development and national policy, and assure her of a sincere welcome into the society of free nations under institutions of her own choosing; and, more than a welcome, assistance also of every kind that she may need and may herself desire. The treatment accorded Russia by her sister nations in the months to come will be the acid test of their goodwill, of their comprehension of her needs as distinguished from their own interests, and of their intelligent and unselfish sympathy.

The fact that self-determination could cut both ways first dawned on Europe with the emergence of three considerable problems at the Peace Conference: the disputes over Fiume, Shantung, and Dantzig, as well as minor squabbles, such as that over the possession of Teschen. Italian and Serbian rivalry over Fiume, Chinese and Japanese disagreement about Shantung, German and Polish claims on Dantzig, suddenly revealed the necessity for self-denial as well as self-determination, and as suddenly made Wilson very unpopular in Europe. But the harm was done. You could not apply self-determination as a universal principle of justice to your enemies and former colleagues and not affect your own imperialistic aspirations. The result has been a gradual subversion of the imperial principle in Great Britain, France, Japan, and the United States, in a long-drawn struggle of which the Peace Conference was but the prelude. Great Britain was the first to suffer its effects and the first to accept them.

In Ireland the revolt against England, which had begun in 1915 and had smoldered throughout the war, could not be put down after the three years of civil warfare which followed the armistice. The result was the establishment of the Irish Free State by the Anglo-Irish Treaty of December 6, 1922. In 1924, the United States received a minister from the Irish Free State and subsequently appointed a minister to Dublin. In Egypt, on the outbreak of the war, Great Britain had declared the country a Protectorate. The result was an Egyptian revolt in 1919, and a prolonged agitation for independence which resulted in the Anglo-Egyptian Treaty of March 16, 1922, ending the British Protectorate and recognizing Egypt as an independent kingdom. A month later the United States accorded diplomatic recognition to Egypt. Following the war there was a long series of uprisings and agitation in India for Swaraj—or self-government, characterized by Ghandi's non-coöperation and boycott policies and flaming into sporadic riots and revolts. In 1918 the Montagu-Chelmsford Commission recommended a system of diarchy, somewhat similar to the pre-war American régime in the Philippines; this failed, and in 1928, a new commission was despatched under Sir John Simon to make new recommendations. In Palestine and Syria the movement for Arab self-determination was complicated by contradictory British promises to the

French, Arabs, and Jews. The Sykes-Picot Treaty of 1915 had promised Syria to France, and the Balfour Declaration of 1917 had promised Palestine to the Jews as a national homeland, while the Arabs had been promised both countries by the British authorities in Egypt. The territories were conquered by the British in 1918, and an Arab kingdom was actually established at Damascus, to be overthrown two years later by the French. In Palestine, a British mandatory government was set up on July 1, 1920, and a British high commissioner was appointed. On September 1, 1923, a new constitution was established, but was boycotted by the Arabs. Subsequently, the establishment of the Arab Kingdoms of Iraq and Transjordania satisfied some of the Arab aspirations.

However, the most interesting change wrought by self-determination has been the partial transformation of the British Empire into a Commonwealth of Nations. The Dominions were given separate places on the Imperial War Council during the war, and afterward sent separate delegations to the Peace Conference and received separate memberships in the League of Nations. They sent separate delegates to the Washington Conference in 1922, and at the Imperial Conference of 1926 were given a legal status equal to that of the Kingdom of Great Britain. Since then, they have negotiated separate treaties and established diplomatic relations with the United States and other powers. Save in her tropical dependencies and Crown Colonies, the imperial element is disappearing from the British Empire and a type of federalism is slowly supplanting it. This is the most significant political development of the post-war age as it is the most important practical result of self-determination as a political ideal.

In the French empire, also, self-determination produced violent and unwelcome results. The Syrian mandate was taken by France, who drove out the Arab King Feisul, bombarded Damascus, and since then engaged in costly guerilla operations against the Arabs and the Druses, which have occasioned fresh bombardments of Damascus and other incidents repugnant to the liberal opinion of the world. In Morocco, the difficult war against the Riffi, which had occupied Spain for a decade, was carried into the French zone by Abd-el-Krim in 1925. This provoked one of the major military campaigns since the war—a drive against the Riffi on a scale comparable to the Boer War and costly in men, money, and prestige to the French administration, which finally, in 1926, extinguished the Riff republic. Since then France has been resting on its precarious laurels, with Moslem North Africa politically unsettled from Cairo to Agadir.

Although these developments of self-determination were not entirely welcome to the United States, in no field has the principle of self-determination been more advantageous to American policy than in eastern Asia, where it has served as a check to Japanese imperialism. In 1919 a Korean rebellion was put down by the Japanese with considerable bloodshed. In China, the boycott of Japanese trade inaugurated by the Nationalist students encouraged the Japanese to end their occupation of Shantung in 1922. Chinese nationalism further served to undermine the special privileges of all powers in China, except Russia, which had the wit to profit by anti-foreign agitation, and has begun to menace Japan's position in Manchuria. Only Soviet Russia and the United States have been unscathed by the Chinese Revolution, which, incidentally, threatens British predominance in the Yangtse Valley and in South China, Japanese influence in Manchuria, Shantung, and Fukien, French influence in Honan and Kwang Chow-Wan, and may affect Russian occupation in northern Manchuria and Outer Mongolia. American endorsement of the principles of Chinese nationalism leaves, in the opinion of some observers, all China an American "sphere of influence."

But the United States was not to pass unscathed through the fire she had kindled. Filipino politicians were quick to seize on the inconsistency of America's keeping their islands in political tutelage. Wilson, alone of American statesmen, was prepared to accept the logic of self-determination in the Philippines. In 1913, he had appointed a Filipino majority in the Insular Commission. In 1916, the Jones Law had substituted an elective Senate for a Legislative Council, and had stated in its Preamble that "It is, as it has always been, the purpose of the people of the United States to withdraw their sovereignty from the Philippines and to recognize their independence as soon as a stable government can be established therein." In December, 1920, Wilson advised Congress that a stable government had been established and recommended that the pledge of independence should be fulfilled. The Filipinos enjoyed home rule from 1914 till 1921, when the Wood-Forbes Mission inspected the islands and declared them not ready for self-government. General Wood was sent out to Manila as governor-general and endeavored to restore order and efficiency to the insular administration. In dismissing a Filipino petition for independence, President Coolidge observed that the Filipinos had not recognized the truth of the theory of the complete separation of legislative, executive, and judicial powers in a democracy, thereby neatly turning the tables by making Wilson's pet moral theory of good government as the condition of self-government.

EUROPE FAILS TO FEDERALIZE

Before branding self-determination as a crime committed by Wilson in the name of liberty, credit must be given for his effort to temper nationalistic autonomy with the principle of federal control. Self-determination became an irresponsible political force only when Europe rejected the proposal for a practical union of her nations on an equal political footing.

Wilson's Fourteenth Point stipulated that "A general association of nations must be formed, under specific covenants, for the purpose of affording mutual guarantees of political independence to great and small states alike."

This was a proffer to Europe of the greatest political discovery of the United States—the art of successful federation—and constituted a germ for a United States of Europe, which, under the new fashions of democracy, might have been a terrible menace to America's selfish ambitions. That risk Wilson gladly accepted for his country. The result justified neither his optimism nor the fears of the American nationalists. With divergent political systems, different languages, faiths, and civilizations, all vigorously developed on a nationalistic basis, the

European states were impotent to combine on any basis save a diplomatic alliance, which served to confirm rather than supplant the uncompromising rigors of national egotism.

The League of Nations, accordingly, far from being the ground-plan of a United States of Europe, became a tangible diplomatic entanglement for the European nations—a sheet of idealistic fly-paper in which the nations buzz and struggle and are clogged in their efforts to go through the motions of national independence. Accordingly, the League is so constituted as to be powerless as a coalition against the United States—the inclusion of the British Dominions and the Latin-American republics would prevent this—and is incapable of becoming a separate sovereignty such as that established by the American Constitution.

Moreover, the League's problems being chiefly European, a case for American abstention was set up at the start. The United States retained a free hand and was not drawn into the mazes of European diplomacy, but has remained outside, proffering helpful advice from time to time to the victims of insufficient faith in the virtue of American ideals.

Not only is America outside the League, but the League is effectively estopped from meddling in American affairs by Article 21 of its covenant, which grants priority to "regional understandings like the Monroe Doctrine." The United States has a free hand in the Americas, and any action on her part to which her elastic and convenient doctrine can be applied is outside the jurisdiction of the League of Nations. Europe has less power to intervene in the Americas than before the war, when the Monroe Doctrine was not formally accepted or endorsed by the European powers.

Again, a further penalty of Europe's failure to federalize is America's power to intervene in Europe through the Latin-American republics which are members of the League. Although, with the exception of Chile, no major Latin-American state is now an active member of the League, three states—Cuba, Panama, and Chile—are members of the League Council, and a larger group is in the Assembly, where they are able to block any action hostile to the general interests of the three Americas, while Canada's influence would undoubtedly be cast in the same direction. On the other hand, the Latin-American republics may not be regarded as the puppets of American policy. Washington could not even rely upon the delegates of Cuba, Panama, Haiti, or the Dominican Republic —which are directly subject to our influence—to vote as the United States might desire; but the spirit of Pan-Americanism, and the fact that the Monroe Doctrine is predicated on an American community of interests, guarantee a reciprocal feeling which would intervene decisively in our behalf in any real threat to American interests.

Finally, the public registration of treaties with the League Secretariat, the publicity which attends meetings of the Assembly, and the assurance that at least one member of the League Council will reveal its proceedings, make Wilson's widowed institution at Geneva a valuable American peephole into European politics. That the League would ever be able to stop a real war is debatable, but that it might serve as a political barometer for such a war is certain. Through the American Legation at Berne and the numerous official, unofficial, and officious American observers at all League functions, the United States can glance into the workings of Europe's volcanic statesmanship and take warning by what is seen through the little window Wilson gave his country into the heart of Europe.

America has received all this, without responsibilities other than her own hostages to fortune—trade, investments, and overseas possessions, her prudence, and the pacific temper of her citizens. Europe's failure to federalize has given America advantages which no other power, save Soviet Russia, possesses; and unlike Russia, the United States is so remote from the center of political intrigue that no immediate concatenation of events can force her to abandon her happy and unhampered position.

THE VAST SIMPLICITY OF WILSON'S ACHIEVEMENTS

Only in perspective does the true character of Wilson's policy appear. There is so vast a simplicity of design in the methods of his statecraft that it has escaped detection. Just as our military intervention, with its assembling of armies on the principle of mass-production and basing their operations in Europe on the remote North American Continent, escaped the attention of the German commanders until "the history of the world was played out in three days," so the huge outlines of Wilson's foreign policy have escaped the attention of its American advocates and its European critics.

A glance at Europe in 1920 as compared to the Europe of 1914 reveals what Wilson really did. The old balance of power is gone, and can scarcely be revived on a worldwide basis without the assent of the United States and

Russia, the two republican federations which prefer to keep aloof from the intricacies of European controversies. All that can be achieved without them is a system of regional balances, in Western Europe, in Eastern Europe, in the Mediterranean, and in eastern Asia, none of which threatens immediate war or menaces the United States.

The old military autocracies are gone—Austria-Hungary, Prussian Germany, Tsarist Russia, are broken. Japan has entered upon an era of far-reaching electoral reforms, and Great Britain is engaged in liquidating her military empire in the Middle East and federalizing her empire. Europe's military, economic, and financial power has been dissipated for at least fifty years. Her subdivision into numerous little new states—mainly republics—has further weakened her military powers. Before the war France was the only republic in Europe; today there are eighteen. Before the war there were twenty-five states in Europe; today there are thirty-five.

Finally, although the easy habit of informal diplomatic ententes is still prevalent in European statesmanship, the hard-and-fast obligations and quid-pro-quo's of secret diplomacy have been seriously invalidated. Europe is today, as before the war, still stored with demoniac forces, fierce energies, incompatible ambitions, but the rest of the world is far better protected against them than ever before.

This is what Wilson accomplished through his dexterous use of the basic principles of American policy. No candid student of international politics can doubt that his achievements have been to the lasting advantage of the United States or that he made America the one real winner in the World War.

Chapter IX

EUROPE ON THE DEFENSIVE

PROPAGANDA

The United States, under Wilson, had attained to its greatest political, military, financial, and economic power. True to its traditions, however, when the emergency passed, it dispensed with its army, dissolved its political affiliations with Europe, and retained only its naval armament, its trade, and its credit, to remind the world that a new power which could no longer be ignored had arisen across the Atlantic.

The first European reaction was a frank endeavor to make use of American resources for European purposes, the second to make America abandon their use for her own. To this end, a concerted world-wide diplomacy was exerted for a decade, ranging from pleas to be "generous" to overt threats against our security. The separate existence of American power could no longer be ignored by Europe's chancelleries. Their first notion that America's naïve power could be easily manipulated soon ended. Disillusioned on that score, Europe endeavored, with greater success, to neutralize American resources and to induce the United States to dissipate its power.

The experience of war-time propaganda had taught Europe that the American people could be deeply stirred by moral flattery and moral appeals. Europe's first propaganda was openly designed to bring the United States into the war—or, in the case of Germany, to keep it neutral—and once America was engaged in the struggle, to win her support for particular European ambitions. Europe's war propaganda was not vicious or dishonest— much of it was entirely straightforward. On this point, it is wise to consider the evidence of one of Europe's most adroit propagandists:

In the psychology of propaganda [he writes], one point is important—not to imagine that people can be converted to a political idea merely by stating it vigorously and enthusiastically or by harping on its details; the chief thing is to arouse interest in your cause as best you can, indirectly no less than directly. Political agitation often frightens or alienates thoughtful people whom art and literature may attract. Sometimes a single phrase, well used at the right moment, is enough. Long-windedness is always to be avoided, especially in private talk. True, propaganda of this kind presupposes culture, political and social breadth of view, tact and knowledge of men on the part of those who undertake it.

Another weighty point is this—propaganda must be honest. Exaggeration is harmful and lies are worse. Some among us thought that the whole art of politics consists in gulling people. Until we stopped them they tried to disseminate "patriotic" untruths, forgetting that falsehoods can be exposed. . . .

A third rule is not to praise one's own goods, like inferior commercial travelers. Intelligent and honest policy must accompany intelligent and honest propaganda.[1]

On the whole, however, the European propaganda in the United States during the 1914-17 period was a matter of phrases and slogans: "plucky little Belgium,"

[1] Thomas Garrigue Masaryk, *The Making of a State.*

"heroic France," "a war for the defense of the rights of small nations," "a war to put down Prussianism." Little or nothing was said about Japan's shrewd rôle in eastern Asia or about the terms under which Italy, Roumania, and Greece were hustled into hostilities. The German propaganda was less honest. It dealt with the "inhumanities" of the British blockade, while Germany's submarines were sinking passenger ships on sight. It complained of Britain's pre-war "encirclement" of Germany, while preparing, in the Zimmermann note, for a German encirclement of the United States. It spoke of "the Russian menace" and condoned the Armenian atrocities. The true motives of European war diplomacy were reflected in the secret war-time treaties for the partition of Germany, Austria-Hungary, Turkey, Persia, China, and the Pacific: the treaties between France and Great Britain for the division of Togoland, the Cameroons, and Turkey; between Russia and Great Britain for the partition of Persia; the Treaty of London (April 26, 1915), in which the Entente guaranteed Italy the acquisition of Austrian territory. On August 18, 1916, Roumania was promised Transylvania, the Banat, and Bukowina in return for her intervention. In February, 1917, Great Britain and Japan arranged for the partition of Germany's Pacific islands and assigned Shantung to Japan. On March 11, 1917, France and Russia negotiated a treaty giving to Russia a free hand in the east of Germany, and to France and Great Britain similar freedom in the west. No less than six secret Allied treaties, from March, 1915, to December, 1918, provided for the partition of the Ottoman Empire. To the Allied Governments it was a war for territorial expansion as well as for self-defense.

The ink was scarcely dry on the Armistice when our European associates began to plan fresh armaments. Admiral Benson at Versailles proposed American-British naval equality and advocated that "Great Britain and America determine jointly from time to time what the strength of the two fleets shall be." The proposal led to nothing. The sinking of the German fleet, advocated by the United States and favored by the British, reduced the French to fury. They said that this fleet was valuable, that its sinking represented the deliberate destruction of property, and they proposed that German reparations should include the cost of the vessels which lay at the bottom of Scapa Flow.

In consequence, having failed to secure the reduction of British armament, America proceeded with her 1916 program, to be completed in 1923-24, on the theory that "The United States should have a navy equal to any that sails the seas." This was the view of Josephus Daniels, Secretary of the Navy, and of President Wilson. The attitude of the British Admiralty was set forth by Mr. Winston Churchill, who declaimed soon after the armistice:

Nothing in the world, nothing that you may think of, or dream of, or any one may tell you; no arguments, however specious, no appeals, however seductive, must lead you to abandon that naval supremacy on which the life of our country depends.

The Japanese Empire in 1920 drew up plans to construct sixteen capital ships, to be ready in 1928, and in 1921, the British Government followed the Japanese and American lead. However, the Washington Conference of 1921-22 put an end to competition in battleships by scrapping seventy war-ships, of which thirty-two were American, and surrendering actual American superiority for theoretical equality with Great Britain.

Thereupon, the United States stopped naval construction. Japan and France, in the following year, took a lead in cruiser construction which promised soon to outclass the two Anglo-Saxon sea-powers. In 1924, Great Britain followed suit. In 1927, when we endeavored to put an end to this ominous building by summoning another naval conference, America was characterized as aggressive by the European press.

American naval power having thus been adequately impaired, the next stage in the game was to turn our financial power against us. Prior to our entry into the war, the French and British had sold large numbers of their bonds in the United States. J. P. Morgan and Company acted as the British purchasing agent and floated British credits up to the amount of $1,000,000,000. When the United States entered the war, the British were facing the prospect of selling $3,000,000,000 worth of American securities in order to preserve their credit. Accordingly the first Allied action was the despatch of "missions" to Washington, with the result that the United States assumed the British and French debts in this country, foreign investments were intact, and the Allies were enabled to borrow freely from the United States Government. At that time both France and Great Britain insisted on the validity of their debts to the United States. They repudiated any suggestion that they were being subsidized by the American Government, but Thomas Lamont has stated that "From start to finish of the Peace Conference President Wilson and his advisers, without exceptions, opposed vigorously and finally any such suggestion or proposition of cancellation." "The question," he added, "in one form or another constantly arose."

The final symptom of the European reaction against America was the effort to divide the American people. Before 1917, the Germans had appealed to pacifist sentiment in an effort to keep the United States neutral. At the same time, they had attempted to cultivate the German-American vote and to stir up the negroes in the South. In exactly the same way, after the armistice the Allies appealed to American public opinion in order to influence Wilson at Versailles. Polish-American, Italian-American, and other racial groups were sedulously cultivated. A great American press agency opened its guns on Wilson because its Paris correspondent had personal reasons for wanting the President to give France the left bank of the Rhine. A concerted Anglo-French drive against Wilson's proposed recognition of Soviet Russia was entirely successful. The net result, however, was disappointing to the Allies. As an unforeseen consequence of their efforts, Wilson was defeated by the American people, and along with him went the Treaty of Versailles and the League of Nations. The harvest of this first effort to manipulate American public opinion in the interest of Europe was international confusion and resentment.

FINANCIAL REACTIONS

Since it had proved difficult to make use of America, the next step was to isolate the United States by a series of financial, economic, and political alignments calculated to encircle North America in a ring of hostile opinion.

The first move in that direction was along the line of debt cancellation. From June 15, 1919, to February 9, 1922, when the Debt Funding Commission was established, no European government made a single move to pay interest or principal. Not until the British debt settlement of June 19, 1923, did any European nation take any action to honor its word. On the contrary, during the interregnum, American tax-payers paid $400,000,000 in interest on the money lent to their war associates.

Immediately afterward, the British Government in the Balfour note of August 11, 1923, declared a policy of limiting Great Britain's total claim against her former Allies and Germany "to the amount necessary to cover the British debt to the United States." By implication, the United States was thus made responsible for every British debt collected on the Continent. The effect was, immediately, to create a European solidarity against America, in favor of Great Britain, and to make any American intercourse with the Continent dependent on the British middleman. Although the Allies, through the Dawes Plan of 1924, put German reparations on the same basis of "ability to pay" which had animated the American debt policy, and although American coöperation both secured the adoption of this plan and financed and administered it, the basic situation of the debts has been, ever since, that America is being paid and that every one else is paying, directly or indirectly, the Government at Washington.

On the Continent the effect of the Balfour note continued to keep Great Britain in the middle position between the United States and Europe until 1927, when the British refusal to disarm at the Tripartite Naval Conference or to encourage the protocol idea in the League of Nations, led to some doubts as to the candor of British policy.

However, the British have managed periodically to remind Europe of the debts. In 1926 there was a violent agitation over the French debt to America, American tourists in Paris were mobbed, and wounded French veterans paraded in protest against collection. In 1927, powerful London newspapers started a clamor about "Uncle Shylock" that produced similar ill-will. The plain fact is that so long as European budgets must make provision for payments to the United States, so long will the debts be to Europe a political problem. To have converted America's influence over European policy into a liability is indicative both of the skill of Europe's diplomats and of the inelasticity of the American statesmen.

With the exception of Great Britain, Europe wants America to cancel her loans, but not to call it cancellation. Europe wants to secure the remission of her debts without parting with a single island, demobilizing a single battalion, or scrapping a single warship.

So Europe is in steady search of a plausible formula for cancellation and is testing American public opinion with most of the arguments which her diplomats tried on the American peace delegation, and with much the same lack of success. This is probably due to one neglected feature of debt cancellation: that cancellation—voluntary and unsolicited—would put the American Government on record as believing that obligations contracted in time of war need not be paid in time of peace.

America is today the richest country in the world, and her credit is indispensable to her political and economic future. If she admits the principle of cancellation, she will have destroyed her public credit as it applies to foreign borrowings. Should we, at some future date, be compelled to seek money abroad in order to finance a war, we would find the world's credit available only at usurious rates. Seen from this angle, cancellation propaganda —whether knowingly or not—is a great danger to our future. Not only would it destroy the one means of political restraint which America can employ in Europe, but it would lay America open to similar demands for cancellation of private loans to foreign governments, municipalities and provinces. In a word, cancellation would tend to close the United States to borrowers and would turn American capital in upon itself.

DIRTY WORK AT THE ECONOMIC CROSSROADS

The culmination of Europe's reaction to the American impact was characteristic. The combination of political authority with economic exclusiveness, which is the logical result of Europe's traditional system, was employed to its full extent. It is exceedingly easy to attribute an anti-American psychology to exclusiveness of the sort which produced the "oil war" and the "rubber war," the continuation of war-time "controls" over essential raw materials, the sudden spread of European "trusts" and "cartels," and import quota regulations for films, oil, and automobiles. All these measures had an adverse effect upon American trade, but they were adopted, primarily, with the object of settling Europe's domestic economic problems. If they hurt the Americans, that didn't worry the Europeans, but that was not their intention. Actually, they were trying to discover some means of political adjustment for a difficult economic situation.

The economic storm began shortly after the armistice in an "oil war" between American and Anglo-Dutch oil interests. Our Secretaries of State, Colby and Hughes, alike protested against the exclusive character of the British oil concessions in the Mosul area and in Palestine. We criticized the monopolistic exploitation of the Djambi oilfields in the Dutch East Indies. The conflict continued outside of governmental spheres in a prolonged duel between the Standard Oil Companies and the Dutch Shell group.

Other raw materials, produced in European, Latin-American, and Asiatic countries, were subjected to governmental "controls," which enhanced the price by limiting the output. Administrative decrees and legislation have imposed virtual monopolies upon Egyptian long-staple cotton, Japanese camphor, Brazilian coffee, Chilean iodine and nitrates, and upon mercury, potash, sisal, and rubber. The Stevenson Rubber Restriction Act, which became law on November 1, 1922, and was maintained until 1928, within three years raised the New York price of rubber from 16.30 cents to 109.50 cents a pound. Its denunciation by Secretary Hoover led to an acrimonious interchange between England and America, and a British observer noted "the profound satisfaction in certain circles at the resentment in America at the artificial raising of the price of raw rubber by the restriction policy. Some Englishmen went about rubbing their hands, quoting the American protests, and boasting that the tribute we were extracting through our control of the rubber supplies more than paid a year's instalment on the debt." [1]

Even more symptomatic of the European reaction against America was the effort to combine European industries in "trusts" and "cartels," or pooled selling agencies. The number of such combinations included at the end of 1927: A raw steel trust, of French, German, Belgian, Czecho-Slovakian, Luxembourg, and Austro-Hungarian producers (formed in September, 1926); a steel rail combine, including British interests, formed in June, 1926; steel tubes (June, 1926), aluminium (August, 1926), enamel-ware (1926), zinc (July, 1926), synthetic silk (January, 1927), copper (October, 1926), with American participation, electric bulbs (1924), wire (February, 1927), as well as pre-war combinations in plate-glass, glass bottles, and borax. Other formidable international combinations included the Swedish-American match trust, the Franco-German potash combine, and the explosives combination of Germany and Great Britain. By the end of 1927, similar combinations were contemplated for zinc selling, cast iron pipe, shapes and semi-finished steel, with negotiations in progress for German, French, and British chemical amalgamations.

An incidental development of the same tendency has been the use of the European quota system to the detriment of American films. In France, Great Britain, Germany, Hungary, Austria, Czecho-Slovakia, Italy, and other European countries, efforts were made to create domestic film industries by restricting the number of foreign films which could be exhibited. An attempt to amalgamate the entire European film industries was made.

[1] Lieutenant-Commander Kenworthy, *Peace or War?*

The surviving war-time system of import licenses was found a convenient basis for economic discrimination. Thus, Lieutenant-Commander Kenworthy noted in his book *Peace or War?* that "the Federation of British Industries, an extremely powerful unofficial corporation of manufacturers and financiers, complains bitterly that American films spread American ideas, and therefore the demand for American goods, in the British Colonies, and demands reprisals and the fostering of a British industry to take the place of the American film monopoly."

Finally, every European country—including Great Britain—came out openly for protection. Tariff revisions, import and export restrictions in the form of total prohibitions, contingents, or government licensing systems, anti-dumping duties, depreciated currency surtaxes, led to a basic revision of the economic policy of Europe which seriously curtailed the expansion of American trade. By 1924, almost every country in Europe had revised its tariff upward, and Great Britain, by the Safeguarding of Industries Act of October, 1921, put a 33⅓ per cent. duty on products competing with British major industries. An effort to foster Inter-Imperial trade resulted in an intensive "Buy British Goods" campaign throughout the Empire. The British Government spent $1,000,000 on publicity for Dominion goods, advertising that "British Goods Are Best." Strong British commercial propaganda in Australia, New Zealand, and the Argentine misrepresented the dangers of the adverse trade balance which such countries have with the United States, and urged them to "Buy Where You Sell" (i.e. from Great Britain). In all, twenty European countries increased their import duties since the war, as have, in the Americas,

British Guiana, Canada, Cuba, Newfoundland, Panama, Paraguay, Uruguay, Venezuela, Ecuador, Haiti, Mexico, and Peru, and elsewhere, Australia, the British West Indies, the Dutch East Indies, Syria, the Union of South Africa, China, and Siam.

Chapter X

THE EUROPEAN COUNTER-ATTACK

POLITICAL ENCIRCLEMENT

With the consolidation of its moral, financial, and economic resistance to American power, the Old World was enabled to proceed with its own program for reconstruction, which implied the eradication of American political influence in Europe and produced the effective isolation of the United States. Here again it would be dangerous to attribute anti-American motives to Europe's actions. They have been, rather, instinctive efforts to enable Europe to recover the place which she had held in the world before the war and which America had stepped into during the ten years of European economic prostration and political preoccupation due to the war.

The first symptom of the political counter-offensive came in the ominous drift toward a war of America against Great Britain and Japan, which was strongly in evidence in 1920-21, and which was stopped by America's voluntary destruction of her battle-fleet by the Washington treaties. The price we paid for peace was the abandonment of naval supremacy in return for the termination of the Anglo-Japanese Alliance. America's belief that this presaged a firm Anglo-American understanding was, however, disappointed in the event; the Geneva Conference in 1927 clearly demonstrated that Great Britain intended to play a lone hand.

The natural Anglo-Japanese resentment at enlarged American naval and political power received incongruous support from Communistic agitation in the Philippines, Mexico, Nicaragua, and China. For seven years the Philippines were the scene of a prolonged agitation against American control, to force immediate independence. In Mexico, the immense economic interests of the United States suffered from radical legislation, which threatened the titles of every American mine operator, land-owner, and oil company south of Texas. Decrees and laws, based on the novel land and mineral provisions of the Constitution of 1917, for a time threatened to involve us in a Mexican intervention, until settled by Ambassador Morrow's diplomacy in 1927-28. The revolutionary faction in Nicaragua, which defied the policy of the United States, received enthusiastic support from radical circles in Latin America and Europe, and our intervention was used as a pretext for an effort to break up the Pan-American Union. In China, the existence of our "colonial slaves" in the Philippines was urged to deter the Nationalists from coming to an agreement with the United States.

At the same time, a vigorous propaganda was waged against the United States from sources as diverse as Russia, Great Britain, Japan, and Mexico. Russian agitation was chiefly academic, aimed to alter America's policy of non-recognition and to criticize her capitalism. Its chief hope was for an Anglo-American war in which the world's two chief capitalistic powers should destroy each other. Anti-American propaganda in Great Britain arose from many diverse sources: simple dislike of the Americans as individuals, industrial opposition to our tariff and shipping policies, Prohibition, irritation at our debt policy, anti-Babbitt mockery, attempts to deflect British emigration to the Dominions. Japanese propaganda was largely designed to combat America's political influence and trade in China, where by talk of American race discrimination, the Japanese sought to turn the yellow world against the whites. As in Great Britain, Japan opposed American dealings with the Soviet republics, hoping by prior negotiations to win Russian support for Japanese policy in China. Although it was suggested that Japanese political designs were back of the Nicaraguan revolution, there was nothing to show that Japan is yet involved in the anti-Yankee agitation in Latin America. The head and front of that agitation has been Mexico, who seeks to make herself the leader of the Latin-American world by undermining the United States in Central America.

The political encirclement of the United States was buttressed by naval dispositions. Naval building has been uninterrupted by Great Britain, France, Italy, and Japan, the four other signatories to the arms limitation treaty of Washington. While Great Britain spent $6.36 per capita on naval expenditure, and Japan—a poor country—$2.02, the United States was spending $2.93 per capita. As incidents in the naval race, France plans to have ninety-one submarines by 1932 and the British Admiralty has set seventy cruisers as its minimum. British naval bases dot the seven seas. There is no part of the world, save the eastern Pacific, to which the British navy has not easy access. Japan, without a world-system of bases, is yet so ringed about with naval bases as to make the western Pacific, the Yellow Sea, and the North China Seas in effect Japanese territorial waters. The United States, alone of the three great sea-powers, found its domestic naval communications controlled by one naval rival, and its communications with its foreign possessions controlled by the other.

Accordingly, the United States decided that its relation to the British Dominions was the solution to its naval problem. We let Canada feel that her west coast is protected by the Monroe Doctrine, that the Panama Canal is a proper Canadian interest, and that her economic position in the Caribbean, Mexico, and Central America tends to identify Canadian interests with those of the United States. The cruise of the United States battle-fleet to Australia and New Zealand in 1925 was another gesture of Anglo-Saxon solidarity in the Pacific. The growing trade relations between the United States and the British Dominions, including the Union of South Africa and the Irish Free State, have come to have a vital bearing on America's naval situation in both the Atlantic, the Pacific, and the Caribbean.

The most ambitious of Europe's moves to combat America's political pretensions have been in Latin America, where Pan-Americanism is being opposed by Pan-Hispanism, by "Latin America for the Latin Americans" sentiment, and by League of Nations propaganda. Pan-Hispanism aspires to reunite Latin America to Europe's 119,000,000 Latins by political, social, and cultural ties, linking South and Central America, Cuba, and the Philippines in a confederacy headed by Spain. The movement originated in Spain in 1846, but its real growth began after the Spanish-American War. Hispanic-American Congresses were held in 1908, 1911, 1912, and 1914. Similar to this movement is that proposed in 1922 by Ugarte, to create a Latin-American League in opposition to the Pan-American Union. The extinction of "foreign loans which mortgage the independence of peoples" is an object of the Ugarte scheme, which works through sedulous propagation of the "Colossus of the North" idea and through opposition to American trade and economic expansion on the single basis of their volume. The League of Nations contact with the Pan-American Union was confined to the attempt made in 1928 to have League officials supervise the Havana Congress. Some League countries were frankly hopeful that the Congress would end the Pan-American Union. The attack on American intervention in Nicaragua was headed by the Argentine and Salvador, the two American republics most intimately influenced by transatlantic political ideas. In order to discredit the United States, the extreme contention was made that no intervention in the affairs of another nation should be permitted under international law. Had this been adopted, it would have opened the door to a renewal of filibustering, subsidized revolutions and "kept" governments, or wars.

THE COMMERCIAL COUNTER-ATTACK

Concurrently with the political isolation of the United States, Europe—led by Great Britain, France, and Germany—developed vigorous competition with America's trade throughout the world. The tours of the Prince of Wales to Africa, Canada, India, and other British Dominions and to British South America—the Argentine, Paraguay, Uruguay, Bolivia, and Chile—were part of the general British trade revival. The "Buy British Goods" campaign, the anti-American film legislation in Great

Britain and the effort to extend it to India, Australia, and New Zealand, were linked to a specious propaganda in the countries where the United States enjoys a "favorable trade balance," in other words, countries where the United States sells more than it buys. This was represented as dangerous to both the Argentine Republic and Australia, but failed to explain the fact that the United States had an adverse trade balance with Japan, which was in no sense a danger to American interests. Rather it was to America's advantage, in that it gave her principal competitor in the Pacific an interest in maintaining good relations with the United States.

Likewise, Germany looks to Latin America and especially to Mexico as a field for trade expansion. Italy is seeking emigration outlets in Brazil and the Argentine. France strives, by a vigorous anti-American propaganda which aspires to create Latin-American boycotts of North American goods, to recapture her share of Latin-American trade. France, Spain, and Italy have sent floating commercial exhibits to Latin America, and by aviation exploits, fast mail and airplane services, plan to bring Latin America closer to Europe than to the United States, and to set up Latin Europe as the middleman in inter-American trade relations.

In all this, Great Britain and Europe are merely trying to promote their own interests. In this attempt, it is only human for them to exploit the clashes of our policy with Latin-American opinion, in such a way as to secure favoritism in Government contracts and to arouse a fear lest North American products pave the way for political intervention. The whole European commercial counter-attack, especially in Latin America, has been designed to restore Europe to its old position as the economic arbiter of the world, rather than deliberately to curtail American power. However, in spite of competition and political agitation, American trade with South America has shown a steady growth since the war, having risen from $370,-000,000 in 1913 to $584,000,000 in 1922, and to $1,000,000,000 in 1926.

UNDOING WILSON'S WORK IN EUROPE

But the principal and most serious element in Europe's counter-attack upon the American system was its undoing —systematically, piecemeal, root and branch—of every aspect of Wilson's effort to demilitarize, democratize, and demobilize the Old World. Diplomacy has triumphed over federation, the autocratic principle over the democratic, the balance of power over disarmament.

The League of Nations has been made safe for diplomacy. Its apparatus has been converted to purely diplomatic uses. The Protocol of 1924 marked the last real effort to encompass the federalization of Europe. Its shipwreck on the rocks of British navalism—when the English refused to permit their fleet to be used to maintain League authority—ended all hope for a United States of Europe. In 1927, a timid attempt to revive the Protocol was promptly squelched by the British Foreign Secretary.

The Locarno Agreements, of October, 1925, set up a definite system of arbitration treaties and mutual guarantees between Great Britain, France, and Germany, with Italian, Belgian, Polish, and Czecho-Slovakian trimmings, dealing with matters of defense which were supposedly covered by the League Covenant. After the armistice, a

French system of military alliances, linking Belgium, Poland, Czecho-Slovakia, Roumania, and Jugo-Slavia, revived the theory of the pre-war diplomatic balance, while Anglo-German coöperation and Anglo-Italian, as well as Italo-Albanian and Italo-Spanish, understandings in the Mediterranean—not to mention the Russo-German treaty of May, 1922—have created a counterpoise to the French organization of Europe's military resources. Wilson's ideal of disarmament proved unacceptable to Europe, as conference after futile conference on the subject demonstrated. Up to 1928, the French said that no disarmament could take place without Russia. In 1928, when Russia proposed immediate and universal disarmament to the League powers, the French accused her of insincerity and said that no disarmament could take place with Russia.

The most striking evidence of Europe's anti-Wilsonism was the wave of anti-democratic dictatorships in Europe and the deliberate repudiation of democracy in several European countries. Since 1917, Russia has been under a Soviet dictatorship which despises democracy as a hypocritical bourgeois device. Since 1922, Italy has been under a Fascist dictatorship, headed by Mussolini, which likewise scorns the entire theory and practice of democracy. Mustapha Kemal has been the dictator of Turkey since 1921. Since 1921, Reza Khan—who made himself Shah in 1927—has been absolute ruler of Persia. Spain has enjoyed a military dictatorship under Primo de Rivera since 1923. Beginning with Venizelos in 1916, Greece has been under a series of republican and monarchist dictators. Roumania for ten years has been governed by the Bratianu family; Hungary, for the same period, has been ruled by Count Bethlen and Admiral Horthy. In 1925,

Pilsudski became dictator of Poland. In Czecho-Slovakia, after ten years of Benes and Masaryk, it is a penal offense to criticize the republic. Austria is under Monsignor Seipel, France under Poincaré, Great Britain under Die-Hard Conservatives, Germany under Von Hindenburg. Save for the Scandinavian countries, there is scarcely a nation in Europe that is not governed on non-democratic lines or by conservative rulers. So much for a world made safe for democracy, when Europe discovered that democracy could not be easily reconciled with her political necessities.

Europe is still a center of military power, with practically universal conscription and large standing armies. Ten years after a war to destroy Prussian militarism, the Continent has over 2,500,000 men under arms, exclusive of the Russian army. The only real reduction has been made in the case of Germany, Austria, Hungary, and Bulgaria, where disarmament is enforced by the terms of the treaties of peace. Europe is still willing to pay a high price for the maintenance of her political system, after a war which cost her 8,500,000 killed and 21,000,000 wounded.

THE MORAL ISOLATION OF THE UNITED STATES

Coupled with the rejection of American ideals, there was a natural tendency to discredit America in a moral sense, as well as politically. Our rejection of the Treaty of Versailles and the League of Nations marked the beginning of this process. The United States was held guilty of a "great betrayal." The betrayal propaganda had its root in Europe's agitation against Wilson at Paris and in the un-American features of the peace settlement. Japan's annexation of Shantung, the unpredictable obligations of Article X of the League of Covenant, and the minor representation of the United States on the Assembly, aroused fear lest America should find itself politically committed to the defense of settlements which were contrary to her interests. The Fiume episode testified to the practical dangers of an attempt to interfere directly with these settlements. Accordingly, America withdrew. The effect was, as Europe later admitted, beneficial in the sense that the Continent was compelled to dispense with our aid and to work out a solution for its own problems without American interference.

However, the failure of the United States to subscribe to the 1924 Protocol for the Pacific Settlement of International Disputes, declaring a "war of aggression" to be an "international crime," led to more "betrayal" talk. Professor Shotwell, General Bliss, and a David Hunter Miller offered unauthorized American support to Europe's efforts to secure American endorsement for the existing political situation, and British rejection of the Protocol was attributed to England's unwillingness to use its navy against the United States. Accordingly, our absence from the League was construed as hostility to its activities.

Similarly, our adherence to the Permanent Court of International Justice at the Hague in 1926 was conditional on our receiving powers over advisory decisions, designed to protect us from any political entanglement in the League's European problems, but the Senate's reservations were met with counter-reservations designed to make us, in effect, a member of the League Council. Again, the United States was accused by Europe, through a Canadian spokesman, of harboring hostile designs. Yet in 1927, when Kellogg proposed to France a multilateral treaty for the "outlawry of war as an instrument of policy," France at first rejected it as incompatible with her obligations to the League of Nations, and denounced the overture as an attempt to offer a substitute for the League. All in all, Europe has succeeded in branding America, in advance, as "an aggressor state," in spite of our naval inertia, our military disarmament and our peaceful policies.

The crowning touch in Europe's reaction against American policies was the steady denigration of American ideas, methods, and civilization. An Englishman who had never set foot in the United States wrote a book characterizing it as a "Babbitt Warren." The execution of Sacco and Vanzetti provided Europe with a heaven-sent opportunity to denounce the United States on racial, social, and political grounds. Our immigration laws made Ellis Island a constant irritant to European public opinion. The construction and operation of our merchant marine led to more bitterness. When the ship subsidy bill was defeated, the British press termed it "the greatest failure in history," and a steady mercantile rivalry lent an economic edge to the anti-American spirit. Europe's liquor and wine interests eagerly joined in on the score of prohibition, and were helped in their ridicule and criticism by the hordes of bibulous Americans who tank up on the Continent every summer.

Most important of all is Europe's cultural war, her natural resistance to "Americanization by demoralization," her dislike of our jazz-bands, our moving-pictures, our slang, our dances, our catchy, ephemeral, and meretricious manners, which are suspect to Europe's traditional culture. Sir Philip Cunliffe-Lister, in a speech concerning our moving-pictures, voiced the British attitude: "What would you say if you had not English literature, and if the whole of your daily press was 95 per cent. foreign controlled? You would say it was an outrage. Yet this medium (the moving-picture) far subtler than the press, more pervading and more insidious, is in the hands of those who are not British." Similarly, G. K. Chesterton, in a speech at the Delphian Coterie dinner in 1927, declared:

Let me say that what I most violently object to is the Americanization of England, but I have no objection to the Americanization of America. . . . I think that you can have much more sympathy with a soldier of a foreign power, who is, after all, only serving his own flag, than you can have with the gradual penetration of your country by *alien corruption appealing all the time only to low material motives.* . . .

The whole of London, a city as national as Paris or Florence, has been wholly Americanized, the look of it has been Americanized. I do not know what more the Kaiser of the Prussian Army could have done if he had occupied London.

Chapter XI

NEW MEN AND OLD POLICIES

HUGHES AND KELLOGG

JUST as Wilson had seemed about to lay his hand upon his heart's desire—an American political pontificate over the world—his arm was plucked back by domestic opposition. Convulsed with fury, sure of his moral authority to speak for all mankind, Wilson denounced his opponents as a "little group of willful men" and called for "a great and solemn referendum" on the issues of the treaty he had signed at Paris and the League of Nations which he had imposed upon Europe. The answer was terribly clear. The Democratic candidate was defeated by a majority of 7,000,000 votes; and four years later the Republican candidate won by an equal plurality. Wilsonian diplomacy was reversed, and the United States faced the post-war era with a free hand.

Accordingly, following the high-spirited and mesmeric diplomacy of Wilson, with his orchestral blending of ulterior material interest with dramatic moral principles, American foreign policy fell into the hands of two new men—Hughes and Kellogg—who, while continuing to follow the basic American policies of which Wilson had been the executor, infused into them a more intimately practical spirit. Evincing from the start a striking grasp of practicalities, Secretary of State Hughes and his successor at the State Department showed that, if the Democrats were superior in the realm of political theory and in the policy of war, the Republicans had a shrewder mastery of the processes of peace. If the two can be fairly contrasted, although their continuity is unquestioned, it is in this respect that American diplomacy under Wilson was predominantly political, while under Hughes and Kellogg it was intrinsically economic. Wilson had proved adept in grasping, interpreting, and solving the issues of the war and of the peace settlement. Hughes and Kellogg were equally adept—and far more self-effacing—in dealing with the difficult problems of peaceful reconstruction and normal economic intercourse. Wilson had been buoyed up by an emergency which commanded the support of the American people. Hughes and Kellogg had to work without this stimulus, and under steady hostility to their aims and methods by the Wilsonian devotees.

Where the rejection by the United States of the League of Nations had left the Wilson Administration politically bankrupt, the Republicans speedily solved the problem by negotiating a simple separate treaty of peace with Germany, in 1922. Where the Democrats had, rather recklessly, offered independence to the Philippines, the Republicans saved the balance of power in eastern Asia from the calamitous dislocation which this would have involved, and restored the principle of American supervision. Where Wilson had advocated a large naval program and a theoretical equality with Great Britain, Hughes secured British assent to naval parity, as well as valuable political and commercial concessions in the Pacific.

A new tariff policy and a new system of commercial treaties were inaugurated, resulting in America's obtaining

an unconditional most-favored-nation status in Albania
(1922-25), Brazil (1923), Czecho-Slovakia (1923), the
Dominican Republic (1924), Esthonia (1925-26), Finland (1925), Germany (1923-25), Greece (1924),
Guatemala (1924), Haiti (1926), Hungary (1926),
Latvia (1926), Lithuania (1925-26), Poland (1925),
Roumania (1926), Spain (1927), Turkey (1927), Salvador (1926), and Honduras (1927)—a revolution in
our commercial policy, which had previously been based
on reciprocity and mutual bargaining.

The Republicans promptly overhauled Wilson's high-
handed course in the Caribbean, which had earned for the
United States much Latin-American suspicion and ill-will.
Santo Domingo was evacuated in 1924. Mexican relations
were placed on a satisfactory basis for the first time in a
decade by the recognition of Obregon in 1923 and the
subsequent support of Obregon and Calles by the United
States, in the face of the Mexican revolts of 1924 and
1927-28. Nicaragua was evacuated in 1926 and was re-
occupied only after a foreign intrigue had threatened the
legal government of Nicaragua with a revolution similar
to those which the United States had discouraged in
Mexico. Hughes carried the Wilson doctrine of legitimate
self-government—"I'm going to teach the South American republics that they've got to elect good men"—to a
logical, almost Quixotic conclusion by promoting the Central American General Treaty of Peace and Amity, signed
at Washington, February 7, 1923, which signalized a
definite American abandonment of the old practices of
filibustering, subsidizing friendly governments or propitious revolutions, and wanton intervention. It bound the
five Central American republics not to recognize a gov-

ernment which came into power through a *coup d'état*
or in violation of the appropriate constitution. It marked
a very definite attempt to combine Central America into
a federal group of states sufficiently strong and stable to
make intervention unnecessary or impracticable. Its chief
defect was that it presupposed that Central Americans
of mixed Spanish, Indian, and negro blood would observe
the same democratic ideals and political methods as the
Anglo-Saxon North Americans, but this was no more
naïve than Wilson's assumption that southern and eastern
Europeans would adopt American political principles and
governmental methods in 1919 simply because we had
turned the scale in the war against Germany.

Hughes and Kellogg were, however, unfortunate in
their keen sensitiveness to all criticism and ridicule. In
this they were unlike Wilson, who had, politically speaking, the hide of a rhinoceros, and who seemed to believe
that any one who disagreed with him was politically
immoral or personally reprehensible.

For example, few episodes were more pitiable than
Kellogg's apologetic and confused attitude toward our
1926 intervention in Nicaragua, when a simple citation of
American interests and treaty rights would have sufficed.
Few statements have been more fatuous than Hughes's
that the Washington naval agreement "absolutely ends
naval competition." Hughes and Kellogg never seemed
able to realize that the function of a statesman is not to
escape criticism, but to serve the public interest, and that
his work, no matter how pure and patriotic its motivation,
must be judged by the harsh pragmatic test. In fact, on
the practical basis, their policy has been excellent, if not

entirely successful. On the other hand, no policy can deserve or expect unqualified support.

On the score of political principle, however, these Republicans were strangely and honestly inarticulate. While sturdily applying the fundamental American principles, their policy was legalistic, quibbling, the logical and lamentable result of entrusting the conduct of foreign relations to professional lawyers. Deprived, in the anarchical condition of international society, of a final court of review, error, and appeal, lawyers in the State Department tend to be argumentative, documentary, and evidential, rather than firm, tolerant, and wise. Instead of seeking to interpret, through the medium of a trained diplomacy, American economic and political aspirations to a world which does not share or understand either, they have tended to a take-it-or-leave-it diplomatic attitude and to appeal to a nonexistent jury rather than to reach a satisfactory settlement. As evidence of this tendency, let one compare the utter and deplorable failure of Kellogg's legalistic diplomacy in Mexico with the prompt success of Ambassador Morrow's bland handling of the same problem. Morrow is not a lawyer. Similarly, one may note that Wilson's irresponsible Caribbean activities were more tolerated than Kellogg's single unfortunate venture in Nicaraguan intervention. Wilson was not a lawyer. To carry the illustration further, Rooseveltian foreign policy was dramatically successful and aroused admiration and sympathy, where Taft's policy in regard to the Panama Canal tolls, Canadian reciprocity, and the Manchurian railways, aroused international resentment. Taft was a lawer; Roosevelt was not.

But in spite of their legal training, neither Hughes nor Kellogg made any clear exposition or formulation of principle designed to render Republican policy popular at home and intelligible abroad. As administrators, they were admirably sane and pacific in a period when the possible rewards of imperialism were unusually tempting and the opportunity for obtaining them never so propitious. They kept the United States from becoming aggressively jingoistic and grasping. It was their misfortune that neither of them understood the value of a pertinent platitude in an emergency and so never endowed their policies with a phraseology which could insure their popularity and facilitate their execution. As Secretaries of State, they succeeded; it was only as statesmen that they failed.

THE BATTLE IN LATIN AMERICA

The Hughes-Kellogg policy toward the Latin-American republics was scrupulous, enlightened, and considerate, but it was robbed of its logical fruits. Those who administered it reaped a harvest of hate, suspicion, and ill-will where they had sought to sow friendship, tolerance, and respect for international obligations and for national sovereignty.

Few attempts at conciliation have been so disastrously received as our effort, in 1923, to settle the Tacna-Arica dispute between Chile and Peru. At one time, it seemed as if the request for our mediation had been a deliberate trap, a subtle attempt to undermine our prestige in South America. Our injudicious efforts to hold a plebiscite aborted, due to Chile's natural opposition to any device which might amputate her actual possessions. A simple-minded proposal for the cession of the provinces to Bolivia, who should pay for them with money borrowed —presumably—from the United States, indicated to Latin-American minds a duplicity in our motives. The Tacna-Arica affair became a costly diplomatic defeat for the United States. We were ill-advised to undertake it, and our conduct of the negotiations provided an opportunity for our South American neighbors and our European rivals to brand our motives as selfish and our methods as stupid.

Toward Mexico the Republican policy was fundamentally sound and its diplomacy hopelessly misguided. American generosity was turned against us, while the proper support of our national interests was branded as imperialism. The Mexican mess had been inherited from Wilson's administration, and as our stake in the natural wealth of Mexico, through oil, mineral, and agricultural investment, was preponderant, it was inevitable that the new constitution of 1917—with its subversion of vested material interests—should provoke a major diplomatic controversy between the two governments. Quite indifferent to the fact that he was apparently tolerating in Mexico what he anathematized in Russia, Hughes recognized President Obregon in 1923. The basis of our recognition was that American property rights acquired before the new constitution should be exempt from its provisions.

That this was not a one-sided agreement was promptly shown by Hughes's attitude toward the de la Huerta revolt against Obregon in 1924. British oil interests backed de la Huerta, while American oil interests gave financial support to Obregon. The United States not only enforced an arms embargo against the rebels but sold munitions to the Mexican Government to enable it to suppress the rising. Obregon was thereupon succeeded by Calles, who asserted that the Mexican Government was not bound by the terms of recognition accorded to the preceding administration. Strenuous efforts were made to enforce the new oil legislation against the American companies, whose investment in Mexico amounted to $700,000,000. Calles demanded that foreigners confirm the rights acquired before the new Constitution, and the Mixed Claims Commission which had been established to settle the damages suffered by Americans and Mexicans in the revolutionary period broke down completely, when the Commission decided that the case of American engineers, lured into the country under Carranza and deliberately massacred by Villa, was outside the Commission's jurisdiction. The Americans withdrew from the Commission and a breach of relations became possible. The application of the laws against the Catholic Church, in 1925, led to another great revolt. Public opinion in the United States was aroused by the persecution of foreign priests, and a religious uprising in 1927, which continued into 1928, was supported by large sections of American public opinion. The United States again came to the rescue of the Mexican Government and again supported the latter's authority against the threat of revolution.

Hence, the sudden outburst over Nicaragua was an unwelcome surprise to the State Department. The Sacasa revolution, of 1926-27, was supported by a semi-official Mexican filibuster, drew its arms and ammuntion from Mexico, and was promptly recognized by the Calles Government. Mexican public opinion was vociferously on the side of Sacasa, and later of the guerilla leader, Sandino.

The entire episode was rendered ludicrous by Kellogg's apparent belief that the Nicaraguan revolution was an attempt to create "a Bolshevist hegemony" between the United States and the Panama Canal. Intervention in Mexico again seemed a distinct possibility until the Senate unanimously voted to arbitrate our claims and the despatch of the Morrow mission brought a new man into the field.

Dwight Morrow, a former partner of J. P. Morgan and Company, was appointed American Ambassador to Mexico in 1927. He soon showed that he had both sense and tact—by his public references to the fact of Mexican sovereignty, which his predecessor had not conspicuously endorsed. Morrow both salved Mexican pride and secured the progressive mitigation of the undesirable Mexican legislation. Lindbergh's flight to Mexico City, early in 1928, paved the way for new leadership in the American world through the coöperation of Mexico with the United States, Argentina, Brazil, and Chile. Consequently, although the Mexican delegates were naturally and comprehensibly eager to curtail America's powers of intervention, at the Havana Conference the Mexicans supported the American delegation on other points and went far to restore Mexican prestige in Pan-American affairs.

However, in Central America and over the question of intervention, the policy of Hughes and Kellogg came nearest to a complete and fatal reverse. The Wilson-Hughes principle of supporting lawfully established governments had been embodied in the treaties of the Central American Conference at Washington in 1922-23, which also provided for arbitral and disarmament conventions between the five Central American republics. From 1915 to 1925, American marines had been occupying Nicaragua, but no sooner were they withdrawn and an election held under the new electoral law which had been drawn up by United States experts, than the revolution occurred. Recognition was refused to the government of Chamorro, which had overthrown the lawfully elected Solorzano and Sacasa. On November 19, 1926, Diaz was accepted as a compromise candidate. A revolt against Diaz, led by Sacasa and Moncada, was ended by American intervention, and the United States pledged itself to hold a fair election in 1928. However, one of Villa's former anti-American lieutenants, Sandino, repudiated the agreement and continued military operations, which were used by European and Mexican and other Latin-American propagandists as the occasion for renewed attacks on the United States. Likewise, a treaty negotiated with Panama in 1925, whereby that republic, regardless of her pledges under the Central American treaty and the Covenant of the League of Nations, undertook to be our ally in any war in which we were a belligerent, incurred world-wide opprobrium. The treaty failed of ratification by the Panaman Senate and was resubmitted to negotiation, although it represented the common sense of the existing political and strategic situation in the Caribbean.

The charge of imperialism was now freely brought against our Latin-American policy. The colossal rush of our investments into Latin-American countries aroused the suspicion that our financiers were plotting to secure an economic and political control of the three Americas. To instance the momentum of our financial drive, our Cuban investments increased by $1,000,000,000 between 1916 and 1926, while our Mexican investments doubled since 1912. In 1912 we had only $2,000,000 invested in Colombia and $3,000,000 in Venezuela; in 1926, the figures were $87,000,000 for Colombia and $75,000,000 for Venezuela. We seemed to be buying up Central America and, under our policy of protecting our property, to be preparing for a systematic extension of our political jurisdiction. Thirty interventions by the United States had occurred in the Caribbean in the thirty years since the Spanish-American war, and American investments in that region had risen to more than $3,000,000,000 in 1926, of which $250,000,000 represented government loans and the political power which such loans confer.

In consequence, the Pan-American Conference at Havana in 1928 came close to being a repudiation of the United States by the Latin-American republics. The American delegation was the strongest which had represented the United States in any international gathering since the Washington Conference. An attempt was made by Argentina to bring up a tariff dispute with the United States; Mexico endeavored to secure the rotation of office in the Pan-American chairmanship; Mexico, Argentina, and Salvador tried to forbid our intervention in the affairs of any American republic under any circumstances whatsoever. The whole was conceived as an attack on the United States, and Europe lent encouragement and support to the secret hope of breaking up the Union and substituting a Latin-American Union which should exclude the United States. The American delegation disclosed, however, that division was a game at which two could play and, in vote after vote, revealed to the world that Latin America was by no means a unit, and that a Latin-American Union would be subject to dissensions far more serious and incompatible than those which threatened the Pan-American body. As a result, the Union was preserved. For all the violence of foreign criticism and domestic agitation, the Hughes-Kellogg policy showed that it was sufficiently grounded in realities to win the support of its supposed victims.

SWINGING THE OPEN DOOR BOTH WAYS

Perhaps the most significant development of the Hughes-Kellogg policy was the new interpretation of the Open Door Doctrine, which resulted from foreign—and principally British—efforts to secure exclusive control of essential raw materials and to enhance their price through political manipulation. The original open door had applied solely to the fair and free marketing of American exports; the post-war open door demanded equally fair and free purchasing of American imports. The problem was, therefore, to convert the open door into a swinging door and not an economic valve.

From the very first, Hughes and, after him Kellogg, was compelled to struggle to assure America an equitable share in the world's raw materials. In this struggle, Great Britain was the protagonist, with Holland, France, and Italy acquiescent in the great game of "milking" the American market. The first incidence of the conflict came in the matter of oil and produced the so-called "oil war" of 1918-28. During the war, the Standard Oil group was engaged in the capture of foreign markets and the acquisition of new sources of supply. At Allied insistence, Wilson had compelled the Standard to abandon its economic offensive and to put its resources at the disposal of the Allies. In consequence, the British had not only "floated to victory on a sea of [Standard] Oil," but had improved the shining hour by quietly collaring all the oil in sight. This promptly produced a collision between the two systems—Europe's economic exclusiveness based on political privilege and concessions, and America's conception of freedom of lease, purchase, and exploitation.

The oil war raged over Palestine, Mesopotamia, Persia, the Dutch East Indies, Russia, Mexico, and Central America, with two groups—the Anglo-Dutch Shell combination and the Standard—predominating. Secretary of State Colby, in the closing days of the Wilson administration, took up the cudgels for the Standard. On May 12, 1920, the State Department's note to Great Britain observed that British actions had "created the unfortunate impression in the minds of the American public that the authorities of His Majesty's Government in the occupied region had given advantages to British oil interests which were not accorded to American companies, and further that Great Britain had been preparing quietly for exclusive control of the oil resources" in the Mesopotamia region. On July 28, 1920, the Department observed that the San Remo agreement, apportioning the Mosul oilfield between British and French interests, would "result in a grave infringement of the mandate principle which was formulated for the purpose of removing in the future some of the principal causes of international differences."

To this, Lord Curzon replied on August 9, 1920, alleging that American influence had been used to secure the cancellation of British oil concessions in Haiti and

Costa Rica. On November 20, 1920, the United States demanded the right to formulate the mandates for conquered German and Turkish territory, as one of the Allied and Associated powers. On February 21, 1921, the United States addressed the Council of the League, demanding an equal opportunity for participation in Mesopotamian oil and a right to pass on the terms of the Mesopotamian mandate.

The quarrel over Mesopotamia was eventually compounded by the exclusion of the Chester concessionaires, who had the only clear title to the Mosul oil fields, and by granting to the Standard and Sinclair interests a quarter share in the exclusive concession granted the Turkish Petroleum Company (the British protégé) by Iraq in 1925. Similar efforts to open up Palestine and Djambi to the Standard were likewise only partially successful. The question of the marketing of Russian oil, in 1927 and 1928, produced a flare-up of Anglo-American oil rivalry. The Dutch Shell interests, led by Sir Henry Deterding, having failed to secure a monopoly for the sale of Russian oil, attempted to boycott the Soviet product. This boycott was broken when the Standard Oil Company of New York and the Vacuum Oil Company arranged for large purchases from the Soviet Government and acquired facilities for its sale in India. The Shell cut prices and the Standard followed suit, but the resulting price-war in India failed to materialize into the world-wide economic battle which this open break seemed to prophesy, and by the middle of 1928, the rival oil companies had come to a general agreement as to the production, purchasing, and marketing of oil throughout the world.

The next great development in the open-door battle

was announced by Hoover, the Secretary of Commerce during both Hughes's and Kellogg's tenure in the State Department. This was styled the "rubber war," due to the prominence given to the conflict of interest between British producers and American consumers of this product. In 1925, Hoover attacked the principle of governmental control of the quantities of production of certain raw materials: the Stevenson Rubber Restriction Act, the Brazilian "valorization" of coffee, Egyptian cotton acreage restrictions, Mexico's sisal control, whereby Mexican production and distribution was restricted and, in the United States, handled by an exclusive sales agency; Japan's control of the silk industry (Japan produces 75 per cent. of the world's silk, and the United States buys 80 per cent. of Japan's silk); the export taxes on Chilean nitrate and iodine; the government-controlled Franco-German potash monopoly; the Japanese government monopoly of camphor, with production by license, refining by the state, and the governmental right to restrict output and to regulate distribution and prices.

The "rubber war" was the most dramatic incident in this struggle. The price of rubber jumped to $1.10 a pound, but after four years of American effort, dropped to 30 cents, inducing the British Government to abandon its restrictive measures. At the same time, the incident drove American interests to seek independent sources of supply. In October, 1925, the Firestone Plantations Company secured a concession from Liberia for the planting of 1,000,000 acres, the investment of $100,000,000, the employment of 300,000 laborers, and the eventual production of 250,000 tons of rubber a year. Likewise the United States Rubber Company, with an investment of $25,000,000 developed 94,000 acres in the Dutch East Indies and 30,000 acres in British Malaya, a total of 7,000,000 trees, and a production of 20,000,000 pounds of raw rubber a year.

Toward the end of Coolidge's second administration, the American counter-measures began to take effect. By the Webb-Pomerene Law, American exporters had been permitted to combine, without violation of the anti-trust laws. Early in 1928, a similar measure to permit American importers to combine in the purchase of products which were subject to foreign control, was temporarily defeated by Congress. However, the Government inaugurated the practice of prosecuting foreign producers of potash and quinine for violation of the anti-trust statute, a step of doubtful juridical propriety but an effective deterrent to private foreign monopoly. The net result of the swinging-door diplomacy, in its new application to the purchase of raw materials, has been to secure American participation—often of a financial character—in the European process of exploitation by exclusive concession or political control of the economic product. In no case has the American principle of a fair field and no favor been accepted. In certain instances, an effort has been made to restrict British oil companies operating in the United States to a position identical to that enjoyed by American companies in British territory, and doubtless this "tit-for-tat" treatment could be extended to every branch of business life. But the prohibition of export taxes by the Federal Constitution makes effective retaliation impossible. Only voluntary associations and coöperative foreign marketing of our wheat, cotton, and copper, could enforce a genuine economic disarmament and reciprocity.

Curiously enough, France, rather than Great Britain, presented the crucial test of American commercial policy. American efforts to negotiate a commercial treaty with France on the most-favored-nation basis failed in 1927. In that year, France had negotiated a commercial agreement with Germany, involving reciprocal concessions which were injurious to American trade. An American effort to secure a satisfactory arrangement with France was met by the threat of differential duties and tariff rates inimical to American interests. When France flatly refused to grant most-favored-nation treatment to the United States, a critical situation developed, and for a time the American Government considered bringing financial pressure to bear on the French. It was understood that the American notes were unusually harsh in tone and completely destroyed the French position on the subject, in view of their official endorsement of the most-favored-nation principle at the Geneva Economic Conference in 1927. French restrictive measures on the American oil and American films and the frank determination of the French Foreign Office to secure the maximum price—possibly, cancellation of the French debt—in return for economic comity, made the negotiation of a Franco-American commercial treaty a contest in endurance.

In consequence, France became a test case for America's open-door diplomacy. On Kellogg's ability to persuade the French to grant most-favored-nation status depended the question whether Europe might become an economic bloc against the United States, which was regarded by Europe's political publicists as the logical "defense" against American industrial predominance. If France suc-

[185]

cessfully resisted the most-favored-nation diplomacy of Washington, there would be no incentive for other European countries—Great Britain, Italy, Spain, and Germany —to maintain similar relations with the United States. The result would be a series of regional economic agreements which would discriminate against American in favor of European products and might turn the open door into a barbed-wire fence so far as our trade with Europe and her colonies was concerned.[1]

To summarize the Hughes and Kellogg handling of our traditional policies is to recognize that they have succeeded on the commercial while failing on the political side. Wilson involved the United States in political interventions in Cuba, Panama, Haiti, Santo Domingo, Nicaragua, Mexico, Europe, Honduras, and Costa Rica: a total of ten interventions in eight American countries and one intervention in Europe, not counting the two in Russia, inside of five years.

Hughes and Kellogg involved the United States in intervention with Honduras and Nicaragua: a total of two interventions in two American nations in eight years. Wilson was hailed as a hero and a great political idealist; Hughes and Kellogg were denounced as cynical reactionaries and imperialists.

It is on the economic side, however, that the Republicans came into their own. In order to effect a political solution, Wilson abandoned immediate American interests in China and Mexico and failed to assure their protection in Europe. The Republicans redressed the balance. The best justification for American foreign policy under

[1] At the time of writing, no Franco-American Commercial Treaty has been completed.

Hughes and Kellogg and Hoover—who is credited with having added $500,000,000 a year to American export trade—are the trade statistics.

Since the end of the Wilson administration, American trade with every portion of the globe, including Europe, has increased. The unnatural growth of the post-armistice period has been deflated and built up again, slowly, coherently, and solidly, to equal and greater volumes. Under the Republicans, trade with South America, Africa, and Oceania virtually doubled in seven years. Our trade with Asia increased by 50 per cent., and with Europe and North America by lesser amounts.

With the exception of Great Britain, we have increased our trade with every part of the British Empire. We have maintained our position in the Caribbean and Central America, and have practically doubled our trade with every South American country except Ecuador and Peru. Our annual trade with Japan has increased by more than $150,000,000. In the face of increasing competition, political animosity, and, in some instances, deliberate misrepresentation and malice, American trade has forged ahead, and without recourse to political manipulation or military threats, has increased until it enjoys substantial parity with that of Great Britain, previously the greatest commercial power of the world.

After the war, Asquith was asked in the House of Commons what the British Empire had got out of the war. His reply was the four monosyllables: "Look at the map!" Hughes and Kellogg could not refer critics of their political course to so convenient a record, but no one who aspires to judge their policy can afford to ignore *The Statistical Abstract of the United States*. There, written in close-printed columns of figures, percentages, and statistical averages, lie the dimensions of an economic expansion which has never been approximated in human history. To have increased their nation's economic power, peacefully, in the face of a politically apprehensive world, is their great achievement. If the world printed its maps in economic rather than political terms, it would reveal the United States as the economic arbiter of mankind.

Chapter XII

OLD MEN AND NEW POLICIES

THE NAVAL SIESTA

In administering the Monroe Doctrine and fostering American commerce, Hughes and Kellogg moved in a familiar element. They were less happy in their efforts to devise new policies or new applications of old policies resulting from the World War. They surrendered American naval power for a settlement in the Pacific. Their attitude toward Europe, with respect to both the war debts and the League of Nations, was ambiguous to Americans and irritating to Europeans. Only in the effort to apply to foreign nations the American conception of property rights were they measurably successful.

The naval policy of the Republicans was by all odds the most daring. In order to dissolve the Anglo-Japanese Alliance and to win renewed international endorsement for the open door doctrine in China, Secretary Hughes agreed to scrap America's battle-fleet and abandoned our right to fortify our Pacific bases at Guam and Manila. Under the naval treaty, the United States scrapped nineteen old warships and thirteen new ones, for a total of 842,380 tons; Great Britain scrapped twenty-two old battleships and no new ones, for a total of 447,750 tons; Japan scrapped twelve old and four new ships, for a total of 354,709 tons. In other words the United States scrapped more than its two chief maritime rivals combined.

It was generally believed at the time that the United States had achieved naval parity with Great Britain. However, the British retained twenty-two capital ships to our eighteen, and were allowed to complete two new battleships —*Nelson* and *Rodney*—which were finished early in 1928. For six years, therefore, Great Britain had a superiority of from four to six capital ships over the United States. The replacement schedules laid down by the treaty would give the United States equality with Great Britain only in 1941. The conference failed to limit cruiser and submarine construction, thereby setting a premium on this type of vessel, since the limitation of battleship strength meant that no superior battle force could be mustered to destroy an enemy's cruisers.

The result was that, in the period between the end of the Washington Conference and the Tripartite Naval Conference at Geneva five years later, the United States was steadily outbuilt at sea. In that period the four League members party to the Washington Conference built or authorized in five years 287 vessels to America's 16, a ratio of nearly 18 to 1. For an equal decline in American sea-power, one must go back to the Republican administrations following the Civil War.

After the Washington Conference, the United States had abandoned all pretense of naval preparedness and took a naval siesta, being content to complete the ten 6,600-ton cruisers of the *Omaha* class, laying down two 10,000-ton cruisers in 1926 and authorizing six more in 1927. Great Britain, in the same period, completed six light and four heavy cruisers, and laid down thirteen 10,000-ton vessels and one 8,300-tonner. Japan completed twelve light cruisers, some of which mounted eight-inch guns, and laid down six heavy cruisers.

The British Admiralty went ahead with plans for the completion of a naval vase at Singapore, to cost $20,000,-000. The base was to be finished in ten years, and with full equipment will cost $38,750,000, of which $10,000,-000 has been supplied by British Malaya, $5,000,000 by New Zealand, and $1,750,000 by Hong-Kong. Moreover, British and Japanese cruiser construction proceeded according to fixed programs, where that of the United States was episodic and uncertain. The Birkenhead Plan, adopted in August, 1925, provided for the construction within five years of sixteen British cruisers (nine of 10,000 tons and seven of 8,300 tons), twenty-seven destroyers, and twenty-three submarines.

In the light of these facts, the Washington Conference appears as a sort of "over-confidence game," in which Secretary Hughes was left holding the bag and hoping he would catch the rabbit. In three months—November, 1921, to February, 1922—the United States gave up the work of years: its 1916 naval program, mostly in terms of ships almost completed. Japan gave up her "eight-eight" program of 1920, mostly in terms of blue prints. And Great Britain qualified her right to naval supremacy.

Yet it is unjust to Hughes to accuse him of reckless folly. He probably understood the functions of the modern cruisers, the technical qualifications of sea-power, and the importance of naval bases. In essence, he weighed an American naval program against American commercial policy and sacrificed military power, in terms of battleships and fortified bases, for a political arrangement designed to stimulate American trade. He broke up the Anglo-Japanese Alliance, which the British were glad to abandon, and left Great Britain with a free hand to swing the balance of power between the United States and Japan. He secured a pledge for the open door and the denunciation of commercial monopolies in China. He secured for China the right to increase her tariff. And he substituted for the existing anarchy a Four-Power Pact of mutual guarantee of the status quo in the Pacific. Finally, although abandoning the right to fortify Manila, which was already one of the strongest naval fortresses in the world, and Guam, which was already isolated by Japanese control of the surrounding islands, he retained the power to fortify the Panama Canal, Hawaii, and the Aleutian Islands.

Actually, at the time there was some belief that the Washington Conference signalized an unofficial Anglo-American entente. This was untrue. Vehement British protests against increasing the elevation of the guns on the American battleships made it evident that in the eyes of the British Admiralty all that had been done was to disarm the United States. The enunciation of the Balfour debt policy, making America responsible for all British collections on the Continent, and the enactment of the Stevenson Rubber Restriction Act, both followed shortly upon the ratification of the Washington treaties. If any Anglo-American entente resulted, it was found in closer political and commercial relations between the United States and the British Dominions.

American naval power was further weakened in this period by the steady decline of the American mercantile marine. In 1900, we had 1,288 steamers of 817,000 tons engaged in foreign trade; in 1920, the figure stood at 5,932 vessels of 9,925,000 tons; in 1926, it had declined to 4,616 of 7,719,000 tons. American shipbuilding likewise declined, until in 1926, only 645 vessels, of a total tonnage of 140,000, were built, in comparison to 639,568 tons of British shipping constructed in the same year. The British share in American foreign trade, which had been less than a quarter during the war period, nearly doubled in volume during the next six years, while the American share slowly dwindled. Each year, the percentage of our foreign trade carried in American vessels decreased. It had been 10 per cent. in 1910 and had risen steadily to 43 per cent. in 1920. It was 36.5 per cent in 1922, 35.7 per cent. in 1924, and 34 per cent. in 1926. In that year, the Americans paid to foreign vessels $65,000,000 for passenger fares and $175,000,000 in freight charges.

By failure to compete effectively on the high seas, we gave Great Britain and other foreign powers an important stake in our continued prosperity and a strong incentive to the maintenance of friendly relations. At the same time, we nurtured neutral shipping connections which might be very useful to us in time of war. The earnings of the European shipping interests constituted a vital element in their national economy, the loss of which would be keenly felt. Our best policy seemed, therefore, to maintain the mercantile marines of other nations, as well as our own.

At the same time, apprehension existed in Great Britain over America's attitude toward the rights of neutral shipping in time of war. In December, 1927, Admiral Wemyss attacked the Declaration of Paris in the British Parliament, urging the abandonment of all nonsense about contraband and blockades and reassertion of the right to sink or capture anything in sight. Likewise, British public opinion was concerned lest a League blockade of an "aggressor state"—*anglice*, a British blockade of Russia—might arouse American resentment. The conflict over the freedom-of-the-sea doctrine became involved in the natural naval rivalry of the two countries. If the United States constructs a powerful navy, will Great Britain in the event of hostilities bar foreign ports to our trade and issue Orders in Council blacklisting American concerns? How, in the next war, can Great Britain dictate to neutral shipping without running into a strong American fleet ambushed behind the legal niceties of this conflict in maritime law?

The most serious criticism of America's post-Washington naval policy has been her failure to face the fundamental commercial issue of sea-power. It was this which wrecked the Geneva Conference, and it is to the credit of the delegates that it was met squarely for the first time since Wilson quietly dropped his "freedom of the seas" point from the immortal Fourteen.

On February 10, 1927, President Coolidge invited Great Britain, France, Italy, and Japan to attend a conference to agree on limitation of cruisers and submarines. France and Italy declined to join, France because she loved the League of Nations, and Italy because of her "unfavorable geographical position." The Conference assembled on June 20, 1927, and lasted until August 4. Nothing was accomplished. Great Britain urged the abolition of heavy 10,000-ton cruisers, the barring of eight-inch guns, and the reduction of battleship tonnage and gun-caliber maximums. The British demanded seventy cruisers for their minimum needs. The United States wanted twenty-five 10,000-ton cruisers, eight-inch guns, and a smaller number of naval vessels all around. Japan played in between the two powers, urging a genuine economy which would enable her to halt her own mounting naval expenditure. In this conference, the British Admiralty reversed its concession of theoretical Anglo-American naval parity. Balfour had said at Washington:

[The American delegation] have, as we think most rightly, taken the battle-fleet as the aggressive unit which they have in the main to consider; and in the battle-fleet you must include those auxiliary ships without which a modern battle-fleet has neither eyes nor ears. . . .

Taking those two as really belonging to one subject, namely the battle-fleet, taking those two, the battleships themselves and the vessels auxiliary and necessary to a battle-fleet, we think that the proportion between the various countries [embodying parity between Great Britain and the United States] is acceptable; we think the limitation of amounts is reasonable; we think it should be accepted.

Balfour later stated, after Geneva, that he did not mean this to apply to cruisers not attached to the battle-fleet. The official British change in viewpoint was better expressed by Winston Churchill after the dissolution of the Tripartite Conference: "We are not able now—and I hope at no future time—to embody in a solemn international agreement any words which would bind us to the principle of mathematical parity in naval strength."

The reason for the Anglo-American split over the size of cruisers and the caliber of their guns was that America's lack of naval bases and the vast distances of the Pacific dictate a heavy class of cruiser for our naval needs. Moreover, the British merchant marine contains more than four times as many fast vessels capable of mounting six-inch guns as the American merchant fleet does. In time of war, such merchantmen could be armed as naval auxiliaries and would enjoy a tactical equality with cruisers mounting similar weapons.

The actual maneuvers of the Conference were of interest chiefly to naval specialists. The only real surprise was the unusually intelligent support given to the American delegation by public opinion in the United States, which had supported the British point of view at the Washington Conference. The effect of failure at Geneva, which was shown to have been due to a change of attitude by the British Government, was to increase American enthusiasm for the navy and to chagrin President Coolidge.

Consequently, the British Government endeavored to allay American resentment. Viscount Cecil, the principal British delegate, resigned from the Cabinet in protest. On November 23, 1927, Bridgeman, the First Lord of the Admiralty, announced that one 10,000-ton cruiser and one 8,300-ton cruiser had been dropped from the 1927-28 building program. American reaction was not at first propitious. On December 6, 1927, the President's message to Congress declared: "The country has put away the Old World policy of competitive armaments. It can never be relieved of the responsibility of adequate national defense. . . . We were granted much coöperation by Japan, but we were unable to come to an agreement with Great Britain."

The final official answer to the British course at Geneva

was announced on December 14, 1927, in the form of a five-year program for the construction of twenty-five 10,000-ton cruisers, nine destroyer leaders, thirty-two fleet submarines, and five aircraft carriers, at a total cost of $725,000,000. This was put forward by the General Board of the Navy as the first part of a twenty-year program which included the replacement of capital ships under the Washington Treaty. It was designed to be to our post-war maritime policy what the 1916 program was to our war difficulties with Great Britain, Germany, and Japan.

In the meantime, pacifist sentiment in America had been organizing to prevent the effective development of American power, and Congress was deluged with hostile propaganda. The political apprehensions caused by the coming election, and the general tendency to believe that the General Board had purposely overestimated our naval requirements, resulted in paring down this total to fifteen heavy cruisers and one aircraft carrier. Even so, it represented a substantial increase in American power to protect our transoceanic commerce and to enforce our naval policies.

In fact, the 10,000-ton cruiser became for the United States the basis of its new fleet. The reason for the original adoption of the 10,000-ton class at the Washton Conference was that the British, in 1916 and 1917, had constructed cruisers of 9,750-tons displacement. In order to save these vessels for the British Navy, the Conference had decreed that any ship over 10,000 tons should be considered a capital ship. They were a British type of vessel and for several years were possessed by the British navy alone.

Such heavy cruisers represent, however, a power of breaking a blockade, highly desirable for a nation whose total sea-borne foreign and domestic trade is now reckoned at $19,000,000,000. Heavy cruisers are also valuable as a means of keeping a blockade of the United States sufficiently far at sea to let raiders slip out of American ports and disrupt hostile shipping. The 1928 program was based on the actual naval problems which the General Board of the Navy was expected to solve in theory lest it become necessary to solve them in practice.

The gist of their problems lay in America's unfavorable strategic position. Our trade with Europe, the Mediterranean, and West Africa, was at the mercy of the British bases of Plymouth, Portsmouth, Scapa Flow, Gibraltar, Sierra Leone, Ascension, St. Helena, and Cape Town. The Mediterranean and the Indian Ocean were, in effect, British lakes on which our ships could travel only with British permission. Our Atlantic coastwise trade was menaced by British bases at Halifax and the Bermudas, while our intercoastal and South American trade could be intercepted from the British bases at Jamaica and Barbados. Japan could harass our maritime communications with the Philippines. Japan and Great Britain might cut our trade with China.

Only in the Caribbean had we sufficient bases to control the vital area of our naval communications. With fleet stations at Pearl Harbor, Samoa, Guam, and on the Pacific Coast, we could hold the eastern Pacific, but were powerless to protect our transoceanic trade, save that with the west coast of South America.

This problem was mentioned but not officially discussed at the Geneva Conference. Without a progressive demilitarization of the world's naval bases—which should be the object of American naval policy—the strategic inferiority of the United States was so marked that only by an overwhelming tactical superiority in heavy cruisers could the United States hope to redress the balance of naval power.

The final irony of the fiasco at Geneva was the extraordinary spectacle of Viscount Cecil, the chief British delegate, who had lectured in America on the "heresy of force" as a means of settling international disputes, upholding the British demands for large naval tonnages and virtually supreme power to exert force on the high seas.

The upshot of eight years of effort by Hughes and Kellogg to assure the freedom of the seas to American commerce through naval equality with Great Britain, was to leave the United States in a position of distinct inferiority and to enable other less naïve nations to increase their own power while hampering ours. The whole episode was characterized by optimism and confidence in the moral validity of American ideas. Its net result was a serious decline of American naval power and political influence, balanced by the undeniable gains of American commerce.

EUROPE AND THE LEAGUE OF NATIONS

The issue of American membership in the League of Nations ended with the election of Harding in 1920. The issue of American cancellation of the loans to Europe ended with the formation of the Debt Funding Commission in 1922. Republican policy toward Europe was, accordingly, a clear reaffirmation of the principle of America's diplomatic disassociation from the affairs of the Old World and an equally clear affirmation of the sanctity of international contracts.

As a result, the Hughes-Kellogg European policy treated the League of Nations merely as a useful organ for international coöperation, not as a valid means for political negotiation. American delegates took part in all the League's general conferences—economics, disarmament, and opium—to such an extent that the United States Government paid to the League Secretariat, for its share of the League's 1927 expenses, as much as did Great Britain. Moreover, in American negotiations with France for the outlawry of war, League membership was recognized by the United States as a binding international obligation comparable to the Monroe Doctrine, and was incorporated as such in the arbitration treaty signed between France and America in February, 1928.

In the same manner, though refusing to consider cancellation, the American Government coöperated in the financial restoration of Europe, throwing, through the Federal Reserve Board, its weight on the side of stabilized currencies and a return to that single standard of financial chastity, gold. The settlement of German reparations began in December, 1922, with Secretary Hughes's speech at New Haven urging the submission of the reparations question to a commission of experts. In the following month, France occupied the Ruhr, but her policy of coercion failed; and on October 13, 1923, Great Britain requested American participation in the commission which Hughes had suggested. On December 11, 1923, the United States Government appointed Dawes and Young as unofficial representatives, and by August, 1924, the Experts' Report, establishing the Dawes Plan, was put into effect. American participation assured the success of a $200,000,000 loan to Germany; a Bank of Issue, independent of Government control, was established; S. Parker Gilbert, an American, was appointed agent for reparation payments, and the problem of German indemnity was taken out of politics.

Very similar to this procedure was the appointment in 1924 of Jeremiah Smith of Boston as commissioner general for an international loan to reorganize Hungarian finance. So thorough was his work that Hungary was released from international control by the end of June, 1926. Smith returned to America, after refusing to accept the $100,000 fee to which he was entitled—as effective a stroke of policy as America's remission of the Boxer indemnity from China. The gold standard had been restored in Austria, through the League of Nations, and in Russia and Italy by internal reforms. France alone lagged in the effort to build post-war Europe on solid financial values.

The Republican debt policy, though firm on the point of cancellation, was considerate in its treatment of the European debtors. Settlement was made on the basis of the debtor's ability to pay, interest was reduced, and a long period for repayment was granted. In consequence of these measures, the actual value of the European obligations was decreased from the original $10,000,000,000 to approximately $4,000,000,000. Every country honored its obligation to the United States, save France, which still hoped for a political—as distinct from a financial—settlement, and Russia, which made no pretense of assuming the obligations contracted by the previous régime. Both the Dawes Plan and the debt agreements, though bitterly attacked by the European debtors and American critics, worked without economic hardship.

While thus intimately concerned in the internal re-organization of Europe's economic life, Hughes and Kellogg successfully reaffirmed the fact of America's political insularity. In two Pan-American Conferences—at Santiago, Chile, in 1923, and at Havana in 1928—they opposed any political or economic organization of the Pan-American Union. American insistence on national sovereignty at the same time scrupulously avoided the appearance of domination over the Americas.

Toward Europe, the same reluctance to underwrite foreign political risks was evinced. In January, 1926, the Senate accepted the World Court, with reservations designed to free the Court from political domination by the League. The League powers' reply, granting the United States the same powers over the Court as shared by members of the Council of the League, was not considered satisfactory. An effort made early in 1928, to resubmit the question to further negotiation, failed to enlist support, save among professional internationalists.

In our policy toward Asia, the break-up of the Anglo-Japanese Alliance had been sufficiently tempting in 1922 to induce Hughes to negotiate a special treaty of mutual guarantee for their Pacific possessions by Great Britain, France, Japan, and the United States. This was, in appearance, an abandonment of political isolation in favor of mutualization; in fact, it was one of those "temporary alliances for extraordinary purposes" which Washington expressly advocated in his Farewell Address. It was, moreover, an alliance based not on reciprocal rights and advantages, but on the duties of mutual responsibility. It was a distinct contribution to the peace not only of the Pacific but of Europe, for the Locarno pacts in 1925 were founded on precisely similar mutual responsibilities. The Four-Power Treaty and the Locarno agreements were, therefore, instances of the successful export of the American ideal of federalism, in which the Hughes-Kellogg policy was one of example rather than formulas. Its object was to secure a general political demobilization of the world, and it was content to entrust international welfare to a sane reliance on the restorative powers of human nature.

In that spirit, the American Government looked with favor on the extension of American foreign loans, not only for productive economic purposes but for governmental uses. In a single year, American bankers granted loans of $1,000,000,000 to foreign governments, provinces, cities, and administrative agencies. In 1921, the State Department induced a conference of bankers to agree to an informal supervision of their foreign flotations. Loans to governments which had not funded their obligations to the United States, and loans deemed subversive to the public interest, were open to objection. This policy was adhered to for seven years with satisfactory results. It amounted to granting a visa to American money, and the only loans of which the Department disapproved were patently incompatible with the public welfare. Secretary Hoover, in 1927, even advocated its extension so as to bar all loans save for productive purposes. Although the system was vigorously attacked by Senator Glass of Virginia, the State Department intervened early in 1928 to prevent the Chase National Bank of New York from handling coupon payments on Soviet Russian railway bonds, and the Treasury Department refused to admit Russian gold bullion to assay. Senator Glass did not protest at this unusual extension of Republican foreign financial policy. That it was successful was shown by the fact under the Wilson administration, American foreign loans amounted to less than $4,000,000,000, while under the Republicans in seven years, nearly $8,000,000,000 more was invested in foreign countries.

The existence of American loans to foreign governments, especially the war debts, conferred upon the United States an indirect control over the policies of foreign governments which the latter could escape only by frank repudiation, at the expense of their national credit, or by friendly coöperation with the American Government. For a time, Europe showed her resentment in a popular hatred of the United States. This, however, proved powerless to do more than stiffen the American determination not to remit the debts without tangible compensation—economic, commercial, political, or territorial—such as had not been offered by any debtor state.

By retaining the bonds of the foreign governments, the American Treasury was enabled to wreck their finances, if necessary, in the face of deliberate default. At the same time, the existence of the war debts served to prevent commission-grabbing American bankers from plunging credulous American investors headlong into worthless European investments or doubtful governmental loans which might be repudiated or destroyed by war or other political action. The war debts were seen to be a defense for the American Government in its dealings with Europe, a weapon in its political armory, and a protection of the American people against those financiers who might desire cancellation in order to enhance the precarious value of their own holdings at the expense of the general public.

As it stands, European nations, provinces, and cities are mortgaged to the United States. American experts have had dictatorial powers over the finances of Germany, Hungary, and Persia; other experts have reorganized Polish and Latin-American finances. The gold standard has been restored, thus protecting American industry from competition in terms of depreciated paper currency. Reparations and war debts have been removed from politics. Eventually, the entire war debts may be handled through independent American banks of issue in the war-debt countries, on the model of Austria, Hungary, and Germany. Or the entire reparations-debt complex may be finally eliminated by a cherished bankers' scheme for an international loan (minus commissions) to be raised in America for the payment of German reparations and foreign debts to the United States. American investments constitute a financial empire of considerable dimensions, though not yet fully subdued, which is a tribute to the diplomacy of Mr. Hughes and Mr. Kellogg. Without involving their government in a single substantial political risk, they have assured to America a financial episcopate over much of the world.

EXPORTING THE FOURTEENTH AMENDMENT

As the natural corollary of the expansion of American foreign investments came the great diplomatic innovation of the Republican administration: the recommendation to foreign nations of the American constitutional guarantee of property rights. The entire basis of the Hughes-Kellogg policy toward Mexico, Russia, China, Central America, and Turkey, was that American citizens should not be deprived of life, liberty, or property without due process of law.

Without asserting the general moral validity of this principle, it were futile for the American Government to encourage or permit the export of American capital to foreign lands. Its enunciation as a cardinal point in American policy was in accord with political tradition, to propose general principles as a solution for specific problems. The annoying duty of protecting American lives and property outside the United States was thus shifted on to other nations, and failure to be considerate of American foreign interests was construed as a violation of the elementary principles of political morality. The United States assumed, for this purpose, a general jurisdiction over its citizens and property, wherever situate, that marked the greatest assumption of authority ever yet enunciated by a member of the family of nations.

The American position was, as in the case of the Monroe Doctrine, first stated by the President in a speech ostensibly addressed to a domestic audience. At the United Press dinner, held on April 25, 1927, at New York City, President Coolidge declared:

While it is well-established international law that we have no right to interfere in the purely domestic affairs of other nations in their dealings with their own citizens, it is equally well established that our Government has certain rights over and duties toward our own citizens and their property, wherever they may be located. *The person and property of a citizen are part of the*

[206]

general domain of the Nation, even when abroad. On the other hand, there is a distinct and binding obligation on the part of self-respecting governments to afford protection to the persons and property of their citizens, wherever they may be. This is both because it has an interest in them and because it has an obligation toward them. *It would seem to be perfectly obvious that if it is wrong to murder and pillage within the confines of the United States, it is equally wrong outside our borders. The fundamental laws of justice are universal in their application. These rights go with the citizen. Wherever he goes, these duties of our Government must follow him.*

This theory of the universal sanctity of American property had been slowly evolved through American experience with Mexico and Russia, where political and social upheavals had destroyed the legal basis of foreign rights. Even before the adoption of the Mexican Constitution on February 5, 1917, the United States had protested against its contemplated legislation regarding land and mineral rights, subsequently embodied in Article 27 of the Mexican organic law.

In February, 1918, Carranza's imposition of a petroleum tax drew from the State Department a warning that "The United States cannot acquiesce in any procedure ostensibly or nominally in the form of taxation or the exercise of eminent domain, but really resulting in the confiscation of private property and arbitrary deprivation of vested rights." Two months later the American Government entered "a formal and solemn protest against the violation or infringement of legitimately acquired American private property rights involved in the enforcement of said decree." In the following August, when the State Department requested Mexico to suspend operation of its decrees, Carranza replied that they were part of the fiscal legislation, and the acting Mexican Secretary of State declared that "The criterion of the Mexican Government in this matter is . . . the simple application of the principle of the equality of nations, frequently forgotten by strong governments in their relations with weak countries." On September 1, 1919, President Carranza addressed the Mexican Congress concerning the "more or less vehement" American suggestions: "The argument used by the American State Department, as well as by the American press, has been that our duties are confiscatory. The Mexican Government hopes the northern republic will respect the sovereignty and independence of Mexico."

It was, perhaps, symptomatic of the Mexico-American controversy of land and oil that it dragged on for nine years, until, in 1928, Ambassador Morrow's endorsement of Mexican sovereignty won a satisfactory adjustment of the obnoxious laws. American property rights acquired prior to the Constitution of 1917 were excepted from their scope. With rare tact, Mr. Morrow announced that the "changes in the Mexican laws and regulations have been made by the voluntary act of the Republic of Mexico."

In its relations with Russia, the State Department was not so successful. In 1917, Washington recognized the Social Democratic government of Kerensky and received its ambassador, Boris Bakmeteff. Since then, it has recognized no Russian government, *de facto* or *de jure*. In the autumn of 1917, the Communists overthrew Kerensky and established Russia's present form of Soviet federation. In the process, foreign property was confiscated and foreign loans to the previous governments were canceled. In 1918 and 1919, moves to recognize the Soviets were made by President Wilson, whose Fourteen Points were actually a paraphrase of the moderate Russian peace proposals of 1917. Ludwig C. A. K. Martens was despatched to New York as Soviet "ambassador." However, radical disturbances in the United States and a genuine concern for the principle of private ownership rapidly hardened the American attitude. Russia owed the American Government $252,000,000, lent to Kerensky, and compensation for confiscated property swelled the total of American claims to double that amount.

Communist propaganda in the United States, China, Mexico, and elsewhere further prejudiced the United States. Hughes actually believed in 1923 that there was a plot to "hoist the red flag over the White House." Kellogg gave credence in 1927 to another plot to insinuate a "Bolshevist hegemony" between the United States and the Panama Canal. On the other hand, the American attitude toward Russian rights was scrupulous and clean-cut. At Paris, Wilson had refused American endorsement to Roumania's annexation of Bessarabia, without Russian consent. At the Washington Conference, the United States assumed a protectorate of Russian rights in the Pacific and secured Japan's withdrawal from Siberia. In 1922, the United States contributed $20,000,000 to the relief of the Russian famine. But a move toward Russian recognition, in 1923, was sternly opposed by Secretary Hughes, and there is no immediate prospect of resumption of relations. American trade with Russia has been encouraged, and official assent has been given to the extension of long-term credits for financing Russo-

American trade; but the efforts to sell Russian railway bonds and to import Russian gold were nullified by Washington. The American Government has adopted a definite attitude. Until Russia provides compensation for confiscated American property and recognizes her debt to the United States, or until the United States abandons its "due process" doctrine, there is no basis for political relations between the two.

In Central America, China, and to a lesser extent in Turkey, Hughes and Kellogg have pursued the traditional policy of protecting American lives and property wherever possible. This element of possibility is the weak point in the old system, which the due-process concept is designed to supplant. It will be remembered that Wilson was much criticized for urging Americans to leave Mexico in 1914, but it was a practical admission that his normal executive powers were insufficient to protect them. In exactly the same way, American residents of China were concentrated in Chinese ports, where the navy could defend them, while Americans in Nicaragua were shielded by the establishment of neutral zones on Nicaraguan soil in which no fighting could take place.

Wherever it is possible, by naval action, shore parties, or marine occupation, for the United States to preserve American property from arbitrary destruction, force is unflinchingly employed for that purpose. For example, a Navy Department pamphlet explains that "One destroyer is kept continually at Samsun, Turkey, to look after the American tobacco interests at that port. . . . The American tobacco companies represented there depend practically entirely on the moral effect of having a man-of-war in port to have their tobacco released for shipment."

The creation of the "neutral zones" in Nicaragua recalls Kipling's prophecy in "With the Night Mail," in which the Aërial Board of Control permitted Crete to go to war so long as it did not interfere with "traffic and all that that implies."

It was, in any case, an anomaly that the professional pacifists should have been the loudest objectors to an American action designed to stop hostilities and prevent loss of life. If an American naval force were at a port threatened by fire or earthquake, and were in a position to save lives at the risk of their own, but refused the task, they would be called poltroons. When they risk the same lives to prevent extensive bloodshed and the destruction of valuable property, due not to natural but to human convulsions, it is difficult to see why they should be regarded as bullies or imperialists.

In effect, the official American attitude toward foreign war and revolution appears to be exactly the same as its attitude toward famines, epidemics, and natural calamities. The legal anarchy of war is repugnant to the American conception of life. In our dealings with the Caribbean, we have practically defined a new political doctrine: War can be waged in localities where American interests are situated, provided that no damage is done to the persons or property of American citizens; provided that the United States may, where possible, intervene to prevent such warfare from inflicting such damage; and provided that the winner of said war or revolution shall bind himself to abstain from actions provocative of renewed disorders. In a word, wars will be tolerated by the United States so long as they do not interfere with American private property "and all that that implies."

Chapter XIII

THE STRUGGLE FOR WORLD TRADE

STATISTICS

EXACTLY as a clever physiologist can prove anything with guinea-pigs, so can a clever economist prove anything by statistics. Statistics must be taken with a great deal of caution. Too often the figures of world-trade are monetary calculations which do not indicate volumes—only valuations. Even so, the element of ownership is invariably omitted. If, for example, an American company owns all the plantations of a Central American country, the figures on imports from that country into the United States are meaningless. They fail to say that the profit goes to an American concern, and that of, say, $300,000 worth of bananas landed at New York, less than $100,000 has been expended in the country of origin, to which, however, the entire sum is credited in computing trade balances. The true meaning of trade statistics is to be sought in dividends. A nation with extensive foreign investments is like a farmer who grows his wheat in one field, raises sheep in one pasture, cattle in another, and chops firewood in yet a fourth tract. To understand international commerce, it is necessary to realize the statistical qualifications.

While statistics are not to be trusted or to be followed blindly, they are a useful means of indicating the relative importance of the United States in the economic world.

Our share of the world's total production and consumption is the best measure of our economic significance.

Of agricultural commodities, the United States produced in 1925-26: one-sixth of the world's wheat, one-tenth of the world's barley, a quarter of the world's oats, a half of the world's maize, a fifth of the world's horses, a tenth of the world's cattle, a fourth of the world's pigs, a tenth of the world's beet sugar, a fifth of the world's tobacco. We produced half of the world's coal, nearly three-fourths of the world's oil, a third of the world's water-power, a half of the world's iron ore and pig iron, steel and copper; two-fifths of the world's lead, nearly half of the world's zinc, over a third of the aluminium, two-fifths of the phosphates, four-fifths of the sulphur, two-fifths of the sulphuric acid, and one-fifth of the synthetic dyes. We produced over one-fourth of the artificial silk, over half of the cotton, a tenth of the wool, nearly half of the electrical goods, nearly three-fifths of the machinery, and almost nine-tenths of the automobiles.

These are the volumes of production which support our export trade. Even more influential on the world are the volumes of consumption which determine the character and value of our import trade. Out of the world totals for 1925-26, the United States consumed over two-fifths of the world's coffee, more than a third of the world's cocoa, over two-thirds of the rubber, nearly a half of the coal, copper, and lead, two-fifths of the world's zinc, more than half of the world's tin and aluminium, a quarter of the world's nitrates, three-tenths of the artificial silk, a fourth of the world's cotton, a fifth of the world's wool, and three-fifths of the world's supply of natural silk.

Such volumes of production and consumption beat down resistance. In values alone, American foreign trade expanded from $500,000,000 in the 'sixties to $2,250,000,000 in 1900, $4,250,000,000 in 1913, and over $9,000,000,000 in 1927. Moreover, for sixty years this trade has been characterized uniformly by "favorable" trade balances which have enabled the United States to pay off its foreign indebtedness and to accumulate the funds for extensive foreign investments. The average favorable trade balance, in the period 1898-1914, was about $500,000,000 a year. During the war period, 1915-20, it soared to $3,000,000,000 a year. During the post-war period, 1921-27, despite the revival of European production and the increase of competition, the average trade balance in favor of the United States was $800,000,000 a year. In all, from the beginning of the war till 1928, the United States accumulated a gross trade balance of over $23,000,000,000—a sum almost exactly equal to its foreign investments, including war loans, of that period.

Moreover, America is freeing herself from economic subservience to Europe. Seventy-five years ago, nearly three-quarters of our foreign trade was with Europe. Before the war, more than half our foreign trade was with Europe. Today, our European trade is little over a third of our total world-trade.

Not only has the direction of our trade changed, but its character has fundamentally altered. In 1850, the bulk of our exports were raw materials and food-stuffs, accounting for nearly seven-tenths of the total. By 1913, less than two-fifths of our export trade was in raw materials; by 1926 they accounted for less than a third of our exports. In 1850, raw materials were only one-sixth of our total imports; in 1913, they were nearly a half, by 1926 more than a half of all our imports. A similar revolution took place in manufactured imports and exports. In 1850, an eighth of our exports were finished manufactures; in 1913, they were nearly a third, in 1926, they were over two-fifths. In 1850, more than half of our imports were manufactured goods; on the eve of the war, nearly a quarter; in 1926, less than a fifth. The United States has slowly been transformed from a source of raw materials and a market for industrial wares into an importer of raw materials and a great exporter of industrial products.

Our gains in the battle for world-trade have been achieved largely by sheer luck, opportunity, impact, and momentum, and hardly at all by finesse, good salesmanship, or technical study of foreign markets. The world has bought from us because our goods were of satisfactory quality and reasonably priced, not because we were clever or likable; and we won the world's market because Europe was industrially decimated by the war.

It is a fact that our success has produced active dislikes. During the war, our business men made little effort to study the tastes and trade regulations of Latin America and the Far East. In consequence, they lost much of their business with those parts of the world shortly after the armistice. General American bumptiousness, discourtesy, unwillingness to "do as the Romans do," and abysmal ignorance of other national mentalities, cost the United States as much in international ill-will as we gained in dollars and cents. Our national contempt for "greasers," "Chinks," "wops," "niggers," and "Japs," was too apparent to win for the United States that good-will which is the better part of trade.

Yet even after much had been lost, American winnings were so impressive and were held so firmly in the face of determined competition that our foreign trade in 1927 was approximately equal to that of Great Britain, the greatest commercial power of the world. In fact, our foreign and coastwise trade is today equal to the entire foreign and inter-imperial commerce of the whole British Empire. Our domestic trade, of over $40,000,000,000 a year, makes the Continental United States the wealthiest single market in the world.

Backed by the complementary forces of mass production and mass consumption, the United States is slowly advancing to commercial predominance.

THE OMINOUS PERCENTAGES

In considering our position in world-trade, it is necessary to remember that what we sell represents the power of our customers over us, while what we buy represents our power over other nations.

Before the war, Latin America was a British commercial stronghold. In practically every country of Latin America, our share of the total trade has risen, while that of Great Britain has declined, in relative importance. Our purchases dominate the export trade of Colombia, Costa Rica, Cuba, Guatemala, Honduras, Mexico, Nicaragua, and Panama, and exert a decisive influence over Bolivia, Brazil, Chile, Ecuador, and Peru. Our sales dominate the markets of Colombia, Costa Rica, Cuba, the Dominican Republic, Guatemala, Haiti, Honduras, Mexico, Nicaragua, Panama, Salvador, Venezuela, and are highly important to the economic life of Argentina, Bolivia, Brazil, Chile, Ecuador, Peru, and Uruguay.

In the British Empire, we buy nearly half of Canada's exports and supply two-thirds of her imports, a quarter of Australia's imports, and a fifth of Great Britain's. We purchase a third of Ceylon's exports, half of British Malaya's, and a tenth of Egypt's. ThePhilippines sell us three-quarters of their exports and buy from us three-fifths of their imports. In 1913, both Great Britain and the United States supplied Japan with a sixth of her imports. In 1926, the United States supplied nearly a third, while the British share had dwindled to one-sixteenth. The United States buys nearly one-half of all Japanese exports. A fourth of Italian imports are of American origin, in Spain and Germany nearly a fifth, in France a sixth. Russia purchases a quarter of her imports from the United States.

From a careful examination of the facts certain definite trends emerge in our economic expansion.

In Latin America we are evolving a virtually complementary exchange of tropical raw materials for our manufactured products. The only element of economic discord in this process is with Argentina, whose wheat and cattle compete with American goods and who is obliged to use her favorable trade balances with England to settle her accounts with the United States. The latter is, in effect, reducing the western hemisphere to a commercial appanage.

Our heavy sales of raw materials and certain manufactures, such as automobiles, create for us in Europe a favorable trade balance of over $1,000,000,000. In order to meet this, European interests sell us the produce of their economic possessions in Africa, Oceania, and southern Asia.

Accordingly, in Asia we create each year an unfavorable balance of $750,000,000—a fact which not only helps Europe to meet her own debts, but tends to create, in Asiatic countries, a desire to maintain friendly relations with the United States. And in Oceania and Africa, we have favorable trade balances which afford an opening wedge for our investments.

That the balance of trade can have a potential political bearing is amply illustrated by the case of the Philippines, which in 1926 enjoyed a favorable balance of $35,000,000 in their trade with the United States. On April 6, 1927, President Coolidge vetoed a bill passed by the Insular Legislature to provide for a plebiscite on the question of Philippine independence. His veto message contained the following observations:

In the calendar year 1926, 761,000,000 pounds of sugar were imported into the United States from the Philippine Islands. The duty waived on this sugar was slightly less than $17,000,000. Of this, $13,000,000, approximately, accrued to the producers of sugar in the Philippine Islands in the increased price thereof.

In the calendar year 1926 Philippine cigars to the value of $5,047,000 were admitted to the United States free of duty. The granting of this privilege meant the waiving of $14,-857,000 customs duties.

In 1926 there was imported into the United States from the Philippines cocoanut oil to the value of $22,000,000. The duties waived on the entry of this oil amounted to $4,900,000. . . .

Briefly, there was waived on Philippine products entering the United States duty amounting to $42,000,000.

The Struggle for World Trade

The total exports of the United States to the Philippine Islands for the year being considered amounted to $71,500,000, and on those products entering the islands, duty of approximately $12,-800,000 was waived. In other words, the duties waived by the United States exceeded the duties waived by the Philippines by nearly $30,000,000.

Do the people of the Philippines realize the effect of these economic facts, and do they appreciate what would be the effect on their progress, their standard of living, their general welfare, of the abolition of the present trade relations?

In fact, trade relations of an extensive and intimate character between the United States and any other nation become a sort of trap from which neither can escape without disastrous injury to its economic welfare. The more intimate the trade relationship, the more inescapable the economic grip. In words almost identical with those addressed to the Filipinos, President Coolidge rejected a Porto Rican plea for fuller independence, in 1928. Forty years ago, a change in the sugar tariff compelled the Hawaiian Islands, in spite of the wishes of the American Government and of the Hawaiian royal family, to enter the American Union. Should America cease to purchase raw silk from Japan, as seems probable in view of the perfection of the synthetic silk industry, no one can prophesy the political consequences in the Island Empire. Should we cease to buy coffee, plantations in Brazil go bankrupt. Should we stop buying tin and rubber from Singapore, British Malaya suffers. Decreasing purchases of nitrates from Chile have already wrought a revolutionary change in that country's attitude toward the United States. For the first time in forty years, Chile is friendly to America, as she begins to realize her economic interest in the United States.

American trade and the tremendous totals which it involves are steadily weaving an economic web throughout the world. No nation can destroy this without endangering its own prosperity.

TRADE AND TARIFFS

For the moment, European economic control of African and Asiatic countries is sufficient to enable the Europeans to use tropical produce in payment for American goods. Thus the sale of European goods in the tropics and the Orient frees Asiatic goods, which, in their turn, pay for the goods we sell to Europe.

This is the economic triangle which, reduced to a single instance, means that a pound of American cotton sold to England buys two yards of cotton cloth, which is sold to Ceylon for a half-pound of raw rubber, which is paid over to America.

This eternal economic triangle is the basis of world-trade and is the highest achievement of commercial credit under the industrial system. It effectively displaces the vicious economic circle, i.e., "You can't expect Europe to pay for American exports unless you accept European imports," which is the argument used against the protective tariff.

In effect, it is both possible and expedient for Europe to pay for our raw materials and manufactured goods—wheat, meat, cotton, copper, petroleum, automobiles, etc.—with the tropical produce required for their manufacture or for other forms of consumption—coffee, tea, cocoa, camphor, silk, rubber, nitrates, potash, and so on. It has even been shown to be practicable, through restrictive legislation and the less widely advertised but equally efficient European cartels and monopolies, to throw the balance of trade against the United States, simply by setting a high arbitrary valuation on goods which are necessary to our industry.

So long as this abnormal situation continues, it is possible for Europe to pay for all her imports from the United States. However, such practices make it profitable for American capital and firms to participate in these economic hold-ups, thus making trade balances a mere matter of bookkeeping. The high prices charged for rubber cease to be so alarming when one remembers that American rubber companies own plantations in British Malaya and the Dutch East Indies, and that the excess profit on the controlled products goes, in many cases, to American firms in the form of dividends.

However, to complete the economic triangle—if only to avoid sending ships in ballast from Liverpool to Singapore to fetch the rubber demanded by New York—Europe must sell her manufactured goods to the tropics, to Latin America, Africa, Oceania, and Australasia.

It is at this point that Europe finds the economic trap closing on her industries. For we compete with Europe in the very regions where she must sell her products in order to pay us. Thus our favorable trade balances in Europe, if not cancelled by the unfavorable trade balances in European dependencies, must be converted into investments, which entail Europe's loss of economic control over her tropical dependencies.

Consequently, in the traditional British markets of

Oceania, the British, after wiping out their own adverse trade balance with the produce of the Middle East, find an annual American surplus of nearly $155,000,000. Everywhere in Asia, Africa, South America, and Oceania, American goods are in competition with European goods, and American capital is engaged in securing economic control. In other words, we tend to manufacture our pound of cotton into cotton cloth and trade it direct with Singapore for the half-pound of rubber, thus avoiding the payment of triple freight-charges, commissions, and other perquisites and emoluments of the European middleman.

In fact, the elimination of Europe as a commercial *entrepôt* has become an inevitable objective of American commerce. Moreover, it is a process which is year by year becoming more of an accomplished fact. In 1850, three-fourths of our trade, both import and export, was with Europe. In 1926, less than a third of our imports came from Europe, and the United States actually imported more from Asia than it did from the Old World.

The European, through his political predominance, still maintains a precarious general supervision of the process of exchange, but is gradually being shouldered out. The silk trade, which once gave Great Britain a firm grip on the destinies of Japan and eastern Asia, has been removed from British control and now passes direct from Tokyo to New York. Similarly the Indian jute trade is held only through British political control of India, and only the status of Malaya as a British Crown Colony made possible the effective restriction of rubber. However, even politics are proving insufficient to maintain a grip on the world's raw materials, as they are vulnerable to financial infiltration. Our investment in controlled products simply diverts to American pockets the profits created by political control, and thus creates new funds for further investment.

Europe's economic dilemma is, therefore, complete. Her efforts to reduce the annual trade balance by enhancing the price of essential raw materials simply makes it possible and desirable for American capital to purchase the source of these raw materials. The profits arising from our investments—now amounting to $750,000,000 a year—simply take the place of the former trade balance, and so increase the net American investment from year to year.

Only war or cancellation can check the growth of our trade and investments. Europe cannot afford to resort to either of these desperate expedients for at least a generation.

Chapter XIV

WHY EUROPE CAN'T COMPETE

AMERICA'S "SECRET"

THE plain fact is that Europe lacks the resources, the industrial organization, and the domestic markets to compete successfully with America in the markets of the world.

Since the armistice, all European countries—especially France, Great Britain, Germany, and Italy—have endeavored to copy or to adapt the mass-production methods of American big business. These efforts seem doomed to disappointment, if not utter failure. No other industrial nation possesses the broad home-market which gives our industry its peculiar strength and stability. All of them are, accordingly, forced at the outset to compete in the world-market and to engage in cutthroat competition, which is ruinous to industrial prosperity. Every effort to escape competition through combinations on the order of the recent European steel trust means an increase in price to the purchaser. This in turn benefits the American competitor, who is only injured by the competition which the combinations are designed to eliminate. Europe seeks economic salvation through mass production and finds that mass production is possible only with an assured market. Attempts to capture such a market reduce prices and enforce consolidation, which raises prices and again enables America to compete.

Europe is now engaged in an economic renaissance

which aims to achieve an American prosperity by the adoption of American industrial methods. Scarcely a week passes but there is news calling attention to the European revival—the "rationalization" of French industry, the vertical and horizontal trust in Germany, the "Fordization" of Russia, the industrialization of Italy, the rise of British protectionism and Imperial preference, steel, chemical, film, and other "alliances." It is characteristic of this revival, as it is typical of the European mind, that most of this is institutional and is imposed on the traditional European economic system, rather than being the natural expression of that system.

Imitation is the most interesting form of flattery, but there is some pathos in the European notion that "America's secret" is machine production and high wages. The true basis of our mass production is, primarily, the possession and free exploitation of large natural resources, which leads in turn to the mass purchasing of raw materials and mass consumption of the finished article. In this economic trinity resides the mystery of our prosperity.

America possesses innumerable raw materials and encourages their rapid exploitation and sale to all industrial interests. Our industry engages in mass production, only after mass purchase of raw and semi-manufactured materials. The market for its product is primarily based on the 125,000,000 Americans engaged in the mass consumption of goods. Without any of these factors, "Americanization" or "rationalization" falls short of prosperity. Europe's political traditions are inimical to the rapid exchange and exploitation of wealth. Economic conservatism, buttressed by governmental authority, is the first impediment to European prosperity. Europe must study the

American policy toward the public lands and apply it without fear or favor to Mesopotamian oil, Malayan rubber, Indian jute, tin, potash, and quinine, if she is to lay the foundation for her prosperity on a broad economic base. She must learn that economic demobilization, if not economic disarmament, is the first step to be taken if she is to compete with America, that it is useless to argue against the policy of ca' canny in the factory if the Government is ca' canny with rubber or films. Voluminous production of raw materials is the better part of American prosperity. It exposes the producer of those raw materials to the changes and chances of the law of supply and demand, and it produces heart-rending hardship, as in the case of the American cotton planters in 1915-17 and the American farmers in 1921-28. But no system of economic production has yet been devised which will eliminate all risk from living. The American idea limits the risk to the most stable portion of the population.

The second element in our system is the encouragement of mass consumption by the payment of high wages. The cheap labor of Europe reduces manufacturing costs, but also restricts profitable exchange to the foreign market. Thus it has been estimated that in "real wages"—the purchasing power of a day's work—where the average Philadelphia laborer receives $1.00, the London worker gets 60 cents, the Parisian 41, the Berliner 40, and the Roman 28. In short, the Englishman must work for a day and two-thirds, the Frenchman and German for two days and a half, and the Italian for nearly four days to get what the Philadelphian obtains for one day's labor. As a result, the American worker is twice as much a factor in purchasing goods as the British, nearly three times as much as the German and the Frenchman, and almost four times as much as the Italian. As there are 42,000,000 Americans "engaged in gainful occupations," 25,000,000 of whom are between the ages of twenty and forty-four—when appetites are strongest and responsibilities greatest—high wages are a vital factor in the purchase of American goods.

The existence of a single, unified, stable American market with an annual turnover of $525,000,000,000 in bank clearings alone, is a further advantage to the American industrialist. He is able to simplify and standardize his production for a market of 125,000,000 people, with approximately the same tastes, who do an average business of $4,000 per capita. This advantage was confirmed by the introduction of the "simplified practice" of the Department of Commerce in 1921. For example, in 1926, seven varieties of steel reënforcing spirals were reduced to three, 190 varieties of sterling silver flatware reduced to 62; 441 kinds of china plumbing fixtures to 58; 102 kinds of stock for wire-bound boxes to 6, and so on. Items of saving, such as these, have merely accelerated a standardizing process which is the logical result of a unified market. Cost of production is correspondingly lowered and the article is better qualified to compete in foreign markets.

Europe, on the other hand, has to manufacture for a diversified market and for differing national tastes. The result is that her inter-European trade has no special advantage or impetus, and that, being constantly liable to political upsets and political risks, it is forced to seek a maximum of immediate gain rather than the creation of a stable market.

As a result, our competition with Europe enjoys the initial advantage of an enormous economic momentum. Against it Europe can raise only the barriers of legislative control, in order to protect her production as well as her consumption, from American domination. This, however, constitutes a denial of the chief element of American prosperity—free exploitation of wealth—and is powerless to prevent the financial acquisition of European property by American investments.

But our mass purchasing is the irresistible factor in our prosperity. The following items were imported duty-free in 1926:

954,817,255 lbs. of rubber, for $339,874,784, principally from British Malaya and Ceylon.

1,433,339,538 lbs. of coffee, at $264,275,310, nearly all from Brazil.

89,169,373 lbs. of tea, for $28,192,298, from Japan, Great Britain and Ceylon.

14,004,593 lbs. of silk, for $390,365,475, nearly all from Japan.

61,009,425 bunches of bananas, worth $34,269,450, mainly from Central America and Jamaica.

424,987,077 lbs. of cocoa, worth $56,815,964, principally from British West Africa and Brazil.

8,431,315,306 lbs. of sugar [dutiable], worth $258,155,475, almost entirely from Cuba.

267,209,564 lbs. of wool [dutiable], worth $82,932,956.

3,973,724,113 lbs. of newsprint, worth $131,488,784, almost all of it from Canada.

The existence of these huge annual purchases is the reason for Europe's inability to dispense with the United States. With our buyers bidding in the sugar crop, the rubber crop, the coffee crop, the silk output, and the banana crop—not to mention her less lavish purchases— no non-American producer in his senses would refuse to sell. And how can the European refuse to pay himself with cheap American wheat, cotton, copper, meat, oil, automobiles, films, and machinery?

The United States has little more than an eighteenth of the world's land and population, but it produces more than a half of the world's iron, steel, copper, petroleum, timber, sulphur, mica, lead, zinc, and cotton, and nearly a half of the world's coal and phosphates. Its national wealth of $400,000,000,000 is nearly half the wealth of the entire world. It controls nearly half of the world's gold supply. And it consumes as lavishly as it produces. It buys from the world as voluminously as it sells.

Our economic system is based on the raw materials, the productive resources, and the consuming habits of the North American Continent. European economic systems are based on colonial raw materials, nationalistic industrial organizations, and the chances of the world-market. Against American mass production, mass purchasing, and mass consumption, Europe can oppose only mass production.

GETTING A LIEN ON OUR COMPETITORS

The almost incalculable transactions of American commerce are backed by the money-power of the United States. It is this which stabilizes the outpouring of American wealth in foreign trade and assures that the goods exported are exchanged for either foreign goods or foreign investments. The result of this system reveals itself in the creation of an informal financial empire on a world-wide scale.

The object of American banking is not to secure foreign investments or financial power, but to make money; the object of American commerce is not to create favorable trade balances, but to sell goods; the object of American tourists is not to introduce a foreign demand for American goods, but to enjoy life.

All these consequences, however, occur, without purpose and without design, and result in our acquiring a lien on our industrial competitors and on their raw materials. The United States exports goods worth more than those which it imports. The difference in value must be accounted for: this is done by converting the balance into foreign investments and by exporting American citizens to reside in or visit foreign lands. Yet the conversion of trade balances into investments results in creating the necessity for payment of interest, which must be paid in either goods or new investments; and the export of American tourists, while reducing the immediate balance of trade, serves to create a foreign interest in American goods, tastes, methods, and ideas, which is subsequently reflected in fresh trade balances. The process thus becomes a vicious circle, and its logical result would be the Americanization of the entire world, if logic were a reliable guide to political or economic processes.

Fortunately for the world and for the United States, logic is only the last resort of fools and Frenchmen. There is no augury that new processes of manufacture, new sources of energy, new social and political ideas, may not overthrow the entire basis of industrial and capitalistic society. Yet the trend of the moment is reliable, in so far as it indicates the growing influence of American finance on the economic life of the globe.

The greatest factor in modern American policy is our money-power, which is equipped to deal with virtually any problem short of deliberate confiscation, and is prepared to make the price of confiscation prohibitively dear. Our private financial dictators have ruled in Hungary, Poland, Persia, and Germany, as they rule today in Haiti, Santo Domingo, Nicaragua, and Ecuador. The settlement of the reparations problem and the rehabilitation of Europe is the work of American finance. No future major step in world-politics, whether it involves the recognition of Russia, the partition of China, or the conversion of the war debts, can be taken without the permission of Wall Street.

The foundations of this power are almost impregnable. American banking is a decentralized, federalized organization of nearly 30,000 National and State banks whose resources—capital, surplus, undivided profits, deposits, loans, discounts, and investments—grew from $25,700,-000,000 in 1913 to $65,000,000,000 in 1926. In addition to these there are the 9,000-odd members of the Federal Reserve System, which was organized in 1914, with total resources in 1926 of over $42,000,000,000. With life insurance policies aggregating over $70,000,000,000, with savings deposits mounting by nearly $2,000,000,000 a year, and with a gold stock of $4,500,000,000—of which $2,500,000,000 was imported between 1914 and 1926—our money power is so firmly rooted in the industrial and commercial life of the world that any injury to American credit would amount to a major international calamity.

Our money seems to be engaged in buying up the world.

[231]

From a foreign investment of little more than $2,500,-000,000 in 1913, our foreign investments today total between $12,000,000,000 and $15,000,000,000—not counting the $10,000,000,000 of war debts owed the United States Government by European powers. In thirteen years (1914-27), Americans lent or invested a net total of $10,500,000,000 in foreign lands.

However, of this total, more than two-thirds has been lent to governmental agencies—states, provinces, and municipalities; of the entire sum invested since 1914, little more than $3,000,000,000 has been invested in private enterprise. For every American dollar invested in profitable or productive private enterprise since the outbreak of the war, $2.30 has been invested in foreign governments. We have lent European governments $3.65; Latin-American governments $1.64; Far Eastern governments $3.63; and Canadian governments $1.22, for every dollar we have put to productive uses in those respective areas. In every year from 1914 till 1927, we invested more money in foreign governments than in foreign business. In 1927, for the first time, we actually placed more money at the service of foreign productive enterprise than we did at the service of foreign political administration.

The spread of American foreign investment proceeds unchecked and there is, as yet, no indication of any power sufficiently grave to halt it. It is estimated that within a generation, American foreign investments may amount to $50,000,000,000. By the time the Allies have paid off the entirety of their war debts to the United States Government, American private investments abroad may amount to $75,000,000,000. At present, the United States invests on the average $1,500,000,000 abroad every year, exclusive of refundings. As interest payments mount, that sum will increase.

TABLE OF AMERICAN INVESTMENTS

Year [1]	Government Loans	Business Investment	Ratio
1914	$ 29,794,000	$ 7,978,000	$ 3.75 to $1.00
1915	734,345,000	69,649,000	10.50 to 1.00
1916	974,099,000	149,230,000	6.50 to 1.00
1917	567,715,000	118,432,000	4.81 to 1.00
1918 [2]	14,845,000	13,270,000	1.11 to 1.00
1919	438,439,000	123,884,000	3.53 to 1.00
1920	372,133,000	147,960,000	2.49 to 1.00
1921	512,000,000	134,296,000	3.82 to 1.00
1922	485,566,000	196,710,000	2.47 to 1.00
1923	295,302,000	118,359,000	2.50 to 1.00
1924	776,735,000	151,757,000	5.14 to 1.00
1925	648,573,000	336,806,000	1.93 to 1.00
1926	594,412,000	550,600,000	1.08 to 1.00
1927 [3]	930,560,000	1,141,393,000	0.81 to 1.00

[1] 1915-26, inclusive, Department of Commerce figures.
[2] War year. War loans of ten billion dollars not included.
[3] Unofficial figures compiled by Dr. Max Winkler.

While the excess of governmental loans over corporate investments creates a glaringly top-heavy financial structure, it is probable that the financial current is setting in the opposite direction. Moreover, governmental loans are desirable, both as a means of restoring political stability and financial integrity, and as giving the private American investor the power to influence the national credit of foreign powers, in the event that they show themselves hostile to his economic interests.

There is, accordingly, a triple power involved in the present status of American foreign finance: the power of the United States Government over European governments, through the war debts and through the State Department's tacit supervision of foreign loans; the power of American investors over foreign governments, through the former's ability to dump the latter's bonds on the market and thereby depress their credit; and the direct participation of the American investors in the creation and development of foreign wealth. The first and the second are, primarily, defensive measures—partly pledges for good behavior, partly the means of making productive investment possible. The third is the actual enjoyment of wealth.

The range of the American dollar is best illustrated by the character of our investments in 1927:

We lend money to public utility, railroad and industrial enterprises in Canada. We finance machinery companies in Germany and Japan; steel companies in Germany and Luxembourg, Bulgaria and Rumania; plantation companies in the Dutch East Indies; oil companies in Australia and the Dutch East Indies; banks and financial institutions in Austria and Germany, Holland and Hungary, Colombia and Australia; hydro-electric companies in Germany and Italy, Norway and Japan; railways in Belgium and Argentina, Chile and Colombia; department stores in Germany and Great Britain; street railways in Germany; rubber and oil concerns in Bolivia; rubber and mining companies in Brazil; textile companies in Germany; automobile companies in France and Italy. We acquire telephone concerns in Austria and Brazil, Chile and Uruguay. We buy public utilities in Brazil; land in Panama and Guatemala. We secure oil concessions in Colombia and Venezuela and rubber concessions in Brazil. We

[234]

buy real estate in Cuba. We finance steamship companies in Great Britain and France, Germany and Italy; sugar companies in Mexico; and even lend money to banks in Iceland.[1]

This deluge of dollars is the natural result of America's favorable trade balance. In the last fifty-two years the United States has accumulated a favorable trade balance of over $58,000,000,000, as against the adverse trade balance of $2,500,000,000 accumulated in the first century of our national existence.

From 1860 till 1914, the United States was a borrowing nation. By 1873, $1,500,000,000 of European capital was invested in the United States; by 1880 the European investment here was $2,000,000,000—three-fourths of it in our railroads; $3,000,000,000 in 1890; $3,300,000,000 in 1899. In 1914, European investors owned between $4,000,000,000 and $5,000,000,000 worth of American securities—about twice our total foreign investment at the same time. The war profits of our industry and finance enabled us to pay off a large portion of our foreign indebtedness; but for the assumption by our government of the British debts, nearly $3,000,000,000 worth of American securities must have been thrown on the market, with corresponding disaster to all values. This so-called "mobilization of American securities" was a practical lesson in the enormous indirect power of money over politics. During the war, $2,000,000,000 worth of American securities were repurchased by the United States, but a balance of $3,000,000,000 worth is still held by European interests and is a powerful deterrent to arbitrary action by the United States.

[1] Dr. Max Winkler, *The Ascendancy of the Dollar.*

The problem of dealing with the American trade balance, interest and other payments to the United States, is intricate. Interest payment may not be postponed, and trade balances can be held in the form of commercial credit only long enough to adjust the flow of goods, cover offsets and other deductions, until a net balance has been clearly established. This balance must then be spent or invested.

The European idea is that the United States should accept payment in goods, but the demand for goods in the United States is measured by definite standards which cannot lightly be ignored. There is no reason why American imports and exports should enjoy mathematical parity. It is rather to our advantage to use the credits built up by our export trade to acquire liens on the natural resources of our European competitors.

By investing our excess capital in European industry we can both harmonize its production to our own industrial needs and obtain access to those raw materials in European possessions which are necessary to our commercial welfare.

There is only one way in which we can avoid the necessity of investing capital abroad in quantities greater than is economically advisable. The export of American tourists is an unfailing means of preventing unwieldy trade balances and heavy interest payments from becoming an embarrassment to us or to our debtors.

Since 1900, our tourist expenditures abroad have averaged over $150,000,000 a year. In 1926, about 365,000 Americans left the United States to help consume the wealth which we had exported in the countries which had received it. Of these 320,000 went to Europe. Their estimated expenditure on the Continent was about $1,250 apiece, or a total of $456,000,000. Adding to this figure the $30,000,000 spent by Americans residing abroad, the $200,000,000 spent by American tourists in Canada, the $15,000,000 similarly spent in Mexico, and the $60,000,-000 of American money spent by aliens normally resident in the United States, in the capacity of tourists, our total tourist bill in 1926 was about $761,000,000. Deducting from this the $115,000,000 spent by foreign tourists in the United States, we still have a balance of nearly $650,000,000 chargeable to the export of Americans in search of the dollars which they had previously exported in the form of goods.

It is obvious that this is not their conscious purpose. They travel in quest of happiness, health, pleasure, instruction, alcoholic beverages, wild oats, or to relieve boredom. Yet their services to American trade are very important. They help to ease the strain consequent on the violent export of American capital. They build up a tourist trade which creates a permanent international interest in the maintenance of friendly and intimate relations with the United States. Travel also gives the Americans a chance to learn about the world and its peoples and thus to participate intelligently in international political and commercial relations. Finally, the tourist creates a demand for American goods wherever he goes, thus helping the American trade which made his journey possible.

Babbitt clamoring for ham and eggs and "an honest-to-God cup of coffee"; Babbitt's son yearning for ice-cream sodas or Eskimo pie; Mrs. Babbitt seeking a dress which will make Main Street envious rather than shocked —through tourists, our clothes, fashions, tastes, and consuming habits are introduced abroad, if only in an effort to cater to the tourist traffic. The tourist advertises and familiarizes the world with American products. Instead of being a red-ink entry on the national ledger, he is actually and ignorantly a servant of economic empire and a means of expanding American commerce. By the very device which enables foreign nations temporarily to resist our economic onset, the world promotes the Americanization of its methods, and adopts the material technique of life which is the means and the object of the American empire.

Chapter XV

EMPIRE ON THE INSTALLMENT PLAN

THE SATRAPIES OF AMERICAN BUSINESS

It is true that the United States Government aspires to no political empire. It is a fact that American business does not engage in foreign trade or foreign investments with the object of acquiring political power. Yet it cannot be denied that our economic expansion inevitably involves a measure of indirect American control over other nations.

This control is not vested in the American Government. It is wielded individually and collectively by the international activities of private American enterprise. It is, in the last analysis, a parallel to the power exerted over our own government by the business interests of the United States. There is no legal or political liaison between Wall Street and the White House; yet the government at Washington is properly solicitous lest its administrative policies react unfavorably on the business life of the nation.

A similar situation is created by the extension of American business to foreign countries. There is no way of disfranchising a million dollars. A foreign investment creates too many personal interests, jobs, and contracts, as well as contributing too generally to the economic life of the political group, to be ignored by its government. A policy which is disadvantageous to, say, the operations of the

United Fruit Company in Jamaica, will not, in practice, be adopted without careful consideration of the effect on Jamaica's prosperity which would result from any injury to a concern with a very substantial stake in the island.

By sheer economic inertia, not to mention the more overt expedients of lobbying, financial pressure on general credit, or—in less orderly communities—subsidizing changes of administration or "influencing" legislators, a large foreign investment can thwart hostile legislation or obtain political favor. In this sense, the activities of American business abroad—again parallel to its influence in the United States—confer upon it an informal political status.

No one can say where the line may be drawn in practice. It is impossible to determine in any case the precise extent to which American business has converted its economic holdings into practical satrapies. In general, it might be inferred that such is the case in Cuba, to a lesser extent in Canada and Mexico, and decidedly so in Central America, Haiti, and Santo Domingo. The fact that it has proved possible for American business to expand so as to dominate the economic life of certain countries directly, and their political life indirectly, without involving the expansion of American sovereignty, is the best testimony to its non-aggressive character.

Merely to record the more important American concerns which have built up these business principalities throughout the world would be wearisome; a summary of their activities, in the barest form, would be material for a good-sized book. The process, however, is of such vital importance that a few selected instances can reveal both its characteristic method—the subsidiary company—and its world-wide scope.

The Vacuum Oil Company, of New York, the oldest oil company in the United States and one of the Standard group, is a case in point. The home company serves the United States, Canada, Mexico, the West Indies, Central America, Panama, Colombia, Venezuela, and the Guianas. Through branch offices at Bombay, Cairo, Buenos Aires, Helsingfors, Hong-Kong, Kobe, Lisbon, and Shanghai, it serves the rest of South America, the Near East, and the rest of Asia, including the East Indies.

Eighteen subsidiary companies organized, respectively, in Spain, Hungary, the Union of South Africa, Denmark, Poland, Gibraltar, Italy, Germany, the Canary Islands, London, Australia, Norway, France, Czecho-Slovakia, Sweden, Austria, and Jugo-Slavia, complete its distributing organization. Northern Arabia and Russia are the only parts of the world where it does not operate, and with Russia it has important oil purchasing contracts. The Vacuum is mainly a refining and marketing company, specializing in lubricants, but its organization is an almost perfect pattern of modern American business technique.

Other oil companies with similarly extensive interests include the Atlantic Refining Company, with oil properties in Latin America, Italy, and Africa; the California Petroleum Company, with large holdings in Mexico, concessions in Venezuela, and world-wide trade connections; the Pan-American Petroleum and Transport Company, formerly owned by E. L. Doheny, but now owned by a syndicate which includes the Standard Oil of Indiana, with 1,000,000 acres of land, refineries, and warehouses in Mexico, refineries in Venezuela, an interest in the Mosul oil field, and extensive marketing connections; the Standard Oil Company of California, the largest producer of

[241]

crude oil in the United States and the third largest re-
finer in the world, with lands in Colombia, Venezuela,
Mexico, and Argentina; the Standard Oil Company of
New Jersey, with thirteen subsidiaries in Belgium, Holland, France, Mexico, Denmark, Germany, Canada, Italy,
Switzerland, Roumania, Brazil, Great Britain, and Portugal, with 2,500,000 acres of oil lands in Venezuela
and Bolivia, shares in the Mosul field, and refineries in
Canada, South America, Europe, and Sumatra. The Standard Oil Company of New York has holdings and plants
in Mexico, operates a candle factory at Tientsin, China,
has over 3,000 small and large agencies in Japan, China,
the Philippines, Indo-China, Siam, the Dutch East Indies,
Straits Settlements, Burma, India, Ceylon, Syria, Turkey,
Bulgaria, Greece, Australasia, and South Africa; controls
subsidiaries in Great Britain, China, and Australia, and
shares in the Mosul oil field. The Texas Company has
selling subsidiaries in Belgium, Sweden, Mexico, the Philippine Islands, Porto Rico, France, South Africa, Great
Britain, and Cuba, produces oil in Mexico and Venezuela,
and through the California Petroleum Company competes
in the Far East with the Standard and the Royal Dutch
groups.

In the realm of tropical production the United Fruit
Company of Boston offers an interesting variant. This
company's ambition is, primarily, to sell bananas. For that
purpose, it owns or leases nearly 2,000,000 acres of
land in Central America and the West Indies, operates
1,571 miles of railroad and a fleet of 100 steamships,
both refrigerator vessels and passenger ships, under four
different flags. Its capital and surplus is $175,200,000
(1926), and it employs 67,000 men. Its medical depart-

ment has been active in combating tropical diseases; it maintains ice plants, bakeries, laundries, electric-light plants, waterworks, sewerage systems, churches, schools, baseball grounds, tennis courts, golf-courses, and swimming-pools. It owns and operates two hotels in Jamaica. It owns sugar plantations and two large raw sugar mills in Cuba, the produce of which is refined and distributed by its subsidiary, the Revere Sugar Company of Boston. It owns the Fruit Despatch Company, a selling subsidiary for the United States and Canada, with fifty-two branches; and a similar English subsidiary, Elders and Fyffes, Ltd., with branches in Great Britain and Europe and a producing division in the Canary Islands. It owns the Tropical Radio Telegraph Company, with stations in Central America, the West Indies, and the United States, to serve the general public as well as the company. It does a direct mercantile business of $10,000,000 a year with Latin America. Its extraordinary diversity as well as its broad policies invite comparison with the East India and Hudson's Bay Companies.

In the financial field, the National City Bank of New York is a fit companion to these business empires. Organized in 1812, the bank has total resources of over $1,500,-000,000, and operates 106 branches in twenty-three foreign countries. Its first foreign branch was opened at Buenos Aires in 1914. In 1915, it acquired the International Banking Corporation. Its head office is at 55 Wall Street; it operates nineteen branches in New York City, two in Argentina, two in Belgium, four in Brazil, two in Chile, eight in China, twenty-five in Cuba, two in England, three in India, two in Italy, four in Japan, one in Java, two in Panama, one in Peru, two in Porto Rico, six in Santo Domingo, and one apiece in the Straits Settlements, Uruguay, and Venezuela. It controls the National City Bank of New York (France), S.A., in Paris, and the Banque Nationale de la République d'Haiti, in Port-au-Prince. Through its control of the International Banking Corporation it conducts investment operations in the Philippines, Spain, and England.

The General Motors Corporation is to the American automobile industry what the National City Bank is to American finance (leaving J. P. Morgan and Company and Henry Ford out of account). In the United States, General Motors includes the Chevrolet, Pontiac, Oldsmobile, Oakland, Buick, La Salle, Cadillac, G.M.C. Trucks, Fisher Body Corporation, Frigidaire Corporation, and Delco Light Company. The General Motors Acceptance Corporation finances its installment-selling. It maintains over 5,000 distributers and dealers in 104 countries. Its overseas investment is $30,000,000. In 1926 it did a foreign trade of nearly $25,000,000. It owns the Vauxhall Motors, Ltd., of London. It maintains 40,000 service stations overseas. It has assembly plants at Melbourne, Perth, Adelaide, Brisbane, Sydney, Buenos Aires, Singapore, São Paulo, Antwerp, Hamburg, Copenhagen, Kobe, Hendon, Wellington, Bilbao, Port Elizabeth, Montevideo, and Singapore, and warehouses at Le Havre and Alexandria. It controls sixteen foreign subsidiary companies. The General Motors Export Company of New York exists solely to handle its overseas trade. It controls the Yellow Truck and Coach Manufacturing Company and the General Motors of Canada, Ltd., of Oshawa, Ontario, which operates two plants, and it has a half interest in the Ethyl Gasoline Corporation. In all, General

Motors controls eight companies in the passenger and commercial car group, fourteen in the accessory and spare parts group, eighteen in the export and overseas group, seven in a miscellaneous group, ten sales companies in the United States, and seven sales companies in Canada—a total of sixty-four corporations controlled by one policy. Its total assets on March 31, 1927, were reckoned at $970,745,574, and in the period from 1919 to 1927 it sold nearly 3,000,000 vehicles.

Similar organizations are maintained by the Ford Motor Company, with factories and assembly plants in the United States and Canada and in Antwerp, Berlin, Copenhagen, Paris, Bordeaux, Cadiz, Southampton, London, Cork, Yokohama, Buenos Aires, Montevideo, Pernambuco, São Paulo, and Mexico City; iron mines in Newfoundland and a 5,000,000-acre rubber concession in the Amazon Valley, as well as by other American automobile manufacturers: the Chrysler Corporation, Dodge Brothers, Durant Motors, Inc., Hupp Motor Car Corporation, Mack Trucks, Inc., Reo Motor Car Company, the Studebaker Corporation, and the Willys-Overland Company.

In the field of ocean transport, one of the most significant developments has been that of W. R. Grace and Company, which operates twenty-six steamers in seven lines, linking North, Central, and South America, on both the east and the west coasts. With nitrate interests in Chile and extensive mining and agricultural properties elsewhere in South America, and an intricate system of agencies and properties throughout the entire world, it is a striking example of an amphibious corporation.

These few companies are not exceptional—they are typical examples of the international organization of

American big business. It should be noted, too, how closely they correspond to the federal type of American political organization. Instead of one company with many branches, a group of companies is welded together, given local autonomy, empowered to deal with separate economic problems, and compelled to coöperate with each other in a general way. Typical of this process is the present condition of the Standard Oil companies, which have been separated since 1912, but which coöperate with each other to prevent unnecessary competition.

To indicate the world-wide effects of this type of American business expansion, one need only consider a few of the bewildering and multifarious facts.

The International Harvester Company has plants and manufacturing subsidiaries in Canada, France, Germany, and Sweden; selling subsidiaries in Argentina, Australia, Denmark, Italy, Great Britain, Latvia, New Zealand, Norway, Spain, Switzerland, and the Philippines.

The Paramount-Famous Players-Lasky Corporation has distributing branches for Paramount Pictures in France, England, Belgium, Italy, Spain, Austria, New Zealand, Cuba, Argentina, Chile, Peru, Porto Rico, Brazil, Japan, the Dutch East Indies, Denmark, Norway, Sweden, Holland, Greece, Turkey, Bulgaria, Algeria, Tunis, Guatemala, Panama, Mexico, Tasmania, and Singapore. It owns two theaters in London and one theater each in Paris and Brussels.

Loew's, Incorporated, has theatrical interests in Canada and Germany, manages 44 theaters in Brazil, and shares in the operation of 110 theaters in Great Britain.

Page and Shaw operate five candy stores in London,

one in Paris, and one in Italy, and maintain 2,000 foreign agencies.

Armour and Company, together with Swift and Company, control nearly half of Britain's imports of meat and have 100 subsidiaries in Europe and North, South, and Central America.

Swift and Company maintain over 500 branch houses and sales agencies, serving practically every important city in the world.

The Manati Sugar Company is the leading producer of Cuban sugar, and owns land, factories, warehouses, railroads, and docks.

The Singer Sewing Machine Company controls 80 per cent. of the world's output of sewing machines. It has foreign factories in the Province of Quebec, in Scotland and Germany, and has a three-fourths interest in the Singer Manufacturing Company, Ltd., of Great Britain.

The International Mercantile Marine Company controls one American, one Belgian, and two British steamship lines.

The Wrigley Products Company now manufactures chewing-gum in Great Britain.

The Lambert Company makes listerine in Toronto, Mexico City, Paris, and Madrid.

The United Drug Company operates, through a subsidiary, 800 drug stores in Great Britain and 36 in Canada, as well as 10,500 in the United States.

The International Nickel Company enjoys what is "almost a world monopoly," owning vast mining properties in Canada, through a subsidiary, which controls 90 per cent. of the world's supply of nickel.

The Vanadium Corporation of America owns the largest known deposit of vanadium ore in the Andes, in Peru, and through a subsidiary controls half of the Rhodesian Vanadium Corporation of South Africa.

The American Chicle Company has concessions for over 5,000,000 acres of chicle-lands in Mexico, Guatemala, and British Honduras.

The Eastman Kodak Company has subsidiaries in Paris, Toronto, London, and Berlin, controls the Kodak-Pathé, and produces 75 per cent. of the raw film output of the world.

The Woolworth Company owns subsidiary companies in Canada, France, Great Britain, and Germany. It operates 1,581 five-and-ten-cent stores in the United States and Canada, 299 in Great Britain and Ireland, of which 57 were established in 1927, and 9 in Germany, where it began retail operations in July, 1927.

The Goodyear Tire and Rubber Company is the largest rubber corporation in the world, using one-seventh of the world's output. It maintains branches and subsidiaries in 135 countries and operates plants in Canada and Australia.

The United States Rubber Company owns, through the General Rubber Company, 134,000 acres of rubber plantation land in Sumatra and British Malaya. It owns 75 per cent. of the stock of the Dominion Rubber Company, with several plants in Canada, eighteen miscellaneous companies in Canada and one in Great Britain, and has selling subsidiaries in Canada, Great Britain, France, Denmark, New Zealand, and South Africa.

The International Telephone and Telegraph Company controls the Cuban and Porto Rican Telephone Companies, has a half interest in the cables linking the United

States and Cuba, owns the All America Cables, the Montevideo Telephone Company, the Chile Telephone Company, and the Mexican Telephone and Telegraph Company. Through a Spanish subsidiary it has a monopoly of all governmental and most private Spanish telephone lines. Through the International Standard Electric Corporation, it has plants at Woolwich, England, Antwerp, Paris, Barcelona, Milan, The Hague, Buenos Aires, Sydney, and—through its subsidiaries—in Tokyo and Pekin. It is also interested in many other foreign corporations.

The Western Union Telegraph Company controls the Mexican Telegraph Company and eight transatlantic cables. It operates Canadian lines under lease.

The Tobacco Products Corporation owns 80 per cent. of the United Cigar Stores and the Happiness Candy Stores, has a heavy interest in Philip Morris and Company, Ltd., owns the Tobacco Products Export Corporation, with interests in the Canadian Tobacco Products Company, Melachrino of Cairo, and Henry Scholey, Ltd., of London, and operates factories in China and England.

These all but wearisome details show why no serious attention should be paid to the formalities of international trade statistics. How can our import and export figures have any real meaning, when American companies own both the sources of supply abroad and the means of distribution in foreign countries? Even though our apparent trade balance is $1,000,000,000, more or less, our actual balance, when the question of ownership is considered, is far greater.

The process of buying up the world is going on continuously. By the time figures are published they are out of date. New subsidiaries have been organized, new companies formed, new projects undertaken. Year by year, American business is conquering new provinces and organizing their economic life so as to forestall competition and preclude commercial fluctuations.

By creating currents of private interest and private profit, transcending rather than conflicting with national aims and ambitions, the satrapies of American business are transforming the world, piecemeal, into an economic federation. We are creating our "empire" slowly, and we are paying for it as we go.

AMERICANIZING THE WORLD'S BUSINESS

The drive of American business is overcoming every artificial barrier erected in its path. Conventional obstacles, such as tariffs, and extraordinary measures, such as import and export quotas of films, rubber, etc., monopolistic combinations, anti-American propaganda, have proved impotent to stop its growth.

No amount of governmental control is sufficient to prevent the investment of our capital abroad, by virtue of which the United States shares in the profits accumulated behind the barriers to its trade. The branch factory system seems to have come to stay and is a frank evasion of the foreign protective tariff. It draws its profits from the patents, good-will, and advertising of the parent American concern to which it pays net dividends. Thus the Ford Company of Canada is enabled to operate within British Imperial Preference and to distribute its cars to every part of the British Empire.

As a matter of fact, Canada is the bridgehead for

American industries which desire to penetrate the British Empire. There are over 700 openly known branches of American industries operating on Canadian soil—such as the International Harvester, General Motors, General Electric—and there are many more with Canadian names, the directorate and management of which are really controlled in the United States. For example, in 1919-20, forty-six new American industries were established in Toronto, as compared with eighteen Canadian and four British concerns. American capital owns one-third of all Canadian industries, one-third of all Canadian mines, one-third of Canadian provincial bonds, one-third of Canadian municipal debentures, an increasing proportion of Dominion Government bonds, much of Canadian timber, outside of the Crown lands, and water-power and real estate. What harm can Imperial Preference do to big American industry under such conditions?

The new technique of our retail business is a further means of economic expansion. Our chains of five-and-ten-cent stores, restaurants, theaters, drug, candy, shoe, grocery, music, and cigar stores, have invaded Canada and Great Britain and are gaining a footing on the European continent. American mail-order houses now do a world-wide business. Our national advertising is changing to international advertising.

The billboards of London proclaim the presence in the land of Palmolive soap, Sun-Maid raisins, Underwood typewriters, Kodaks, Ford cars, Gillette safety razors, Wrigley's chewing gum and the goods of the United States Rubber Company. . . . One can stand on a near-by street [to Shaftesbury Avenue] and see within a few blocks the "Pen Corner" with the Waterman fountain pen and Dixon pencil stores; American Art Metal furniture in another window; and the offices of Armour and Company, the Ingersoll Watch Company, Kodak, Ltd., the Dennison Manufacturing Company, F. W. Woolworth and Company, Texas Oil and six other American concerns. On London newsstands American magazines, published in England, are displayed along with British publications.[1]

Mr. Clark proceeds to quote the publisher of *Le Petit Parisien:*

"I shave with an American safety razor; on the breakfast table I find grapefruit, a typical article of an American breakfast. When I go to my office I ride in an automobile, a French machine, but my gasoline is American and has been put into the tank by an automatic American pump now to be found in every garage in France. In addition, my chauffeur tells me that a certain American oil is the lubricant that suits the engine best. At the office among the newspapers I read are two American ones printed in Paris. Then my stenographer brings me my letters written on an American machine and I sign them with an American fountain pen.

"Next comes telephoning—of course, it is all American!— and we have in our building more than 500 telephones connected up through your new automatic system. Moreover, the major part of our equipment comes from America; linotypes from New York, the stereotyping plant from Brooklyn, rotary presses from New York and Chicago, delivery trucks from Detroit. To all these you may add that the paper on which the *Petit Parisien* is printed is made in our own paper mill, which is so thoroughly American that I had to bring over from America fifty men in order to get it started."

The Americanization of international business is backed by domestic chain-store systems doing an annual business

[1] Evans Clark, "Uncle Sam Now World's Business Man," *New York Times*, April 29, 1928.

of nearly $2,000,000,000, by mail-order houses with sales of almost $600,000,000 a year, by 300,000,000 lines of national advertising in American newspapers, and by enormous volumes of installment selling and financing.

The films are another means by which our business evades the world's barriers. In the period 1926-28, Europe suddenly discovered that the export of American pictures bore a direct relation to the export of American goods. Designed solely to attract "cash customers" to the box-office window, they incidentally succeeded in advertising our merchandise. They showed American products, clothes, and methods, many of which immediately recommended themselves to the unsuspecting spectators. They began to mold the world's taste in dress, furniture, automobiles, and so on.

Incidentally, they developed great trouble-breeding propensities. They demolished the myth of the "sahib's" sacrosanctity in India and Africa and undermined European political prestige in the East. Moreover, the haphazard employment by Hollywood of Japanese and Mexican "villains," French and Italian "seducers," and similar irritating assignments, have needlessly offended foreign nations. It would be interesting to know the exact number and character of the foreign protests filed with our State Department against specific breaches of good taste and etiquette and offenses against national *amour-propre* in the exhibition of American films in the United States. The instance of a Broadway exhibitor who stationed men dressed in the uniform of the French Foreign Legion outside of the theater where *Beau Geste* was being shown, drew the attention of the American and French authorities to a flagrant breach of international law.

The consequence of these nationalistic and economic motives has been the enactment of European legislation restrictive of American films. The object is primarily to establish European film industries and incidentally to advertise European goods. But it is unlikely that even the arbitrary provisions of Europe's film quotas can seriously affect American markets. Of our $2,000,000,000 worth of exports to Europe, only a quarter consists of finished manufactures. In Asia and South America, on the other hand, American films are not subject to European political control and may be expected, in view of their long headstart, to meet European competition without difficulty. Here again, the United States has the advantage. American films take their chief profit from the home market; exhibition abroad is largely incidental. No European country, however, has a domestic market for its films sufficiently important to support the national industry. Europe must, therefore, manufacture for export, and in the export field it finds its production carelessly shouldered aside by the less expensive American films, which do not need the market and can afford to operate at lower prices. Thus, in May, 1928, when the French film industry attempted to compel our cinematograph companies to buy French films for the privilege of exhibiting American pictures in France, the Americans quite calmly prepared to withdraw altogether from the French market and compelled the ambitious Gauls to modify their entire scheme for rehabilitating the French industry at the expense of the United States.

Films are not the only American export which ties in with American general foreign trade. Certain types of our products are so dynamic as to alter the entire civilization of the importing nation and to remodel it on the American patterns. These are the exports which lead first to new orders, then orders for spare parts, then orders for accessory products, then a demand for our engineers, machinery, and methods of management.

The export of our automobiles is followed by orders for spare spark-plugs, crank-shafts, magnetos, and tires. Then come orders for gasoline and lubricants, filling-stations, and eventually concrete-mixers and road-building machinery, hot-dog stands, and traffic apparatus. The export of American tractors is followed by a general demand for all types of American farm machinery, pumps and reaping-machines, threshers and binders, grain elevator and milling equipment. The export of railway cars and locomotives is a prelude to orders for American docks, cranes, ware-houses, rails, automatic couplers, air-brakes, coaling devices, structural steel, and bridges. The employment of American engineers in mines, factories, or highway construction leads to a demand for American mine apparatus, pumps, industrial machinery, and tools.

In 1926, we exported nearly 15,000 cream separators, over 45,000 harvesters, nearly 69,000 motor trucks, nearly 240,000 passenger cars, and 118,500 automobile engines. In the same year we exported over $85,000,000 worth of spare parts for agricultural machinery and $36,-000,000 worth of spare automobile parts. In 1926, we exported 450 locomotives, 249 railway cars, and about 5,000 freight cars, but also over $5,000,000 worth of spare railway parts. We exported $85,000,000 worth of electrical machinery and $180,000,000 worth of industrial, construction, mining, and textile machinery. We exported over 27,000 cash registers and over $500,000 worth of spare parts for them, 328,000 typewriters and $891,000 worth of spare typewriter parts. The increases in volume over our pre-war export of similar goods ranged from 50 to 1,000 per cent.

Most interesting of all is that group of cultural exports which defy statistical analysis but which contribute to the foreign demand for our products. The films are an important item in this intangible export of Americanism, but there are others: our books, plays, jazz, musicians, dances, tourists, Lindbergh, sportsmen, and sporting achievements. England has in some instances barred American actors and musicians from her shores, on the ground of native unemployment. France ransacks the West Indies and South America to find a substitute for the Charleston and the Black Bottom. High political and ecclesiastical authority is invoked to discountenance our habits and manners. Our films, besides being restricted by import and other quotas, are denounced as "inartistic." However, the tide of Americanism rises, and, much as the dominance of English literature in the United States coincided with British dominance of our market, so the spread of our "culture" is helping to extend our control of the world-markets.

Again, our business technique and mechanical civilization offer such conveniences that they invite imitation. The originality and utility of American business architecture encourages the erection of skyscrapers in London, Paris, and Berlin. Our office furniture, desks, chairs, filing equipment, dictographs, typewriters, adding machines, mailing machines, addressographs, and cataloguing devices, are transforming the business methods of the world. Finally, our domestic architecture, our vacuum cleaners, our electric dishwashers, our porcelain bathtubs, our open plumbing openly arrived at, our O-Cedar mops and our floor-polishers, which set so distinctive a stamp upon our daily life, are yet so neutral and useful as to invite universal adoption.

These are the things which Sinclair Lewis satirized in *Main Street* and *Babbitt*, both of which were popular abroad. *Main Street* was published in 1922. Since then our exports of earthenware plumbing fixtures increased from under 40,000 to over 90,000 in 1926. In the same period our exports of gas-stoves tripled; we exported nearly 30,000 more steel filing cases in 1926 than we did in the year when *Main Street* appeared, and nearly 50,000 more motor-driven household devices. Our exports of enameled lavatories and sinks increased from 41,000 to 52,000, and we distributed over 65,000 electric fans to foreign peoples. These articles of daily use and convenience are among America's cultural exports and must be reckoned as part and parcel not only of the annual trade balance but of the Americanization of the world.

And the process is as unintentional as it is inevitable. The Americans have no desire to impose their civilization on the world. When touring abroad they are as apt to resent signs of the modernization of "Old World charm" as they do the hordes of other American transients from whom they can find no escape, whether in Venice, Paris, London, Moscow, or Constantinople. They would like the Old World to stay "old," the peasants to remain "quaint," the "antiques" to sell at unsophisticated prices. They find Western Europe attempting to inject itself with our industrial monkey-glands, peasants doffing smocks for overalls and driving Fordson tractors instead of dogs, oxen, and Rosa Bonheur-ish Percherons. They seek the wine of the country and are offered cocktails and champagne *goût américain*. Not the least amusing of modern paradoxes is the fact that the Americans, in their foreign relations, are destroying the very things which they desire, and that in their restless quest for change and novelty they are engaged in Americanizing the world, not only against its will but contrary to their own desires.

Part Three

THE FUTURE OF AMERICAN EXPANSION

Chapter XVI

THE STAKES OF WORLD-POWER

THE PRICE OF FAILURE

In appraising the future of American expansion, it is
necessary to distinguish clearly between what is going to
happen and what we should like to have happen. It is by
no means sure that the economic forces now let loose upon
the North American Continent will prevail over the rest
of the world as they have done in the Caribbean, but it is
probable that they will modify the economic practice and
the daily life of other nations. There are many reasons
for regretting this trend toward international standardization and the assimilation of manners and ideas. As individuals, we wish England to remain English, France
French, Japan Japanese; we resent, equally with them,
the "Americanization" of London, Paris, and Tokyo. We
wish to see no skyscrapers in Rome, no chewing-gum on
the Strand, no ice-cream sodas at the Café de la Paix.
Yet as a nation we are slowly pressing out on the world
and are inarticulately striving to remake it in our national image.

Therefore, our present position in the world is highly
critical, both for ourselves and for other nations. Such
economic power as we now possess has in the past tended
to confer political empire on its possessor. Although we
are ourselves the product of European imperialism and

although our early history is a long record of aggressive expansion, we have reached a stage where we find physical empire incompatible with our domestic institutions and repugnant to our individual moral beliefs. Our problem is, accordingly, to make our economic expansion harmless to the political rights of other nations and to induce other countries to make their political practice considerate of our economic interests.

Because our material interests correspond too precisely with our moral professions, we are inclined to approach the world in an irritating and self-righteous manner which assumes that because a thing is good for us it is right for everybody. Actually, it is by no means certain that some of our dogmatic beliefs are generally true. Our belief in democracy should not blind us to the fact that in other parts of the world other forms of government work equally well or better than ours. Our righteous enthusiasm for the open door need not convince other nations that it is to their interest to accede to our commercial desires. On the other hand, it is reasonably clear that we have the right to promote democracy as a measure of defense in the western hemisphere, and it is evident that the traditional alliance of business and politics in foreign lands—and increasingly so in the United States—is fraught with danger of war and is pregnant with international ill-will. Who that remembers our outburst over British rubber restriction can doubt that the marriage of business and government is a menace to international friendship? What person who studies the shipping question can fail to realize that the operations of the United States Shipping Board are heaping up unnecessary animosities for our traders?

The Stakes of World-Power

Some of our institutions are excellent and may eventually win adoption; others are so frankly selfish that their acceptance by other nations would be merely the measure of our power; some are, possibly, entirely vicious and should be abandoned by the United States as soon as their impracticability is demonstrated. American economic federation need not imply the root-and-branch elimination of all foreign ideas and methods; rather it should connote a readiness to readjust our own ways of thinking to those of other nations. If we are out for economic domination, we can achieve it measurably. If we are out for physical conquest, it is possible that we should create a political empire comparable to those of Europe. In neither of these processes need we concern ourselves overmuch with the ways and traditions of others. But if we recognize that our real interest is "honest friendship with all nations," we must learn to consider the rights of others, to modify our own preconceived notions of ourselves and other nations, and to make mutual peace and general prosperity the real tests of our foreign policy.

Unfortunately, we live in a highly competitive world. It is still every nation for itself and the marines take the hindermost. We have the right and the duty of self-preservation no less than other powers. In spite of many of our professions and beliefs we are being slowly impelled toward a perilous eminence of power by the immensity of what is ours to defend, no less than by the immensity of what we may acquire. We stand, as it were, upon a high place from which we may see the kingdoms of the world, and we should ponder whether we stand to lose our own soul in the prospect which opens before us.

Realistic considerations are shaping our statesmanship,

and the thought of what we stand to win or lose in the next three generations is becoming a vital element in our policy. To survey the world is not to covet it, but as we consider the surge of political and economic rivalries we can only wonder how long we can withstand the pressure which is put upon us.

Politics is a game which is played for high stakes. We have hitherto striven to avoid the game and to acquire the stakes by economic means, but the time is approaching when we shall have to learn to play the game and to consider shrewdly the chips which we have cast upon the board. At worst, we might be deprived of our independent political existence. A disastrous war, or the silent but equally deadly processes of peace, may result in unemployment, undernourishment, starvation, pestilence, and national disintegration, similar to the ordeals to which Germany, Russia, and China have been recently subjected.

We might, through conquest or diplomacy, lose our power to manage our own affairs, shape our institutions, or control our destinies. We might find our finances subjected to a Dawes Plan, our legislation subject to foreign veto, or our entire political life paralyzed by the gendarmerie or army of occupation of a victorious conqueror. Such a fate seems fantastically improbable, but it is no more fantastic than what is recorded of China under the "unequal" treaties, Italy under the Habsburgs, Armenia under the Ottomans, Korea under the Japanese, the Philippines under the Americans, or India under the British.

We should naturally stand to lose our wealth, which is now reckoned at nearly half that of the entire world. The usufruct of this wealth—in the form of national income—amounts to more than $90,000,000,000 a year. To tap our income, or to acquire our wealth, would be a logical move in the efforts of other countries to curb our unwelcome predominance. To approach the fortress of our vested capital, to use the current of our economic dynamo, with its billion-dollar power energies, the world might attempt to deprive us of our tariff autonomy, our foreign trade, our coastwise shipping, and our control of the Panama Canal.

Drive after drive has been launched against our tariff from industrial Europe and has won approval from certain of our commercial, financial, and agricultural interests. At the Havana Conference, the Argentine Republic strove to introduce the principle of tariff reduction into the Pan-American Union. Our foreign trade of $9,500,000,000, as compared with the British foreign trade of $10,500,-000,000, is the object of aggressive competition throughout the world. Our domestic seaboard trade, now limited to vessels of American registry, is another prize which might be acquired by our foreign rivals. No accurate valuation of our coastal trade can be made, as it requires no formal clearances, but the total has been put at $11,000,-000,000. With American vessels carrying $3,000,000,000 worth of merchandise in transoceanic trade, it is apparent that our stake upon the high seas is worth winning.

The means by which this trade is conducted is also a legitimate stake for the victors. Aside from our Lake shipping, we have an ocean fleet worth $781,000,000 which might be destroyed, captured, or surrendered as the price of an unsuccessful bid for power. This fleet includes 1,270,000 gross tons of passenger ships, over 11,000,000 deadweight tons of freighters, 3,500,000 deadweight tons of tankers, and 112,500 gross tons of refrigerator ships. Finally, our defeat would inevitably mean that control of the Panama Canal would pass into the hands of our victors and that our intercoastal trade would be subject to the will of our foreign rivals.

On the social side, we should also be prepared to modify our liquor laws and our immigration policies. Our prohibitory legislation is repugnant to British distillers, German brewers, and French and Italian wine-growers. We should not forget that the opium wars forced the importation of a dangerous narcotic on China. If we lost in the race for power we should be prepared to scrap prohibition for the convenience of foreign liquor interests. Likewise, our control over immigration might be wrested from us, in fact if not in form. Japan once adopted a policy of absolute non-intercourse with other nations. Admiral Perry's naval mission induced Japan to modify her policy. The price of downfall would be a corresponding change in our own. It is, perhaps, significant that we did not restrict immigration until after Europe had been enfeebled by the war.

In the same way, the safeguards of American labor, our standard of living, our very jobs, might be subordinated to the needs of such exporters of labor as Italy and Japan, if we were conquered in war. There is, finally, our vital social heritage, the 120,000,000 Americans who hope to live in comfort and to die of old age. If we were conquered, there is no reason why the American stock should not be supplanted by other breeds. Three or four hundred million Japanese, or from 250,000,000 to 300,-000,000 Italians, could probably live on the same resources which we require. We must face the possible ex-

[266]

tinction of our race if we are overcome in a struggle for power.

In fact, "Chinafication" or "Haitianization" is the fate which might await us in our adversity: foreign control of our customs, our justice, our social life, and our political institutions; foreign troops in our seaports and at our capital; foreign naval bases along our coasts; the trade of New York, New Orleans, and San Francisco in the hands of our commercial rivals; our banks and revenues mortgaged to the service of foreign bonds, loans, and indemnities; foreign missionaries teaching our children to think along foreign lines; and foreign policies and subsidies ready to support domestic factions so as to keep us disunited and impotent to resent our predicament. The world has so dealt with China and we have so behaved in Haiti.

What we stand to lose in a bid for power is so considerable that we should never lightly appeal to the test of force or invoke the argument of the sword, before which all laws are silent. The policies of power are too perilous for our use.

THE SPOILS OF PEACE

The rewards which await the policy of peace are dazzling. If the price of failure is high, the spoils of peace are higher still. If we can learn to adjust our interests to the rights of others, we stand to knit the world into an economic federation to which war would be the supreme calamity and to spread a Pax Americana over the greater portion of the globe. If we can take the nations into partnership with us, it is our manifest destiny to control the world as it has never been ruled before: informally, unobtrusively, invulnerably. Through our trade and our investments we can develop a denationalized economic federation which can be directed by finance. To this end, we should not only convert our trade balances and interest payments into foreign loans, but should encourage foreign investments in the United States, thus mutualizing our prosperity. Whatever we do, wherever we advance, we should pave the way with our goods, our money, our labor, energy, and organization. Whatever control we exert over the world should be solely through our ability to gratify its needs for prosperity and peace. And we should be willing to let the world acquire the means to participate in our own prosperity and the control of our own economic power. *Unless our power is mutual, it is doomed to go the way of that of Carthage, Rome, and Spain.*

We must, moreover, be careful to appreciate in advance the natural limits of our possible influence. Extensive as our resources are, advantageous as our geographical position is, nature has set definite bounds to our economic expansion which we cannot surpass without peril of sure punishment. Our fundamental power will always rest on the North American Continent. We may widen the base of our commercial activities until we have developed the resources of the South American continent, but our economic fatherland will consist primarily of Canada, the United States, Mexico, Central America, and the Caribbean area.

The development of this hemisphere should require at least a generation of effort. For South America—through Europe's political, economic, and cultural predominance—is a fortress as well as a treasure-house, but its principal interests lie with North America, once the battlements of political prejudice are scaled, for no other nation has the financial means to encompass it.

When we have organized the resources of the western hemisphere, we may best bring our latent transoceanic power to bear. From this power, Europe is immune. The Old World will never be commercially dependent on us and will always exert an influence over us in proportion to its needs for our raw materials. Our influence will, accordingly, be strongest in the southern oceans. We shall find our customers in New Zealand, Australia, and the Pacific islands. Western Africa may also fall under our commercial influence, no matter whose the flags that fly over the sweltering deltas of the Congo and Niger. From the Straits of Gibraltar to Durban, Africa can be made an American sphere of interest. Our interest in Morocco goes back to the Algeciras Conference. We have recently developed a new commercial interest in Liberia. The Department of Commerce has opened an office at Accra. The Gold and Ivory Coasts, Nigeria, the Congo, Angola, German Southwest Africa, Rhodesia, and the Union of South Africa may in time become associated with the commerce of North America instead of that of northern Europe.

At the same time, we may expand our north Pacific power from the broad continental base which extends from our Alaskan possessions to our naval sally-port at Panama. We may come to dominate the trade of the Japanese Empire, maritime China, eastern Siberia, and the Dutch East Indies as far west as the Straits of Malacca. Our commercial federation would thus embrace the entire Pacific basin, the three Americas, and the basin of the south Atlantic.

These are the natural geographical frontiers of our economic expansion. Trade, save along special lines, pushed west of Singapore or east of Gibraltar, would be economically inexpedient and would be difficult to defend from competition. Europe, Russia, Central Asia, India, and Siberia are regions which will lie, at least for a century or so, properly outside of our direct commercial influence. The rich basin of the Indian Ocean, with its ring of British territory and protectorates from East Africa north to Mosul and thence east to Thibet and south to Singapore, is the natural economic sphere of the Eurasian countries. It may become accessible to our commerce, but will never be any considerable part of our economic zone.

Nature has traced the bounds of our utmost expansion. These are the "natural frontiers" of economic America: from Greenland to Gibraltar in the North Atlantic; from Tangier to Durban, including the river basins, in the south Atlantic; thence, skirting the Antarctic, westerly to Cape Horn and Melbourne; from Melbourne northwest to Singapore; from Singapore to Vladivostok and the Aleutian Islands; and from Alaska east to Greenland. What lies within that ring may be made an American sphere of economic influence.

The spoils of peace are so much richer than the possible rewards of any war or of any bid for exclusive economic control that it is difficult to believe that any nation in our position could ever abandon the substance of peaceful prosperity in order to grasp for the shadows of political predominance or for the equally misleading rewards of financial exploitation.

However, if we are to avail ourselves of this opportunity, we must first envisage the apparent obstacles which stand between us and the consummation of our desires, and must devise the means by which the barriers can be not so much overcome as avoided. This course between the Scylla of imperialism and the Charybdis of exploitation is difficult to follow, with the political forces of Europe pressing us into the great game of politics and the economic forces of our financiers pushing us toward a "Caribbeanization" of the world. Only by the wisest sort of economic statesmanship and the firmest observance of our traditional principles of political conduct may we achieve the sort of destiny which will preserve our proper interests without trespassing on those of other nations.

Chapter XVII

THE NAVAL TANGLE

OUR STRATEGIC INFERIORITY

THE years which have passed since the Armistice have served to reveal very clearly the existence of a group of strategic, economic, political, and psychological conflicts of interest between the United States and Europe. The past decade has merely succeeded in joining the issue, leaving its solution to the future. One school of thought believes that only through a general Americanization of the world will the dispute be settled; another believes that the best hope lies in the political integration of the United States to Europe through the League of Nations and similar organic treaties. Actually, there is no reason why either extreme course should be followed. Human nature precludes the violent transformation of either Europe or America. Most probably, what will happen is a reasonable compromise between the two systems. Europe will adopt some of our views, and we shall adopt some of Europe's. Therefore, everything depends on the spirit in which we approach the questions which await our settlement. Time will cure many things, but only wisdom can enable time to function beneficially. In this, in spite of many superficial irritations, both Europe and America are at one. Neither desires to force the international pace. For us, the important thing is to refuse to regard as insoluble the unsettled problems of international society. To attempt to meet them by direct action would be to exaggerate their importance. Indeed, to regard them as real obstacles would be to concede a dangerous degree of conflict. We should, rather, trust to our national destiny, tempered with reasonable precautions, to render irrelevant or obsolete the barriers which today impede our harmonious relations with the rest of the world. We need not assume that armed conflict or physical collision are inevitable, simply because our interest is not at the moment identical with that of another nation.

This is particularly true of the naval strategic situation in the Atlantic, the Caribbean, the Pacific, and the China Seas. The science of naval strategy would suggest that British naval bases control our Atlantic coasts and the eastern approaches to the Panama Canal. From the technical point of view, Halifax and Bermuda are pistols leveled at our heart, while Barbados and Jamaica are impediments to our intercoastal trade. Furthermore, all strategic access to European waters is dominated by the British navy and by the British bases in Europe—so that a long-range blockade of our transatlantic commerce would be entirely feasible, even without the British bases in American waters.

The important consideration, therefore, is that these British bases are dangerous to us only in the event of an Anglo-American war. Hence it is vital that we should not contemplate such a war. Once we concede that they are perilous to our interest, we find ourselves committed to the doctrine of a naval rivalry between England and America. These bases undoubtedly are embarrassing to our naval strategists; unquestionably, the General Board of the Navy would heave a sigh of relief if they were demilitarized, dismantled, or in our own possession. Reckoned in conventional terms, the British navy has a life-and-death power over our European commerce and almost as great a measure of strategic control over our trade through the Panama Canal. However, to reckon in conventional terms is to exaggerate the danger we should avoid. It should be, rather, the goal of American statesmanship to find some qualification which may render British naval power compatible with our own and with our legitimate interests.

We inherited this Atlantic problem and have never been able to solve it. Our strategic disadvantage is so obvious as to justify our claim for naval parity with the British Empire, although our commercial interests and political responsibilities are demonstrably less urgent than those of Great Britain.

In the Caribbean, on the other hand, we have been able to solve some of the strategic problems as they have arisen and have partially matched our commercial expansion and political interests in that region with the naval power to defend them. And in the Pacific we have been so forehanded as to carry our naval influence to the coasts of Asia. With naval bases at Panama, San Diego, San Francisco, and Seattle, and with no foreign bases on the west coast of South America, we control the trade of our western seaboard. Our base at Samoa assures us of the power to communicate with Australia and New Zealand. The fortifications at Pearl Harbor guarantee us substantial predominance in the eastern Pacific.

In the western Pacific, we have at Manila a strongly defended naval fortress and at Guam a naval station which partially secures our trade with the Philippines and the East Indies. We have, however, abandoned the right to fortify these two bases further, and with islands mandated to Japan lying athwart our transpacific communications, the Japanese navy could harass our East Indian trade and sever all intercourse with eastern Asia.

Our greatest naval problem in the Pacific, however, is distance. The wide intervals which separate our bases and our insular possessions impose upon our naval engineers a heavier type of cruiser than that which is adequate for British and Japanese purposes. British and Japanese bases are closer together and a lighter vessel is sufficient for their normal needs, but if we are to give our Pacific trade a measure of protection and if our battle fleet is to operate in Pacific waters, we should insist on a type of vessel which has fuel capacity and seaworthiness for a wide cruising radius. This elemental need brought us, at Geneva, into an impasse in which the dictates of geography seemed to assign us an aggressive purpose.

Accordingly, it would be wise for us to concede that other naval powers have equally urgent, special requirements of their own which may impel them to follow a different course from ours; we might refrain from assigning them an aggressive intention when they are simply acting according to their own necessities. We need not admit that we have any fundamental controversy with any other Pacific power. While we cut our naval uniform to the measure of our interests in the Pacific, they have a clear right to do the same. There is no occasion for naval rivalry to obscure our fundamental naval purpose.

The underlying purpose of our maritime policy is simply to permit our traders to compete on equal terms with those of other nations. It was this which brought us to the Philippines, giving us a commercial base at Manila and a ring-side seat on the South China Sea. It is there that the naval drama of the future will be played out, and to the winner will go the lion's share of the trade of eastern Asia. Here Great Britain, Japan, and the United States face each other: Japan with a ring of bases from Formosa to Sakhalien and a dominating position over Fukien, Shanghai, Shantung, and Manchuria; Great Britain with bases at Singapore, Hong-Kong, and Wei-hai-wei, and a grip on Canton, South China, and the Yangtse Valley. France in Indo-China, and Holland in the East Indies, also play an important part in the naval game.

If we play it as a naval game, we have lost at the out-set. In the strategic sense, we may trade with Asia only on British or Japanese sufferance. The value of Manila as a center of Asiatic commerce is comparable to Hong-Kong, but as a naval base it is inferior to Singapore. Our future position in the China Seas, accordingly, will depend largely on how completely we can ignore the strategic aspects of our position and can develop our commercial advantages.

Unless we are prepared to make an ambitious bid for world-power which would alarm and alienate the rest of the world long before it could win us a more favored position, we should frankly recognize that neither in naval strength nor in merchant shipping are we in a position to oppose British or Japanese sea-power. In the Mediterranean, the Indian Ocean, and generally in African waters, we trade merely on the strategic permission of Great Britain. At any time that the British navy decides to bar us from these areas, it has the power to do so. The commercial heart of the world—the basin of the Indian Ocean—is protected by a series of British naval citadels, in the Mediterranean, the South Atlantic, the Indian Ocean, the Red Sea, and in India, Ceylon, Malaya, Australia, and New Zealand. Our fleet could no more conduct naval operations in those regions without British assent than in the North Sea or the English Channel. Gibraltar and Singapore stand as the portals of a naval empire which we cannot enter through naval force.

THE ANSWER TO STRATEGY

We can, of course, set out to build the largest navy in the world. We can multiply our naval bases and solicit naval alliances in Europe, in South America, and in Asia. We can match armaments with armaments, alliances with counter-alliances. We can encourage our public opinion to regard Great Britain and Japan as implacable rivals and can enlist popular support for the largest navy in the world. If we are childish enough to fight fire with fire, to deal in reprisals, and to prepare for a naval conflict, we can possibly muster a force sufficient to overpower all effective opposition.

Yet none of these measures would afford us any abiding security for our commerce or any guarantee of future peace. They are fraught with as much peril as a failure to make any provision for our naval protection would be. Strength invites disaster, no less than weakness. We have experienced too many of the discomforts and perils of economic prosperity to be reckless of the danger which lies in military preponderance.

Our best course would seem to be to maintain a "treaty

navy"—one tactically comparable to that of Great Britain—and to press for a general limitation of armaments. We have tried both methods with rather inadequate results. Having failed to secure further disarmament by international agreement in 1927, the Coolidge administration then proposed the construction of seventy-one warships, as the first of four five-year programs, contemplating a total expenditure of nearly $3,000,000,000. This was designed to maintain our power at a parity with that of Great Britain, and had the full backing of the administration and of the General Board of the navy, but a pacifist lobby pared the program down to sixteen ships in the House of Representatives, while the Senate neglected to vote on the proposal at all. On the other hand, it is probable that before the five signatories to the naval treaty of Washington meet in 1931 to consider revision of the treaty, which expires five years later, the program of the General Board will be substantially authorized.

It will probably be used, however, as a base to bargain for further disarmament rather than as a means to provide the United States with a fleet able to defend our interests in the Caribbean, strong enough to prevent the Chinese turmoil from embroiling us with any other power in the Pacific, and tactically equipped to disrupt commerce in the Atlantic in the event of war with any European nation. It is our policy to regard our navy as a means to secure rather than to maintain peace.

With reference to our merchant marine, we should rid our minds of any political complex. A merchant vessel should be regarded as a means for transporting merchandise economically rather than as material for a future naval reserve. If we have any belief in the theory that government and business should be separated, we should take the Government out of the shipping business as soon as it is possible to operate private American shipping with profit. The formulation of a fixed policy, comparable to the protective tariff, to support a mercantile marine, is not beyond the intellectual powers of Congress. Whether by shipbuilding loans at low interest, by mail or mileage subsidies or other means, it should not be difficult to keep our flag flying and to assure reliable shipping services in time of peace, rather than naval auxiliaries in time of war.

If we are really worried about the chances of war, we might well continue to acquire a merchant marine "in our wife's name," that is to say, American-owned vessels of British, German, Italian, Cuban, Panaman, Honduran, and Chinese registry. In this connection, it is interesting to note that in September, 1927, there were eighty-four American shipping companies owning 650 foreign-flag vessels, with a tonnage of over 4,000,000 deadweight tons. These ships in time of peace are exempt from the restrictions of our shipping laws and in time of war would be exempt from seizure by an enemy and from other violations of neutral rights. Moreover, we have invested $125,000,000 in foreign shipping companies, thereby obtaining a share in the profits of our ostensible competitors.

Through our direct and indirect interest in vessels under foreign flags, we are reinsured against the chances of war. If war is the only justification for a merchant marine, this triple shipping policy provides a sure defense. Private capital invested in foreign shipping, foreign vessels owned by American corporations, an American merchant fleet supported by public policy: the whole would

[279]

be a baffling combination for a naval adversary. On the other hand, by permitting foreign shipping as now to handle a disproportionate share of our commerce, we may remove the chief incentive for a naval war. British ships carry a larger proportion of our foreign trade than our own vessels do. An Anglo-American war would cost the British, for a time at least, this valuable business, and could give them little more than they already possess. It is undeniable that naval auxiliaries are useful to a fleet in time of war, but to create a merchant marine for the purpose of obtaining naval auxiliaries is a weird perversion of national policy, especially if that policy is aimed to render naval war "unthinkable."

Exactly the same sort of consideration should govern our attitude toward the British bases in American waters. Our interest is to neutralize those bases against ourselves. We might, of course, try to get the British to dismantle Halifax, Bermuda, Jamaica, and Barbados at the Conference of 1931. But it is most unlikely that any British Government would consent to the demilitarization of these valuable possessions, unless we agreed to demilitarize the Panama Canal, which we would decline to do. Just as the Panama Canal is useful to us, as a means both of extending our own commerce and of controlling the commerce of others, so the British bases are useful to Great Britain as supports to British commerce and as curbs on our own. We cannot expect to keep the Caribbean an American naval lake and to demand that the British withdraw. They have as much right there as we have; in fact, they were there before us.

There remains, therefore, only the possibility of rendering these bases harmless to us by less direct political means. It would certainly be a relief to us if Britain's American possessions were transferred to Canadian administration. Canada's interests in the British West Indies are commercially and financially considerable; their transfer to Canada would be an act of devolution, well deserved by the Dominion for her sacrifices in the World War, and perfectly consistent with similar tendencies in other parts of the Empire; no problems of flag, sovereignty, or allegiance would be involved. Their possession by Canada would remove the only strategic barrier to Anglo-American friendship and would end a technical nightmare for our more articulate naval theorists. Canada's interest in the Panama Canal is second only to our own, and, in connection with her growing West Indies trade, might stimulate a Canadian naval expansion which would be as beneficial to the coöperation of the United States, Canada, and Great Britain as our own naval expansion in 1898 was to Anglo-American friendship.

Such a development, however, requires as its major premise the maintenance of cordial relations between the United States and Great Britain. The British Government would never consider a course that would give her nothing and take away a measure of her naval power, unless it were apparent that the power would not be required in her dealings with this hemisphere. In that case, there would be no valid American reason to fear the British bases in these waters, and the measure would be dictated solely by considerations of administrative expediency. In sum, the cultivation of a firm Anglo-American friendship is, for us, the best and most lasting defense against the armed might of the British Empire. To challenge British power on the seas openly or to resent secretly the means by which this power is maintained is short-sighted folly.

The American answer to strategy is, fundamentally, to ignore it, and to cultivate instead such intimate and amicable relations with our two chief naval rivals that there need be no occasion to appeal from the common-sense arguments of mutual interest to the incalculable dictates of force.

Chapter XVIII

ECONOMIC INCOMPATIBILITY

THE CONFLICT OF PRINCIPLES

BEFORE we can dispel the motives which might induce other sea-powers to exert their force against us, there is a perplexing group of problems which must be met and mastered by sound economic statesmanship. There is no reason to pretend that Europe's business interests are identical with ours; yet there is no irreconcilable divergence between them. What exists is a sort of economic incompatibility which must be solved by mutual adjustments of principles and methods.

If they are not solved, there is little doubt that international relations will be poisoned by the same sort of economic rancors as those which preceded the World War. A letter to a radical paper from one of the American "Army of the Unemployed" stated the problem with the stark logic of an empty stomach:

The reason why there is an unemployment situation is just because business at large is slow, and this again is quite natural. It is not like anarchists say, the capitalists; but it is the bad ability of our American diplomacy, which does not realize that it went the wrong way about our foreign policy. There is only one thing to abolish unemployment and the only remedy is—War.

We need a war with some foreign power in order to get new markets for our products and lift up industries.

What the stupid brains of our diplomats could not do by psychological understanding toward other countries we must let our guns speak for. Or in other words, if Love does fail use Force. So in my opinion it would be quite justified to declare war, on all those countries which slow down our industrial market and so create unemployment and danger to more than 10 million of human beings.[1]

Actually, the case is by no means as simple as dialectics so cruel would suggest. The world is already buying from America far in excess of its means to pay, and the difference is being expressed in terms of foreign investments. Moreover, though our trade has experienced a phenomenal expansion, it is not displacing the trade of other nations. Thus in 1913, 14.7 per cent. of Argentina's imports came from the United States and 31.1 per cent. from Great Britain, whereas in 1925, 23.4 per cent. came from the United States and 22.6 per cent. from Great Britain. On the surface, this would suggest that we were supplanting British trade. Actually, in that period British exports to Argentina increased by nearly 20 per cent.

There are, however, very definite economic dissonances between the United States and Europe which will have to be harmonized before the two dominant continents can achieve a mutual prosperity. The chief of these is the system of government controls over raw materials. The whole system of state-fostered cartels, selling agencies, and European trusts—of which the Soviet Gostorg is the archtype—is at variance with American methods. We have made an attempt to combat this system by the short-sighted device of imitation. Exporters are permitted by

[1] Robert S. E. Foerster, *The New Masses,* June, 1928.

the Webb-Pomerene Law to combine for foreign trade, and by 1926, fifty-five such export groups had been formed and goods valued at more than $200,000,000 have been sold through their agencies. Legislation is pending in Congress to permit similar import combinations for the purchase of "controlled" raw materials. Moreover, our participation in several of the European groups indicates a willingness on our part to profit by this economic device.

This willingness is at variance with our traditional attempt to separate government and business. An acceptance of the theory of state sponsorship of trade would imply a psychological revolution which may in time lead to serious complications. We have found British resentment at our debt policy affecting the price of rubber. We have seen the French desire to compete in Latin America take the form of vigorous political opposition to the Monroe Doctrine. We have witnessed Japanese eagerness to exploit the resources of China creating a disproportionate resentment at our immigration policy. On the other hand, we have seen our own willingness to profit commercially by Russia's misunderstandings with Great Britain. And we have witnessed a determined effort by the American farmer to enhance the price of his product through Government authority.

We cannot build solid economic relations on the sands of political caprice. Unless we persuade Europe to adopt our attitude toward business, we shall run the risk of seeing normal commercial rivalry degenerate into political animosity. The case is the more serious in that we are, ourselves, adopting a political psychology toward economic questions and are tending to abandon our principles at the first sign of conflict with those of Europe.

The adoption of the European viewpoint is especially grave when we consider that the most desirable portions of the world are already parceled out to our commercial competitors. The prescriptive principle of *beati possidentes* —blessed are those who possess—suggests that the owner of a territorial dependency has the right as well as the power to assign its economic resources to his own interests. Thus Iraq, under British control, awarded the best part of Mosul oil to British interests. Thus Manchuria, dominated by Japan, is a happy hunting-ground for Japanese traders. Thus American interests predominate in Haiti and the Philippines.

Save for Liberia, all Africa is under European control. All of Asia, save Persia, Siam, and inland China, is owned or controlled by Europe and Japan. Australasia and the Pacific are, with the exception of a few small islands, in European control. Only in Latin America the land has not been preëmpted by Europeans. Elsewhere, Europe is on the ground floor, and our own tenancy, however achieved, must be without prejudice to Europe's title. If we admit that the economic life of tropical dependencies is the proper subject of political manipulation, we shall have slammed the open door in our own face.

In only one area of Eurasia is our business immune from European influence—in Soviet Russia. There, however, we contemplate a discouraging set of economic heresies which have hitherto baffled the intelligence of our statesmanship. Our civilization is predicated on private property, Russia's on communism. Our Due Process Doctrine makes the confiscation of foreign property by the United States impracticable even as a war measure; Russia has confiscated American property. We believe in free competition; Russia believes in state monopoly. We try to separate business and government; in Russia they are identical. We uphold the sanctity of contracts; the Russians have repudiated theirs. The economic psychology of Soviet Russia is, accordingly, the most formidable obstacle to the commercial pacification of the globe. Until the two countries devise a means of adjusting their divergences in business methods, Russia will be regarded as outside the economic pale.

ECONOMIC ADJUSTMENTS

We should be wary of assuming that these economic incompatibilities are devised for the purpose of stifling our commercial growth. Europe's economic institutions are organized, in every instance, for the single purpose of solving her domestic problems. The simple fact that our interest is not identical with that of Europe is responsible for our naïve and egotistical assumption that what is not to our advantage is caused by envy or dislike of the United States.

Our preoccupation should be not to combat Europe's methods, but to seek to harmonize and identify our interests with hers. The first step in this process is to reassert our major economic doctrines: the open door, the separation of business and state, the protective tariff, and the most-favored-nation policy. These form the basis of our commercial relationships with other nations and should be enunciated in our effort to mitigate future economic misunderstandings.

To maintain our trade in the markets of eastern Asia,

[287]

the open door is essential. The Philippines now serve as a Far Eastern warehouse for our merchandise and insure prompt delivery of orders in China, Japan, Malaya, and the East Indies. Without the open door in China, the Philippines are not especially important to us economically and could well be abandoned.

With regard to the marriage of politics and business abroad, our wisest course would seem to maintain our own tradition of trade without political strings. The genius of our economic life has resided in the free exploitation of raw materials and the widest competition. American investment in the foreign sources of raw materials is a perfectly adequate defense against what might seem an effort to milk the American market. Thus our capital has recently been invested in Malayan and Sumatran rubber plantations, and other sources of supply have been organized in Liberia, Brazil, and the Philippines. Moreover, our ability to pay high prices will simply result in bidding up the cost of raw materials until other consumers cannot afford to buy as heavily as the processes of mass production require. To put it bluntly, so long as we get the rubber, we will manufacture the tires, and the game will not be worth the candle for the proponents of governmentalized business. In the same way, the import quotas, on such typical American products as automobiles, may easily be avoided by establishing, with American capital, branch factories in the quota countries, through which the sales profits and patent royalties will go to the United States while the labor costs of assembly and distribution will go to the country of their location.

If it is our intention to protect the American producer,

[288]

who is also the ultimate consumer, we shall maintain the principle of the protective tariff. Indeed, with Great Britain adopting protection, the last practical argument for free trade has disappeared. For the next generation at least, we shall live in a protectionist world. Behind the wall of a tariff we can assure a relative economic stability and can temper the blasts of supply and demand to the needs of American business.

Conversely, in our commercial treaties, we should secure unconditional most-favored-nation treatment for our goods abroad. Thus we shall be in a position to benefit from future tariff reductions and to anticipate the possible creation of a European customs union.

Whatever the character of our administration and whatever alterations there may be in our tariff schedules and our foreign policies, the basis of our commercial treatment of other nations should be conditioned by our traditional commercial policies. We cannot substantially modify any one of these principles without necessitating the most complete revision of our entire economic practice. Inasmuch as our greatest contribution to the world has been in the realm of business and industrial technique, there is no occasion for diffidence in supporting the principles which have underlain our business growth. If we have anything to offer the world, it is in this sphere.

FINANCIAL MANEUVERS

Our real problem will be to demonstrate to the world that it stands to benefit by reconciling its business psychology with our economic methods. For unless our economic institutions are compatible with the general interest of mankind, there is absolutely no reason why they should be tolerated.

The test of our intentions will be in the use we make of our financial power. We can aspire to turn the world into a sort of banker's paradise, floating enormous foreign loans, mortgaging foreign governments, and pledging the revenues of foreign nations to serve unextinguishable debts. We might try to reduce mankind to a financial servitude of the sort envisaged by Communist critics of our civilization.

This would be shamefully unnecessary, since we can support our real interests by a spirit of accommodation and financial humanity. For example, it is in our power to convert Japan into a willing partner by extensive investments in Japanese industry. Japan is entering on a period of great economic stress, due to the chronic crisis in the raw silk industry. We have more to fear from Japanese unemployment than we have from the Japanese navy. If we use our wealth to prevent a disaster to Japanese industry, we shall stand both to participate in the economic welfare of the Island Empire and to terminate any economic conflict of interest with the Japanese. If we use our capital wisely, the next generation may see a complete reversal of American-Japanese antipathy and the development, in its place, of the most intimate economic, financial, and social relations between the two countries.

Toward Europe, on the other hand, our financial policy should be tempered with caution. We should invest in European industries to enable the Continent to complete her economic restoration, and thus prevent the likelihood of war or other political disturbance. But at the same time, we should remember that the political risks of European investments are high. A European war would wreck the entire economic structure, and a social revolution might result in nationalizing our European investments. Our loans to European governments should be primarily for the purpose of maintaining political order and financial solvency.

Our financial policy toward the British Empire should be a blend of coöperation, participation, and competition. We should continue to coöperate with British finance in promoting the stability of Europe, particularly in the restoration and maintenance of the gold standard. We both want a stable, prosperous Continent rather than one wrestling with inflated currencies and fluctuating exchanges. We should also use the London money market as the easiest avenue for investment in Britain's tropical empire, and thus participate in its orderly and prosperous development. At the same time, we should continue to compete in British markets. By a careful balancing of coöperation, participation, and competition we might break down the economic barriers erected by the sanctions of British imperial power and substitute for them our own principle of free competition and exploitation.

In this regard, one of the greatest single obstacles to be overcome is the official British opposition to our financial and economic relations with Russia. British hostility to Russia is the gravest deterrent to fruitful Russo-American coöperation. This fact need cause us no surprise, in view of the obvious conflict of interest between the two powers in Asia. Whether we approve this conflict or not, it exists and is, for us, decisive. The British are closer to us—geographically, commercially, racially, and ethically

—than the Russians are, and if we were compelled to choose our friends between them, we should unhesitatingly prefer the British. Therefore, our road to Moscow lies through London.

This does not imply that we should follow the British lead blindly or subordinate our interests to those of Great Britain. It simply means that we ought to make sure in advance that any steps which we might take toward a rapprochement with Russia will not inspire British hostility toward us. We must disarm British suspicion before we attempt to collaborate wtih the Soviets. However, as soon as it is possible, we should go into Russia, because there lies the greatest undeveloped region on the face of the globe. Russia's economic prosperity would do more to assure political stability, peace, and international welfare than any number of League of Nations Covenants, World Court protocols, Locarno treaties, and pacts for the outlawry of war.

In short, the guiding spirit of our financial policy should be to promote the prosperity of every part of the globe where political conditions or economic distress threaten international ill-will or social disorder. A prosperous Europe is less of a menace to us and to our trade than a Europe with a low buying power and a high political blood-pressure. Japan or England in the grip of unemployment are more to be feared than any number of Japanese and British war-ships and naval bases. A Russia estranged from the western world and distracted by a sterile economic system is a greater threat to international security than all the battalions in the Red Army.

With Japan as the ally, Europe the beneficiary, England the partner, and Russia the opportunity of our financial resources, we need anticipate no serious difficulties in weathering the storm and stress of the next two generations. Economic incompatibilities will be more easily reconciled by mutual benefits than by mutual animosities. The experience of the last decade reveals many readjustments which seemed fatally impossible at the time of the armistice—Franco-German economic coöperation, for one. The next ten years should see the majority of the economic rancors of the present relegated to the limbo of defunct controversies. If it does not, we shall have to blame only ourselves and the short-sightedness which might make us prefer our immediate advantage to the future prosperity of the world at large.

Chapter XIX

POLITICAL CONFLICT

THE POLITICAL IMPASSE

No American need apologize for his political institutions. In the brief period of our national existence, in spite of our transformation from an agricultural to an industrial community and notwithstanding the incorporation into our political life of millions of aliens, the fundamental principles of our government have been adequate to our needs and have undergone a constant development which should in time remedy many of the admitted defects of federal democracy. At the same time, there is no warrant for our despising other forms of government and political principles alien to our own. Democracy is still on trial before the world, and the monarchical ideal is deeply rooted in human nature and satisfies the needs of millions of people.

Yet it is neither scornful nor apologetic to recognize that there are political conditions elsewhere which are incompatible with our own and which may, in time, produce such clashes of interest as to prevent the establishment of international solidarity. In fact, the strategic and economic obstacles to our growth are only the phenomena of underlying political institutions and psychological concepts. We can appreciate the strength of the ostensible barriers to our national aims only by considering the underlying conditions which make them possible.

It would be futile to discuss our political conflicts without keeping clearly in mind our own political interests.

[294]

These are, primarily, the maintenance of federal democracy in the United States. Next in importance is our need to prevent the Caribbean and Central American region from coming under the control of a non-American power. The exposure of the Mississippi Valley to invasion and the vulnerability of our intercoastal as well as foreign trade through the Panama Canal make this essential to our safety. It is the only justification for our high-handed attempts to maintain orderly self-government by force in the region between us and the Canal. Our third interest is the defense of the western hemisphere against non-American interference, as stipulated in the Monroe Doctrine. Our fourth interest is the preservation of friendly relations with the British Empire. We are located almost precisely in the center of the group of self-governing British nations, and any threat to their political existence or economic prosperity is a menace to ourselves. Our final and only legitimate interest in the rest of the world is the maintenance of peaceful, friendly relations with all nations and the discouragement of war and of warlike combinations which might injure our trade or threaten our existence. It is for this reason that we watch both Europe and eastern Asia with intimate interest, for experience has taught us that we cannot be indifferent to events in either region. Toward Russia, our sole interest is to use it as a counterpoise to possible European or Asiatic combinations which might become a menace to our own security.

In Europe, we must face a political and economic coalescence, through the League of Nations, in the lands between the Russian border and the Atlantic Ocean. The psychology underlying this effort to combine Europe is partly anti-American, that is to say, it arises from Eu-

[295]

rope's sense of economic inferiority in the face of America's mass production, and of political distraction in the face of our national unity. Europe's general repudiation of democracy—as demonstrated by her dictatorships and her secular tradition of centralized government, a tradition supported by the European ecclesiastical organization —is a less serious consideration.

We were misled by Wilsonian self-determination into an unnatural interest in Europe's domestic politics. It is out of the question that we should accept for European democracy any responsibility such as we have assumed in the Caribbean. American marines will not intervene in Portugal, Italy, or the Baltic states to "shoot men into self-government." It is natural for us to be interested in the progress of Continental democracy, but the first premise of the Monroe Doctrine is that so far as Europe is concerned, for us the de facto government shall be the rightful one. The effort to impose our political ideals on the Old World was short-sighted and mischievous, and the effort to prevent their collapse would be impertinent and ridiculous. If our assumption that democracy is superior to autocracy—a belief supported, in part, by the verdict of the World War, in which the democratic nations prevailed over the autocratic empires—be correct, then in the long run nothing can prevent the democratization of Europe, as a condition of her own survival. The first need of a democracy is for patience, and this applies to its foreign intercourse no less than to its internal development.

A more acute type of political conflict is the development of Latin-American nationalism on an anti-Yankee basis. In Mexico, Costa Rica, and Argentina—to select three widely divergent types of state—racial and national patriotism has been invoked to oppose the spread of our influence. Much of this opposition is merely the natural consequence of deep racial, cultural, linguistic, and religious cleavages. Some of it may have been deliberately fostered by foreign agencies for commercial and political motives, but the native residue is impressive.

The political cleavage goes even deeper. Latin-American political thought is based on the conception of an absolute sovereignty foreign to our idea of mutual rights and duties between nations. Latin-American statesmen have endeavored to erect juridical standards which would render their countries immune from any foreign intervention, no matter what the provocation. In 1868, the Calvo Doctrine maintained that intervention, whether military or diplomatic, was not a legitimate device for enforcing private claims growing out of contracts or arising from civil war, insurrection, or mob violence. The only recourse for the creditor, it asserted, must lie in the law court of the debtor, from whose decision there might be no appeal. In 1902, the Argentine Minister of Foreign Affairs advanced the Drago Doctrine: "The public debt cannot occasion armed intervention nor even the actual occupation of the territory of American nations by a European power." At the Havana Conference in 1928, our delegates were compelled to unusual exertions in justification of our intervention in Nicaragua, the Salvadorean and Argentinian representatives asserting that "no nation may intervene in the internal affairs of another nation."

The clash between our theory that international rights are conditioned by international duties and the Latin-American belief in an absolute national sovereignty is at the heart of the challenge of Latin-American nationalism to our influence. This conflict has had few practical repercussions. While a few of the southern republics turned to Spain for loans in 1927, and while Salvador, Guatemala, and Honduras formed an *entente cordiale* regarding our course in Central America, our trade with the Latin-American nations continued to prosper, and in 1927 nearly $500,000,000 was lent them by the United States. We supply nearly a third of all South American imports, doing an annual business of $1,000,000,000 with the twenty American republics. In every Latin-American nation save Paraguay, the United States is the principal source of imports. Political divergencies have not impaired the economic relations which we are creating in the western hemisphere.

Far more dangerous to our real political interest is the precarious state of self-government in Central and Caribbean America. Tropical America has shown a tendency to lapse into an administrative autocracy indistinguishable from monarchy. The problem of the United States has been to prevent the collapse of democracy in that region. Dictatorships, revolutions, *coups d'état*, palace revolutions, partisan intrigues, corruption, and looting of the public treasury—these have been qualifications of the validity of the democratic dogma which require wisdom and sympathy if we are to justify republican institutions to the world. Hitherto, for the failure to maintain self-government in the region most vital to our own political security, we have offered no remedy save the irritating insistence that self-government shall be given another chance, backed by our force and our prestige, until—as Wilson said—the Latin Americans are taught "to elect good men." It has not, apparently, occurred to us that there may be some inadequacy in a democracy which requires constant intervention to maintain its forms.

Farther afield, our policy is bogged in the quicksands of eastern Asiatic turmoil. With China convulsed by banditry, revolution, and civil war, with Manchuria and Mongolia mere pawns in the conflict of Russo-Japanese policies, we must confine our interventions to the basic principles of the protection of our nationals, the preservation of the open door, and the maintenance of Chinese integrity. Our attempt to lay the foundation for a progressive development of Chinese prosperity and self-government, through education, hospitals, missions, and diplomatic good offices, lies in ruins. The failure of our social panacea—education—leaves us temporarily baffled. Under the circumstances we can only await events, in stupefied expectancy, hoping for a turn in the situation in which the responsible elements in China may appreciate our benevolent intentions.

In this connection, we should be well advised to regard as one of our most formidable foes the spread of immature, imitative, and ill-digested nationalism in India, China, Egypt, and the Philippines. Self-government is an art to be mastered quite as much as it is a creed to be professed. We are not yet ourselves so proficient in democracy that we can afford to cast stones at other types of government. Nothing could be better calculated to discredit democracy than the antics of some of its self-confessed adherents in eastern countries, where neither religious, economic, cultural, nor social institutions afford a firm foundation for political self-rule. We should return to our first principles and remember that not the desire for national liberty, but the power to achieve and maintain it, has been the criterion of our foreign policy. The sooner we develop a healthy skepticism toward the self-styled democrats of Asia, the better for us and for the down-trodden coolies, peasants, and fellaheen who are the victims of their vociferous leaders.

Between us and the Orient lies the Japanese Empire, an institution which we must learn to understand before we can comprehend the character of Oriental politics. The imputation of divine descent to the Mikado, the military and naval traditions of the Choshu and Satsuma clans, the persistence of feudal ideals, the lack of sovereign powers by the Japanese Diet, and the practice of government by the Genro, or elder statesmen, forms an imperial institution which we have not yet tried to comprehend. With the best will in the world for stable relations, we have not felt altogether easy in the face of the spread of Japan, within a single generation, from a small island group off the coast of Asia, to an empire, acquired by the sword, which controls Korea, Manchuria, eastern Mongolia, Shantung, and Fukien, and which has spread southward across the Pacific to the Equator. As the largest of the self-governing nations in the Pacific basin, we have felt a sense of apprehension in confronting a political organism so foreign to all our concepts of government, and so successful.

Finally, Russia—which is of strategic importance to our security—is at present completely cut off by the incompatibility of her political institutions. Russia repudiates democracy as completely as capitalism. She regards the Filipinos, Cubans, Nicaraguans, etc., as our "colonial slaves"; she has no sympathy for our political ideas or for our economic methods. However, as one of the great federal republican unions of the world, Russia's incompatibility is not necessarily inherent in her political constitution. It is by no means certain that her political life will remain permanently estranged from our own. As in the case of Europe and China, we must wait for Russia to evolve.

In this connection, it is as well to admit that socialism, both national and international, is among our political opponents. In the national sense, our radical socialists are hostile to our traditional policies. They frankly prefer their political and economic ideals to those of America, and make no secret of their intention of altering our institutions. In the international sense, the radical socialists add fuel to the anti-American flames whenever possible. This is partly because ours is a capitalistic country, but also because our "new capitalism" of mass production, high wages, and scientific management offers a tangible alternative to the somewhat cheerless promises of revolutionary socialism. Only by further justification of our institutions, through a more general division of the rewards of industry and a solution of the recurrent scandals of over-production and unemployment, can we prevent this radical hostility from becoming a serious embarrassment. Already, in Mexico, South America, Europe, and China, it has helped to inflame the world's masses against the political interests of the world's most wealthy nation.

THE POLITICAL MASTER-STROKE

Generally, we should guard ourselves against the temptation to deal narrowly with any given situation. To strive to play off one European nation against the next, to dominate rather than conciliate Latin America, or to back Oriental peoples as though they were horses, would be short-sighted and unnecessary. Our best course is to develop the principle of "live and let live" into a positive policy. There is room in this world for many types of nation and many kinds of government. A general uniformity would show a lack of imagination most dangerous for the future welfare of the race. If we are to fall back on any policy, it should be the one which gave us birth: nationalism. By recognizing the rights of other nations to a separate development as well as existence, we can both protect ourselves from future interference and disarm suspicion that we contemplate an assimilation of the globe.

Our fundamental move in this direction must be in relation to the British Empire. In this our object should be simply to disarm that Empire as against ourselves, while increasing its economic and political cohesion as against external aggression. We should adopt a tacit Monroe Doctrine for the English-speaking world, regarding as an act unfriendly to the United States any attempt to alienate the sovereignty or independence of the British Dominions. Lest this seem far-fetched, it is well to remember that one of the underlying motives for our declaration of war against Germany in 1917 was our fear of the break-up of the British Empire.

While supporting the political integrity of the British Commonwealth of Nations, we should favor its development in the direction of Dominion self-rule. In other words, we should encourage the evolution of the Commonwealth in such a manner as to make the United States the political center of gravity for the self-governing nations of the English-speaking world, without disturbing the administrative relations between Great Britain and her African and Asiatic dependencies.

For this reason we ought to be especially scrupulous not to espouse the hasty nationalistic movements of the Orient. We should learn to differentiate, to distinguish between genuine and false nationalism, between real and spurious democracy, between slogans and self-government. For England's achievements in civilizing Africa and Asia we should learn to evince admiration, and we should rid ourselves of the demagogic itch to interfere with matters of which we have had no experience. Great Britain has a host of intricate and difficult problems, in the Mediterranean, in northern Africa, in Arabia, Persia, India, Malaya, and in tropical Africa, which are entirely outside our comprehension. We have seen how easy it is for people to point the finger of scorn at what we believe to be our necessary activities in Central America; we should beware of like ignorant and irresponsible criticisms of any other power.

On the other hand, we should learn to watch for the progressive transformation of the British Empire into regional groupings. It has already been suggested that Anglo-American relations would benefit through the transfer to Canada of administrative control over Bermuda, British Guiana, British Honduras, and the British West Indies. We may yet see the transfer to the Union of South Africa of Britain's other South and East African holdings up to the Egyptian border, as forecast in 1927 by the British Secretary of State for the Colonies, in a speech at Cape Town. And we may witness the transfer of Britain's Pacific possessions to Australia and New Zealand, leaving to Great Britain's individual control the Indian Peninsula and the Middle East. These future developments would not necessarily bring us any ease. On the contrary, they might lead to a greater assertiveness toward us on the part of the great Dominions. But that is in the nature of political growth and is a development which, if we are prudent, we will accept with as good grace as that which the British evinced toward our own emergence into world-power.

Whether or not it seems to our immediate advantage, we should encourage Latin-American nationalism rather than regard it as an obstacle to our policies. We should have clear warrant in fact and in international law for any intervention we undertake in the Caribbean region, and we should maintain the sovereignty of Latin-American republics with the utmost circumspection. On the basis of nationalism we may build a practical Pan-American cooperation and also demonstrate to Latin America that we have no design of political empire. In this regard, the sympathy, as well as the patience, with which we deal with the nations between us and the Panama Canal, will serve to justify our methods and to illustrate the character of our motives. Any ambiguity in policy or indecision in action in that part of the world will exact a heavy forfeit of misunderstanding in Europe, Asia, and South America.

Much as we have reason to distrust European combinations, we ought not to discourage the confederation of Europe in the League of Nations. The sense of nationalism in Europe is too strong to permit any League to function purely as an anti-American body. We should maintain a cordial contact with the League of Nations, perhaps through the appointment of a special diplomatic representative at Geneva. By full coöperation with the League in all general, though not political, international problems—such as we have already given in the case of disarmament and similar questions—we can rid European alarmists and our own emotionalists of the notion that we are hostile to the League or have designs on its authority.

We need not fear that the League will become the focus of a hostile coalition. Our endorsement of nationalism provides the solution to this problem. Only one course recommends itself in this respect. If we encouraged German or Italian nationalistic aspirations, it would be in the full knowledge that neither power can stir without British consent. If we encouraged French nationalism, we should know that France would strive to make use of us in her own European policy. A general recognition of European nationalism would, therefore, be preferable to any policy of backing the ambitions of any one nation. A group which couples Italy and Yugo-Slavia, France and Germany, Poland and Lithuania, Roumania and Hungary, will not be very dangerous to the United States.

As the largest single nation in the world, we have least to fear from nationalism; as the best organized and most powerful federal state, we have least to fear from genuine federative impulses. We can best prevent coalitions and combinations hostile to our interests by promoting the unity of Europe. The League of Nations, with America out of it, seems to be the most practical move in this direction. And if European nationalism is stronger than the League, it will not be in any sense our fault or our desire.

While setting ourselves against premature Asiatic democracy, as likely to embarrass our foreign policies and to discredit our domestic institutions, we should regard with sympathy all well-founded Oriental nationalism—as in the case of Japan—without reference to the form of government it may prefer. This will set up a strong dyke against European, Asiatic, and Russian imperialism. Responsible nationalistic movements in the East will be the best guarantee of eventual peace in that region. But if we invoke nationalism in Asia we must be prepared to apply it in our Asiatic possessions, the Philippines.

We should even apply it against the Filipinos, by the partition of the islands between the Christian Filipinos and the Moslem Moros. Then we could end our control under a Platt Amendment type of treaty which would confirm our naval and commercial rights and would acknowledge our right to suppress disorder, to protect life and property, and to prevent the disproportionate inflation of the insular debt. As a final gesture, in acknowledgment of the Hispanic civilization of the islands, we might secure the admission of the Philippine republics to the Pan-American Union and enlist the western hemisphere in a mutual guarantee of the territorial integrity of the islands.

Our "political" policy should begin and end with nationalism. We have no responsibility toward democracy, no duty to maintain any type of government anywhere. The world is large and contains many diverse peoples. As soon as we realize that our course in the Caribbean is dictated entirely by considerations of defense and that the same consideration underlies the Monroe Doctrine, the world will rid itself of the fear that it got rid of Prussian militarism only to fall prey to an equally aggressive Americanism.

Chapter XX

PSYCHOLOGICAL IMPONDERABLES

BARRIERS TO UNDERSTANDING

THE most serious obstacle to international harmony is the difference of national psychologies. America is not Europe, and there is no reason why she should be or think like Europe. Europe is not America, and her institutions and ways of thought are quite distinct from ours. We expect a Chinese to act on different principles from our own, but are surprised whenever Europe behaves in a way which is at variance with our beliefs. Conversely, Europeans tend to misinterpret our actions by assigning them motives which would apply in Europe but which do not always apply here. No nation is like another, least of all those which superficially resemble each other. French psychology differs from Italian, and the Canadians differ from us. Because we speak a variant of the English language, and many of our laws and institutions are of British origin, it is commonly assumed that Great Britain and the United States are fundamentally alike, whereas the British mind is actually closer to the Continental than it is to ours.

In the long run, national policy is determined by national psychology, and before we can hope to understand the real character of the various strategic, economic, and political incompatibilities of the world, we must appraise some of the psychological incompatibilities and set ourselves the task of reconciling them.

The first consideration is that we are not a politically minded people. We are inclined instead to think in terms of broad and annoying moral principles. What political-mindedness there is among us is an actual handicap, for it is largely the product of our composite population and of the division of our electorate into racial groups. This division is not so great as foreign and domestic politicians suppose—witness the overwhelming majorities for our exclusive immigration laws in 1921 and 1924—but it is sufficient to poison much of our current political thought. Irish hatred of England is kept alive by the Clan-na-Gael on Irish rather than American grounds. The Italians, the Poles, the Yugo-Slavs, and the Germans are constantly threatening to act as units on issues which affect their native countries. Although much of this hyphenism automatically cancels itself, it leaves the American public especially vulnerable to foreign propaganda, and the large foreign communities here provide convenient bridge-heads for the dissemination of foreign political views.

Our general ignorance of foreign problems, coupled with respect for the average successful hard-working immigrant, combines to give the latter's political prejudices greater currency than they deserve. Since 1880, 27,000,-000 immigrants have entered the United States, and even with the restrictive laws, at least 330,000 more are admitted every year. In the United States there are over 1,000 newspapers published in thirty-eight languages other than English, and there are more than 20,000 foreign-language organizations in the country. This situation is a constant temptation to foreign governments and a con-

stant irritation to our own. Whereas a thorough ground-
ing in international politics is a first requisite for the formation of an intelligent public opinion, even now our
school books are edited with direct reference to the prejudices of foreign groups in such American cities as Chicago.

A greater barrier than our ignorance—for that, after
all, can be cured—is our inclination to race prejudice.
The mutual dislike of the Anglo-Saxon and the Latin results in insolent terminologies—spick, dago, greaser, wop,
frog, or, to roam further afield, hunky, Polack—which
prevent any real sympathy between North and South
America or between the United States and most of Europe. Similarly, our settled black-white prejudice is a
tremendous handicap in dealing with the numerous colored races of the world in India, Africa, the Caribbean,
and the South Seas. We call any man with a colored skin
a "nigger" and dismiss him as an inferior. This is fatal
to the development of harmonious trade, political, and
cultural relationships. Finally, we share the prejudice of
the Occidental against the Oriental and are rewarded by
dislike and resentment. To us the Chinese is a Chink, the
Japanese a Jap, and the Malay and the Hindu simple
niggers. Our relations with the greater part of the human
race are poisoned by vulgar prejudices which have already exerted a depressing influence on our foreign policy.

The original cause of this attitude is that members of
these races came to America in menial positions, as immigrants, and that while their social position did not command respect, their economic competition earned dislike.
The most virulent of the negro-lynching mobs are re-
cruited from the Southern poor whites, whose labor was
supplanted by the blacks. Our race prejudices are thus

legacies of our unfortunate importation of black African slaves and our equally unfortunate policy of the unrestricted immigration of cheap labor. We shall have to pay a heavy price before this racial account is fully liquidated.

Other psychological barriers to mutual friendship with the world are less to our discredit. We are firm believers in the theory of individualism, whereas Europe trusts in an authoritarian principle of government. Caesar and Napoleon, Frederick the Great and Bismarck, Lenin and Mussolini, are Europe's political heroes. This ideal, which is enshrined in the vast and powerful European beaurocracies, is antithetic to our own belief in popular sovereignty and local self-government. The ideal of communistic, autocratic Bolshevism, as contrasted to our individualistic, democratic industrialism, sums up the cleavage between European and American political psychology.

In Europe, the state is superior to the people, in theory. In America, the state belongs to the people, again in theory. In Europe, the state accords and defends popular liberties. In America, the people put restraints on themselves and on their liberties through the state. In actual, everyday life, the European is far freer than the American, for centuries of experience have taught the Old World that there was a great deal of truth in the old Roman formula of "bread and circuses," whereas we have not yet learned that the state has its limitations and that the minority has rights which the sovereign—even the sovereign majority—ought to respect. This is a difference which only time can alter.

There are, in consequence, absolutely distinct European and American attitudes toward government, a subtle but clear differentiation all along the line between the responsible European authorities and the irresponsible American electorate. It is for this reason that Europe and America are suspicious of each other's motives and afraid of each other's methods. The European attributes to us a Continental type of foreign policy, while we cannot understand why the Old World doesn't scrap its armaments, dethrone its monarchs, and form a United States of Europe. Each has a mentality so distinct as almost to require a distinct political terminology. Words which are innocent in Europe are here considered wicked—take "imperialism." Actions which to us seem innocent are significant to Europe—take our intervention in Nicaragua for another example. It is doubly unfortunate that Europe and America share the same languages, for our connotations for European terms cannot be translated, even when the terms themselves are identical. Imperialism is to Europe a natural and necessary political process. We do not understand it and in consequence consider it immoral. To us, government is very like the governing board of a rather rowdy country club, to the European, government is comparable to the general staff of an army. To us, the Constitution is a written document as tangible as a legal contract or the articles of an incorporation. To the Englishman, the British Constitution is the whole body of laws, liberties, traditions, and usages which go to make up his political system.

At the moment, Europe believes that with power and opportunities similar to those of the United States, a nation tends to set out to dominate the world politically. Accordingly, Europeans are inclined to suspect our national actions of concealing a deep-seated design to achieve

[311]

dominion. We think it incomprehensible that our disinclination to acquire further political responsibilities, and our dislike of conquest, should not be recognized and praised by others. Accordingly, Europe suspects "American hypocrisy" and we are repelled by "European cynicism," and so the chasm of misunderstanding widens until only tremendous exertions can harmonize the two in an effort to secure mutual peace and prosperity.

Our financial psychology is another element in the general problem of understanding. We are the wealthiest nation in the world, and we suspect every other nation of scheming, by hook or by crook, to get some of our wealth away from us. The world, on the other hand, resents and dislikes our financial and economic power and concludes that we must be sordidly materialistic, that "the ledger is our Bible," that we are international loan-sharks and congenitally grasping.

Actually, Europe's financial complex is as discouraging as is our own. It carries the European peasant's characteristic attitude toward money into the sphere of international policy. If ever a breed of men were parsimonious, it is the European peasant. He will fight for a sou, and this is not to his discredit. Centuries of penurious and grinding toil have given him a peculiar respect for money. We have had things easy. The very casual good-will of our commercial and individual methods is an element of discord. To the Old World peasant, failure to haggle to the last decimal point is almost as a sign of imbecility. When our tourists carry our traditional lax methods into Europe they are despised as fools and treated accordingly. We conclude by condemning the European as a penny-pincher; he retaliates by scorning us as spendthrifts. The money-complex is one of the most stubborn psychological obstacles to be overcome in the next few generations.

The first stage in destroying the invisible barriers to our participation in world-civilization will be a clear distinction between our traditional political isolation and our equally traditional social coöperation. While developing our own social forms and cultural methods, we have drawn heavily on the older civilizations of Europe and the East, and we have taken part in every movement for general human progress. In the future, in all matters of religion, science, art, health—in short, in all matters pertaining to human welfare and happiness—we should continue to collaborate with the rest of the world. We are a young nation, inclined to be cocksure and self-satisfied; Europe has been living a long time, and has acquired a much surer knowledge of the art of life.

We must remember that the world at large feels that it has little to learn from us and that it can certainly teach us many things. Faith, art, science, and good works have no boundaries and should involve no national passions. Save in matters of political alignment, we should be internationalists, seeking out the good of every land and acquiring it for ourselves, through study, imitation, and creative adaptation. The Americanization of Europe is impossible without the Europeanization of America.

The narrow boundary between political insularity and provincial isolation must be clearly defined. Otherwise we may fall prey to a colossal self-satisfaction which will gradually alienate us from the rest of the human race,

[313]

until the act of war merely confirms the enmity which the arts of peace have engendered. In our anxiety to convert the world to the methods which we have found best for ourselves, we should not forget that we can learn much more than we can teach and that the merit of our ways will be measured by their ability to withstand the competition of other ideals. Ours is not the first revelation or the final dispensation, nor does all grace reside on our side of the Atlantic. If we can but temper our natural pride in our own devices with a little humble willingness to learn from others, we shall have done everything possible to anticipate and disarm the hostility which our wealth and our success may arouse among less fortunate peoples.

Therefore, our final and our greatest victory will be over ourselves and over parochial ways of thinking. To follow the path of peace, we must cultivate an intelligent rather than emotional knowledge of world-affairs. It is not enough to hear the spokesmen of foreign viewpoints declaim at fortnightly banquets and at Institutes of Politics. It is not enough to read the foreign news despatches in our press. It is not enough to proclaim our good intentions to the rest of mankind if we do not know how the world will interpret those intentions. We have a crying need for a sense of comparative national psychology.

We should learn from the racial groups in our country to appreciate foreign points of view and alien political ideas, without identifying our viewpoint with theirs or adopting their ways of thought. So we may apply to our advantage the racial complexity of our population and may benefit from the current of foreign propaganda which is now confusing our public opinion. To serve as nuclei for those American parties on which we shall ultimately depend to maintain satisfactory relations with other nations, we should rely on the friends and relatives of the aliens who have come to us to build up colonies of American sympathy in the lands of their origin and to interpret our institutions to the world. This program involves the adoption of a more sympathetic and dignified attitude toward the aliens in our country, and the effective collaboration of our foreign-language press in educating them in the meaning and character of our institutions. It is about time that a belated respect for the good opinion of mankind put an end to our scorn of the immigrant and that a respect for the value of our own citizenship terminated our truculent and almost forcible insistence upon his Americanization.

While learning to appreciate foreign psychology, no greater disservice to the world could be done than the adoption of the foreign political attitude toward economic matters. We are a part of the world, and we have the right to try to contribute to it one of our principal political discoveries. The marriage of policy and economics has begotten wars too often in the past for us to abandon our effort to remove business as completely as religious interests from international relationships.

It is legitimate for our diplomats to promote the general business interests of this country and to protect particular American companies and individuals from injury to their duly acquired rights. But beyond this we should not go. We should not negotiate for a particular concession or contract for a particular American concern. We should not, as a government, ask for exclusive economic rights anywhere. In our possessions and in the countries measurably under our influence we should refuse to disqualify for economic opportunity any one by reason of his political status. We should segregate our business expansion from any political aggrandizement. We should eschew empire.

The world is ruled by significant trinkets—flags, scepters, decorations—which are dear to the human heart. No nation can bear to have its dolls broken. No people will tolerate disrespect for its dreams. When our flag is insulted, our battleships arrive on the scene no less promptly than those of any other country. The patriotic mysteries may be as illogical as those which bind the members of a secret society, but they may not lightly be despised.

Our interest in the world is to influence without governing, to collaborate without acquiring, to expand without conflict, to prosper without compulsion. We should not lay a finger on the flags, governments, cultures, civilizations, languages, and loyalties of the peoples of the world. Even where our interest is so transcendent as to render these only the forms of independence, we should recognize that form is the essential of political society. We might, in argument, be willing to admit to the radicals that the United States is ruled by Wall Street, but we would never permit the functions of government to be transferred to the banking houses. For we would not admit that the rule of Wall Street would be final. Other forces might arise which would exercise the real power of the country, and to prevent a bloody revolution, if for no other purpose, we could not permit the present source of power to destroy the future forms of national sovereignty. Respect for the national rights of others should be the first law of our political conduct.

Chapter XXI

THE FUTURE OF AMERICAN POLICY

THE idea of power without empire will seem an anti-climax to those whose minds have been molded by the last fifty years of international politics. Others may conclude that the ideal of peaceful predominance connotes no abnegation but implies the acquisition of an invisible economic empire, subdued and ruled by finance. Actually, it means that we shall be compelled neither to give up anything nor to force our will on others.

It is true that we stand to gain from the world, on the economic side, peaceably and piecemeal, the prizes which have in the past been considered the appropriate reward for victory in warfare, but it is also true that we shall give the world similar prizes. In short, instead of destroying the reward in the struggle for power, we shall produce and divide, by mutual effort, rewards of greater and more abiding value.

The first token of this process will be the general elimination of artificial restraints of trade. Protective tariffs may continue and anti-dumping duties remain on the statute-books, but such special measures as political controls or private monopolies of essential raw materials will disappear. As our trade increases and trade balances mount, hundreds of thousands of Americans will take advantage of our export of wealth to travel and gain experience of the world, in Asia, Africa, Latin America, and Australia, as well as in Europe. These tourists will not only stimulate a foreign demand for our products and teach us the needs and tastes of other nations; they will also bring back to this country foreign tastes and ideas and will increase our demand for foreign goods, thus inadvertently contributing to the world's general economic prosperity.

As our goods and citizens go abroad in ever-increasing volumes, our independent shipping power may expand to correspond to their needs. Our mercantile marine, passenger and freight, modernized and with methods of operation as efficient as those which prevail in other American industries, may become able to compete with those of other nations. Once we have succeeded in obtaining the power—through national control of insurance and the adoption of a national shipping policy—to send our goods where we will and to pick up return cargoes as we need them, the general tone of our national economy should improve. We should not, however, expect to render ourselves independent of foreign shipping. Efforts to secure maritime supremacy or to capture the world's carrying trade would lead to conflicts of interest with Great Britain, Europe, and Japan, and would produce a rivalry and bitterness far out of proportion to the benefits secured. It is part of our business tradition to let the "other fellow" make money too.

Another gain for the peace of the world will come through the increase of our imports. Our heavy purchases of raw materials—oil, rubber, tin, tea, coffee, nitrates, silk, wood pulp, wool, cocoa, etc.—will build up a set of "American parties" in Japan, China, India, Russia,

[318]

Argentina, Brazil, Australia, Canada, South Africa, Mexico, and Chile, comparable to the silent "British parties" which function so powerfully in the eastern and southern United States, in South America, Europe, and in the British Dominions. Through these groups, motivated by natural self-interest and the need for future prosperity, political disputes may be prevented from destroying international stability.

The final development will be the opening of financial fields which have hitherto been dominated by the mortmain of nineteenth century imperialism. Russia, which is today a *terra incognita* for American investment, should eventually respond to our capital, as soon as British and Japanese political anxieties are abated and we have mustered the nerve to acknowledge her political existence. Modern China, which still lies under the shadow of international economic and political rivalry, is another opportunity for world coöperation. China is emerging from the "sphere of influence" stage. Japan controls Manchuria, Shantung, and Fukien; France is supreme in the South; Great Britain is master of the Yangtse Valley; Russia rules in northern Manchuria and Mongolia. Eventually, through the Consortium, which guarantees us a share in all future Chinese developments, and through the open door, the theory of a clear field and no favor may win ground in the Far East, and it may become possible for our wealth to join with that of Europe in the reconstruction of China.

Africa is essentially a preserve for European capital, and in general the entire Indian Ocean area—including the Near and Middle East—is marked with "No Trespassing" signs. We should be cautious in dealing with this natural European dependency. Africa is far closer to Europe than South America is to us. Europe has quietly adopted her own Monroe Doctrine for Africa and the Middle East—any non-European intrusion in that area would shake the political foundations of the Old World.

Thus it is to be noted that of all the American money invested abroad in 1926, not one dollar was invested in Africa or in India. The only manner in which we can help develop these regions without arousing political resentment is by working through London and Paris and Rome.

POLITICAL LIKE-MINDEDNESS

Our fundamental policy will continue to be "honest friendship with all nations" and respect for national sovereignty. In practice, however, we will tend to more intimate and cordial relations with those countries which are most akin to ours. Accordingly, our policy in the future will, as in the past, fall into two halves—one for the Americas and one for the rest of the world.

Working through the Pan-American Union, without direct reference to the sanctions of the Monroe Doctrine, we should extend our friendly influence throughout the western hemisphere. A policy of practical collaboration with Mexico, Cuba, Argentina, Brazil, and Chile should serve to maintain the political peace and economic order of the three Americas. Moreover, in this process we should welcome the informal collaboration of Canada, whose interests in this hemisphere are so nearly identical with ours. In this case, the American system may come into being as a daring experiment in international friendship, based on broad considerations of mutual economic and political interest, in the face of cultural, racial, linguistic, and social divergences.

Our normal friendship for "like-minded" nations may help maintain peace in the rest of the world, through a spontaneous development of the balance of power.

The natural growth of close commercial and social ties with the British Dominions, whose origin and problems are so like ours, should insure us against the possible naval and political hostility of Great Britain. Being so closely linked by business and racial ties to England, we should coöperate with England in our dealings with the Continent of Europe. The source of our general civilization and much of our population being Continental, we should support Europe as against Russia. In spite of our numerous present disagreements, Russia is nearer to us in blood and tradition than Asia, and should be supported by us in its general relations with Japan. On the other hand, Japan is engaged in an industrial and political evolution which should eventually make her more adaptable to our form of civilization, and should also be supported in her general relation to the Far East. Although China is now impotent, its future emergence into vigorous nationalism may compel us to support both Japan and Russia against China, which of all great countries in the world is the least congenial to us.

The normal direction of our sympathies should serve to set Europe against Russia, with British support, thus keeping the Continent preoccupied in the solution of its own political problems and turning Russia's attention away from Europe to eastern Asia. There, by an equal support of the natural Japanese interests in the same area, we can stabilize Russia and Japan in a balance which our maintenance of Chinese integrity can keep from turning into an alliance.

The rough identity between America's and Russia's Chinese policies—the chief difference being one of motive—should establish Russia as a foil for any revival of Japanese imperialism, just as we supported Japan in 1904-05 as a counterpoise to Russian imperialism. Russia is thus the center of the Eurasian political system which we desire to keep in harmony, and only by shifting the weight of the Soviet Union to East or West, as circumstances demand, can peace be maintained.

For us, China and Europe are the two most important areas in the non-American world. Their approximate unity and prosperity are essential to our own welfare. We must, however, approach these vital areas by way of the maritime powers of Great Britain and Japan. These two, acting in concert, could prevent any of our trans-oceanic policies from becoming effective. If either of them obtains the sovereign power over Europe or China, our own safety might be endangered. If either of them were conquered by a Continental nation our peace would be at an end. Accordingly, we should remember that Russia's interest in Europe and in China is as great as our own and may legitimately be invoked to support our own policies.

At the moment, a seductive avenue is opened by the idea of an alliance of the United States, Great Britain, and Japan, to dominate Europe and Asia and to divide the world in a naval triumvirate. This policy would be fatal to peace. It would throw Europe and China into the arms of Russia and would pave the way for a Eurasian coalition which would overshadow the power of the British Empire and could brush the Japanese out of Asia. On the other hand, an open American-Russian *entente* would be equally perilous. Russia is too weak to be an immediate asset to our foreign policy. Such a combination would provoke Great Britain and Japan to renew the Anglo-Japanese Alliance on an openly anti-American basis. They might also be encouraged to undertake an aggressive policy against Russia in both Europe and China, before either the United States or Russia could develop their power.

Accordingly, our efforts now—and for many years to come—should be designed to prevent the formation of any hard-and-fast Eurasian grouping. Only by a natural and informal use of the balance of power, eastward and westward toward Russia, can we postpone the outbreak of a new world war until it is obvious that such a war is entirely unnecessary.

DEMOBILIZATION

If we can extend our prosperity and render other parts of the world more productive, without resort to war, trickery or threats, we shall have advanced the cause of disarmament and have justified our pacific ideas and methods. Despite the imperfections of democracy and the arid aspects of the republican form of government, the New World can fairly take pride in its relative freedom from armaments, wars, political alliances, annexations, and imperialistic aggression. Despite a few early instances, forcible annexation is not usual with American nations.

This is the Pax Americana, which relies on laws and education, rather than on police and armaments, to maintain international peace. In contrast to a Europe and an Asia under arms, a few thousand marines in the most critical political area of the Western World suffice to prevent the development of really dangerous international conflicts, and even the existence of these forces is justified more by our own interest in future security than by any immediate necessity for their police activities. If we can encourage the world to reduce its armaments to a similar scale and to employ them for similar purposes, we shall have contributed materially to international welfare.

The second possible contribution we can make to the general welfare is the demonstration that political self-consciousness is not indispensable to human safety. By her traditions, character, and necessities, Europe is essentially political. Politics and politicians have, outside of America, developed a special caste, known as statesmen, individuals expert in the intricacies of international society and trained to employ diplomacy to compass the national interest. We have ceased to develop such specialists. We have no foreign policy in the conventional European sense, no alliances, no secret engagements or understandings. We have, instead of statesmen, only legislators and office holders, who are praised or despised according to their apparent merits and without respect for their class or persons. As a nation, we are politically demobilized.

Should Europe decide that it was possible to follow this example, to demobilize her economics and to alter her political traditions, there might be an end to the conflict of diplomacies, the "spheres of influence" and "peaceful penetrations," which bred war so inevitably in the period from 1870 to 1914, and which may breed war again in the future.

[324]

The Future of American Policy

There is no reason why Europe should imitate any of our methods or adopt any of our ideas, unless their success has first been demonstrated. Our greatest service to the world, therefore, will be to have faith in our own institutions. We are still conducting an experimental form of government, and the world can benefit enormously by our mistakes as well as by our successes. If we abandon our beliefs at the first sign of danger, there will be no means of knowing whether a government such as ours can long endure. We believe that we have succeeded in exorcising some of the political demons which have hitherto beset the world. The only test of whether it is possible for a democratic republic to survive and prosper without powerful armaments or highly organized political self-consciousness will come through our own conduct. If we cannot prove it, no nation will attempt a political demobilization on a like scale. If we succeed, the world will not long refuse to share in our success.

Chapter XXII

"THE NEXT WAR"

THE CHANCE OF CONFLICT

WAR always represents the failure of policy. For the United States, war is even the negation of policy. American policy is peace. Peaceable intercourse with other nations will require the utmost vigilance by the American Government and the intelligent support of public opinion, or it will be difficult to avoid political self-seeking and to disarm political resentment. The broadest type of economic statesmanship, rather than the old dollar diplomacy, is demanded. Otherwise, there will be serious danger lest our natural economic expansion should degenerate into national pugnacity and culminate in another great war. Only by seeking to increase international interdependence to such a degree that war would be obviously fatal for every country concerned can the peril be abated.

Already the economic materials for war have accumulated between Great Britain and the United States, but the mutual interests of the two powers have prevented its possibility. We are competing with Great Britain on the high seas, both with merchant shipping and with naval armaments. New York has supplanted London as the financial capital of the world. Our foreign investments are larger than those of Great Britain at their maximum. We are acquiring an increasingly great proportion of the trade of eastern Asia, South America, and the British Dominions. We are engaged in a world-wide struggle with British interests for essential raw materials. We have refused to coöperate with Great Britain in her effort to dominate the Chinese situation through force of arms, and we have declined to enter the general anti-Russian alignment, into which Anglo-Russian rivalry in Asia is forcing the British Empire. Our doctrine of self-determination has challenged the imperial bond in Ireland, Egypt, and India, and is transforming the status of the self-governing Dominions. We have helped break the Anglo-Japanese Alliance on which the security of Britain's Asiatic interests depended, and we have refused to enter the League of Nations by which Great Britain seeks to prevent the outbreak of another European war. In every corner of the world and in every department of international intercourse we are treading on British toes and are arousing British resentment.

Yet there is little likelihood of war between the two nations. Such a war, in itself, is not "unthinkable." Similarity of race, language, and civilization has never prevented hostility; it has even facilitated conflict. We have already fought two wars with England and one war with our own fellow countrymen. The reason why an Anglo-American war is the least likely of political developments is simply that our common interests have become far more important than our points of difference, and that each nation is in a position to inflict irretrievable injury on the other.

The current economic squabbles between the two countries are, at the most, over a few hundred million dollars. Each year there is a direct trade between the two countries worth more than $1,000,000,000, while the general business and financial turn-over amounts to well over $500,000,000 more. British investments in the United States are worth $2,000,000,000. American tourists spend $50,000,000 a year in England and as much more in Canada. In 1927, British vessels carried nearly 800,000 passengers to and from the United States and earned at least $300,000,000 in freight charges on our import and export trade. American investments in the British Empire stand at over $4,000,000,000, and our trade with the Empire accounts for 40 per cent. of our exports and a third of our imports. Nations with so much to lose do not go to war lightly.

Moreover, an Anglo-American war would be mutual suicide. Great Britain could stop our overseas trade and disturb our communications through the Panama Canal. From Nova Scotia and Bermuda air bases she could threaten our eastern cities, while her navy could capture our Philippine possessions and shake our strategic hold on the Caribbean. The United States could threaten Canada and the British West Indies, and our navy could despatch raiders into the Atlantic which would disrupt British commerce and destroy British trade. Japan and Europe would be the only winners in such a struggle.

With the best will in the world for war, neither nation could afford it. Their interests have become so intertwined that war could only come through an act of folly unique in the history of the two countries. This is the sort of peace which can be created by America in the course of its simple economic expansion. It leaves the United States as much a prisoner of peace as it does any other nation. In exactly the same way, the fact that we purchase nearly a half of all Japan's exports and supply a quarter of her imports has created a situation in which an American-Japanese war—which appeared distinctly possible eight years ago—is becoming preposterous.

In consequence of the economic interdependence which we have fostered, every nation is enabled to contend for its economic and commercial policies on their intrinsic merits. In this sense, "the next war" is being fought today, but it is being waged along the line of traditional foreign policies and not along the line of alliances. So far as we are concerned, the doctrine of the open door is involved in many unusual restraints on trade; the Monroe Doctrine is being subjected to critical opposition in Europe and Latin America; our efforts to support the freedom of the seas, our Caribbean interests, and our Pacific policy by the construction of an adequate navy is being opposed as "aggressive"; our policy of diplomatic disassociation has been construed as hostility to the League of Nations in Europe and as parochial selfishness in the United States; our war debt, tariff, immigration, and Prohibition policies are the targets for world-wide criticism and dislike. A torrent of propaganda, here and elsewhere, is designed to induce us to abandon our own interests in the interest of other nations or to render us odious to the entire world.

There is nothing in this to arouse our anger. This is "peacefare." It is natural for every nation to seek to make its views prevail. Propaganda is part of the price of peace. We take part in propaganda no less than any other power. When Lindbergh and Will Rogers are sent to Mexico as guests of Ambassador Morrow, we call them ambassadors of good will. They are also, in the broad meaning of the word, propagandists for American policy.

In peacetime, we must take our chances with the rest of the world and trust to the merits of our institutions to support our interests. For the world does not forget—what we do not yet suspect—that it is in time of peace that nations rise, ripen, and rot. Power is a growth which is unknown until it has been proven by war. Yet it is the paradox of power that the very possessions which, in an emergency, insure strength, tend to sap strength if the emergency is not forthcoming. Prosperity, which is the goal of American policy, is also the menace to American power.

Europe is an athlete, trained lean, weary after his last fight, but with great recuperative powers. If we cannot master our prosperity, we may be regarded as a short-winded, timid, bespectacled fat man, who will soon become too corpulent to protect himself from a hardier adversary's jabs to the wind. Yet the Old World has a haunting fear that old age and exhaustion would preclude her victory and that the battle would go to the New World.

Accordingly, Europe will do everything possible to prevent our being drawn into another war. It might teach us too much and encourage us to rely on force rather than fair dealing in our relations with the world. The last war surprised Europe by its revelation of our power. Up to 1916, the Continent had regarded us much as in 1898, as an unwelcome upstart which had defeated a second-class European power under conditions overwhelmingly in our favor. In 1919, Europe feared that we were a giant who might seize the political mastery of the world. There was talk of an Anglo-Saxon hegemony and numerous political forecasts of an Anglo-American or

American-Japanese war, in which the most powerful survivors of the World War were obligingly to eliminate each other in a struggle for supremacy.

Since that time our international course has shown the world that we value our power lightly, do not intend to use it, and are almost unaware of it. Europe's interest is to prevent our using our strength to our advantage. Our policy is to refrain from resorting to force so long as it is humanly possible. Both the Old World and the New are, therefore, united in proclaiming that war is unwise and unnecessary and undesirable. In consequence, the chances of our being involved in hostilities with a major foreign power are exceedingly slight.

WORLD-POWER

We cannot compete with the world in diplomacy so long as we have nothing to offer or accept in the diplomatic line. We are not in the market for an alliance, and we are not engaged in selecting an adversary. Therefore, the world will have little interest in what our statesmen say or our public opinion believes, and will regard only what we do.

If we are to support, as well as to proclaim, our policies, it will not be through their intrinsic justice or the purity of our intentions, but through the national power —military, economic, or financial—which we can put at the service of our purposes. The freedom of the seas, as a diplomatic dogma, has fared badly with the British navy in control of the seas. The Monroe Doctrine, as an avenue for British trade, has fared well by virtue of the same navy. The doctrine of the open door met with little success for sixty years. When we had taken the Philippines and could muster troops and warships in the China Seas, the open door became a valid international principle. As Admiral Mahan observed, "The function of force is to enable moral ideas to take root." To get a hearing in the world, you must be strong—or desperate.

It would, however, be foolish to accept an arbitrary basis of physical force as the measure of strength. The ability to build battleships is more important than the possession of a fleet. So long as we dispose of economic and financial power, our military force is a secondary consideration. We cannot deny the facts of our present power. Unless we destroy our factories, discharge our workers, and give away our wealth, we are destined to be strong.

Our problem is to use our power with consideration for the rights of others. Strength is the greatest of national responsibilities. Prosperity is its measure, as well as its object. Wealth has its obligations. Mere economic expansion can become a numbing tyranny, if it is directed by purely selfish motives. We might succeed in achieving as spectacular and temporary an influence as that of Portugal and Holland in the days of their glory, but unless we discipline our power with consideration for other nations, it will be a delusion at home and a calamity abroad. We should learn to make our power convenient and necessary to the world at large, to let America become a luxury which the world would not do without, to serve rather than control the nations. If we cannot make our power as useful to others as to ourselves, our policy will be weak in its most vital part and will collapse at the first hint of our adversity.

"The Next War"

We cannot expect to avoid all armed conflict in the course of the next two generations, but we should recognize that any war is hostile to our interests, and we ought to make every effort to prevent the outbreak of a general conflict.

War of any sort will signalize the breakdown of our policies, even if we are not directly involved. We endeavored in 1914 to preserve peace in Europe and in 1916 to end hostilities, having realized the danger to ourselves from the controversies of others. We cannot remain indifferent even to small wars in which we do not participate. The huge costs of modern warfare wipe out the values of foreign investments, inflate currencies, jeopardize trade everywhere, and result in lower purchasing power and fewer customers—to put matters economically. Every war has a tendency to spread politically. Even our Civil War came close to involving Great Britain and France in hostilities. Although we had nothing to do with the causes of the last war, we were dragged into it by the events which it set in train. Our basic interest in world-power is world-peace.

We should throw our political, economic, and financial influence on the side of peace. On the other hand, we should be very cautious before we subscribe to any treaty for outlawing war, lest the removal of the sanctions of force from international society should create an anarchy of national egotism and irresponsibility. We should, instead, throw our political influence in favor of any course which promises to maintain the general peace, even if that course implies a little warfare.

[333]

We should, therefore, remember that we shall always fight in defense of our political institutions, the Monroe Doctrine, and the Panama Canal. Violation of the open door or the freedom of the seas would induce us to prepare purposefully for a test of strength. If we renounce war as an instrument of national policy, it is because we resent war as a legal conception that abrogates all international contracts. Mr. Kellogg did not propose to abandon *force* as an instrument of policy.

We do not propose to scrap our armaments. We can still resort to diplomatic negotiation and to arbitration of disputes. We can still invoke reprisals, retaliation, political, diplomatic, and financial pressure, and severance of diplomatic relations. And if other means fail, we can still resort to intervention to attain our ends. What we propose is to get our way without paying the usual price in terms of broken treaties and canceled obligations. If the Kellogg treaties succeed, it will mean that we have devised a way to eat our cake and have it, too, in respect to war. Closely considered and stripped of emotion, the outlawry of war is one of the shrewdest pieces of national selfishness which any nation has yet advocated.

Therefore, no treaty outlawing war will ever be stronger than a scrap of paper in the face of a genuine emergency. The moment that it injured its vital interests, any nation would be ready to denounce it. The pursuit of policy and the struggle for power will continue without respite, for war is only one of the many instruments of policy. The world may have gained by abandoning the legal consequences of war, but force will remain, as heretofore, the underlying principle of national policy.

Rather than trust in a peace prescribed by treaty—and

[334]

nearly every treaty of peace ever signed stipulates a "firm and perpetual peace" between the "high contracting parties"—we should so develop our prosperity as to make war impossible without us and war against us equivalent to commercial ruin for others. We should give the world so large a stake in the maintenance of American prosperity as to make our downfall as calamitous to our foes as to our friends.

We are dependent on the world, and the world is dependent on us. We can best serve the cause of peace by confirming and increasing this economic interdependence. We should strive by every means in our power to render our commercial expansion harmless to the political rights of others and, as a proper consideration, to persuade other nations to render their political institutions harmless to our legitimate interests. American expansion should produce, not an American empire, but the economic confederation of mankind.

The greatest test of our policy will be the death's-head at the feast of power, the writing on the wall of our prosperity: the realization that nothing under the sun abides, that empire is the prelude to disintegration, that weakness alternates with strength. While, therefore, we are economically and industrially on the up-grade, we should put from us the thought of domination. Through our wealth and prestige, we can obtain the substance of power without condemning ourselves to maintain the forms of power in perpetuity.

The time will come—not, perhaps, for several centuries, but come it will—when our power will slip away from us and we shall be superseded by nations of a greater vitality or superior resources. If we have not burdened ourselves with the trappings of imperial sovereignty, we shall be under no compulsion to fight for our prestige or to preserve an obsolete political condition. We can quietly let go colonies which we have never annexed. We can peacefully surrender provinces which have never owed us allegiance. We need fear no insurrection from races whom we have never conquered. Our work will be done. For nations, as well as for men, it is an art to grow old gracefully. Our present self-control will be the best defense against the violence of those future rivals who would be forced to destroy us were we to achieve world-dominion.

We stand today at the threshold of our strength, able to choose our own course and to set our own goal. If we assumed that we are perfect and that we have nothing to learn, it would be as much a calamity as it would be for us to believe that we were altogether worthless and with nothing to contribute to the world. If, however, while holding fast to our own individuality, we seek to discover the good in others, we may share in a meeting of minds with the world which will be the prelude to a new age of peace for this perplexing planet.

Index

Index

Index

Bliss, General, 166
Bridgeman, Rt. Hon. William Clive, 196
British Cinematograph Films Act, 74
British Dominions, U. S. relation to, 160, 321
British Empire, partially transformed into commonwealth of nations, 136; American commerce with, 217; American financial policy toward, 291; American tactics toward, 302; regional groupings of, 303
Bryan-Chamorro Treaty, 100, 110
Business, American, political aspects, 239-250
Business and state, 262; separation of, 30, 73-78, 285
Business technique, American, imitation of, 256
"Buy British Goods" campaign, 155, 161

Calhoun, John C., 84
California Petroleum Company, 241
Calles, Plutarco, Elias, 176
Calvo Doctrine, 297
Canada, attempt at annexation, 84; identity of interests with U. S., 160; as bridgehead for American industries in British Empire, 250; transfer of British American possessions to proposed, 281
Canal zone, acquired from Panama, 97
Cancellation of war loans, Europe's efforts for, 150-152, 199
Caperton, Admiral, 111
Caribbean, America's power in, 6, 16, 94-104; Wilson's policies in, 110; Republican policies in, 171; naval bases in, 198, 274; precarious state of self-government dangerous to American interests, 298; nationalism, American encouragement of, 304
Carranza, Venustiano, inauguration, 110
Catholic Church, Mexican laws against, 176

Cecil, Viscount, 196, 199
Central America, American interventions in, 101, 186. *See also* Latin America
Central American Court of Justice, 101
Central American General Treaty of Peace and Amity, 44, 171
Central Europe, Balkanization of, 130
Chain stores, 251, 252
Chase National Bank, 204
Château-Thierry, Battle of, 127
Cherokee Indians, 81
Chesterton, Gilbert Keith, cited, 168
Chile, attitude toward U. S. influenced by nitrate trade, 219
China, American commerce in, 61, 63; Wilson's policies in, 112; exploitation by powers, 113; Japan's Twenty-One Demands, 119; nationalism, 137; protection of American property in, 210; failure of American intervention in, 299; opportunity for world coöperation, 319
China Seas, area of world's greatest tension, 16; future position of U. S. in, 276
Chinese Consortium, 113
Churchill, Winston, cited, 147, 195
Civil War, as a test of union, 37
Clark, Evans, cited, 252
Clay, Henry, 84
Clayton-Bulwer Treaty, 97
Cleveland, Grover, and the annexation of Hawaii, 41, 91
Coastal trade, 265
Cocos Island, 12
Colby, Bainbridge, 153, 181
Colombia, Roosevelt's dealings with, 97; intervention in, 101; indemnity to, 103
Commerce, American, attempts of Great Britain to strangle, 54; European counter-attack on, 161-165
Commercial doctrines, American, 52-64
Commercial treaties, 170

Index

Index

191; speech on reparations, 200; belief in Communist plots, 209

Hungary, financial reorganization, 201

Immigrants, political prejudices of, 308; need of a more sympathetic attitude toward, 315

Immigration, 266

Imperial Conference (1926), 136

Imperial War Council, 136

Imperialism, principles of, 3-18; American sentiment about, 311

Import trade, 213; statistics, 228

India, agitations, 135

Indian Ocean, 12, 270

Indian wars, 80-81

Individualism, American belief in, 310

Industrial combinations, in Europe, 154

Industrialization of Europe, 225

Institutions, American, 263, 294, 325; maintenance of, 10

International Banking Corporation, 244

International Harvester Company, 246

International Mercantile Marine Company, 247

International Nickel Company, 247

International police power, 49

International standardization, 261

International Telephone and Telegraph Company, 248

Internationalism, 313

Interstate Commerce Commission, 77

Interventions, in Central America, 101, 186; in Europe, 186

Investments, foreign, 29; in Latin America, 178; table, 233; nature of, 234. See also Loans, foreign

Iraq, 63, 136

Ireland, revolt against England, 135

Irish Free State, establishment of, 135

Italy, trade expansion in Latin-America, 162; Fascist dictatorship, 164; imports from U. S., 217

Jackson, Andrew, 81, 85

Jamaica, operations of the United Fruit Company in, 240

Japan, sea-power, 14; imperialism, 27, 137; opening of to foreign commerce, 62; Twenty-One Demands to China, 119; part in World War, 122; war with U. S. threatened in 1920-21, 157; anti-American propaganda, 159; navy, 191; American financial policy toward, 290; American relations with, 321; improbability of war with U. S., 329

Jefferson, Thomas, warning against entangling alliances, 67

Jones Law, 138

Jugo-Slavia. See Yugo-Slavia

Jute trade, 222

Kellogg, Frank B., proposal for outlawry of war, 167; foreign policies, 169-187; belief in Communist plots, 209

Kellogg treaties, 334

Kenworthy, Lieutenant-Commander, cited, 154

Kerensky government recognized, 208

Knox, Philander, 113

Knox-Castrillo Convention, 100

Korea, 62; annexation, 113

Lambert Company, 247

Lamont, Thomas, cited, 148

Land-power, 15

Lansing, Robert, 132

Lansing-Ishii Agreement, 117, 120

Latin America, political ideals, 23; U. S. policy toward, 44; intervention in, 95; membership in League of Nations, 141; anti-Yankee agitation, 159-160, 296; European trade with, 162; Hughes-Kellogg policy, 173; trade with U S., 217, 298; nationalism in, 304

Latin-American League (proposed), 161

Law, Roman, 21

Lawyers as statesmen, 173

Index

Index

Tobacco Products Corporation, 249
Tourists, American, expenditures in Europe, 236
Trade balance, 214, 235
Trade statistics, 212, 249; American, 187
Transjordania, 136
Treaties, war, 146
Treaty of Amity and Commerce with France, 52, 59
Treaty of Guadeloupe Hidalgo, 87
Treaty of London, 117
Treaty of Nanking, 62
Treaty of Portsmouth, 70
Treaty of Washington, 56
"Treaty navy," 277
Tripartite Naval Conference, 150
Triple Alliance, 115
Triple Entente, 115
Tripoli, Bey of, 54
Trusts, European, 225; American. See Anti-trust laws
Turkish Petroleum Company, 182
Tyrrell, Sir William, 109

Ugarte, Manuel, 160
Ukrainia, 133
United Drug Company, 247
United Fruit Company, 240, 242
United States, economic power, 2; economic expansion, 28; interventions in Latin America, 49, 95; European menace to, 107-124; financial reactions against, 149; unpopularity in Europe, 150; moral isolation, 165-168; financial control over foreign governments, 205; future of expansion, 261; consequences of defeat to, 264-267
United States Army, 126
United States Bank, 75
United States Navy, 53, 126, 128, 197; cruise to the East in 1925, 160; compared with British, 190; policy in regard to, 278
United States Railroad Administration, 126
United States Rubber Company, 183, 248

United States Shipping Board, 77, 126, 127, 262
United States Steel Corporation, 76

Vacuum Oil Company, 241
Vanadium Corporation, 248
Venezuela, interventions in, 101
Vera Cruz seized by American navy, 102, 110
Villa, Pancho, 102

Wages, as a factor in American prosperity, 30
Walker, William, 87
Wall Street, political influence of, 316
War, outlawry of, 167, 334; American attitude toward, 211; as a cure for unemployment, 283; chances of, 326-336
War debts, Republican policy, 201; as a defense for the American government, 204. See also Debt cancellation
War Industries Board, 126
War of 1812, 54, 84
Washington, George, warning against entangling alliances, 66
Washington Conference (1922), 57, 147, 191
Wayne, "Mad Anthony," 80
Webb-Pomerene Export Trade Act, 76, 184, 285
Wemyss, Admiral, 193
West Indies Company, Dutch, 24
Western Union Telegraph Company, 249
Wilson, Woodrow, message to Russia, 41; policy toward Central America, 43; speech to Latin-American journalists, 50; on American neutrality, 71; policy toward Mexico, 103; international policies, 107-108; war message, 125, 129; struggle for self-determination, 131-139; Russian policy, 134; attitude of Philippine independence, 138; simplicity of his achievements, 142; defeat of, 149; efforts to

[347]